MIND, CULTURE, AND ACTIVITY, 7(1&2), 1–3
Copyright © 2000, Regents of the University of California on behalf of the Laboratory of C

INTRODUCTION

Vision and Inscription in Practice

The study of how people—both actors and the social scientists who study them—construct, see, and classify the consequential phenomena that define their lifeworld has been an enduring topic in the analysis of human action, cognition, and social organization. Quite frequently investigation of such processes focuses on the structure of carefully isolated, self-contained systems, such as kinship or color terms, which are presumed to have their primary organization in the mental life of an actor. By way of contrast, all of the articles in this issue investigate how vision and classification are accomplished through public discursive practices in which objects, images, diagrams, talk, the body, standards, encompassing activities, and so on play a central role. All of the articles contribute to a growing body of work focused on how action, cognition, and activity are socially organized in scientific and workplace settings (see, e.g., Engeström & Middleton, 1996; Hutchins, 1995; Lynch & Woolgar, 1988; Rogoff & Lave, 1984; The Xerox PARC Workplace Project initiated by Lucy Suchman; and the articles that appear in *Social Studies of Science,* and earlier work by the authors who appear in this issue).

In addition to the Vygotskian perspective on activity, the articles in this issue also draw on American pragmatism, the approach to the social organization of human interaction pioneered by the Chicago School sociologists, ethnomethodology and conversation analysis as analytic points of departure. In the opening article, Lucy Suchman examines the relation between activity theory and ethnomethodology. She emphasizes the reflexive relationship between objects, practices, setting, and accounts of what is occurring that are brought together by participants in a "contexture" of mutually constitutive details. Note, as Lynch and Jordan point out in their article, how this notion of reflexivity, in which actions and objects elaborate and are elaborated by the settings and activities in which they are embedded differs, from perspectives on reflexivity that focus exclusively on the self-referential properties of language itself. All of the articles in this issue provide examples of this reflexivity by investigating how relevant vision and classification are organized by juxtaposing quite disparate phenomena, including artifacts, inscriptions, language, displays made by the body, underlying standards, and so on so as to make visible for participants the unfolding structure of relevant events, such that they can accomplish in concert with each other the consequential activities that make up the lifeworld of their community.

Suchman herself investigates the work practices, different kinds of representations, and visual technology of engineers designing a bridge. In the following article, Chuck Goodwin provides a new perspective on color classification, one of the classic topics in cognitive and linguistic anthropology, by looking at how archaeologists, rather than relying upon just the color lexicon of a particular language, use an artifact, a Munsell chart, to code the color of the dirt they are excavating. Rather than simply acting as a representation, the Munsell chart, which contains both structurally different kinds of sign systems appropriate to alternative tasks, and holes so that the dirt being classified can be placed in the same visual field as the color samples, provides an historically structured framework for the production of meaningful action.

Both Yasuko Kawatoko and Naoki Ueno examine events in the same work site, a factory that produces large quantities of precision metal parts through the use of computer-controlled lathes. Kawatoko begins by looking in detail at how the lathe operators juxtapose a range of different kinds of documents and artifacts to both program their lathes and build a perceptual field where relevant events in the process become visible. The layout diagram used to represent the actions of the lathe provides an interesting comparison to the instructions described by Lynch and Jordan in their article. In the second part of her article, Kawatoko looks at how a common standard plan is used in very different ways in different sections of the plant such that it is able to organize multiple, perspectival visions of the "same" events, and thus becomes a key artifact for the coordination of a division of labor. Both her article and Ueno's look at standarization as situated practice and are thus quite relevant to the issues raised by Bowker and Star in their article. Ueno used the factory's standard plan as one part of a sustained investigation of the technologies through which social organization, society, and activity are rendered visible. His analytic framework, with its emphasis on how vision is shaped by tools, inscriptions, and situated practices, although oriented to different kinds of addressees, applies equally to a painter's use of tools to draw perspective, scientists making phenomena visible in the world they are examining, workers at the lathe plant making their work and activities visible in a differentiated fashion in alternative settings, and the methods used by both participants and social scientists to make visible macro–social structure and the objects that are the focus of activity. The way in which these practices vary from setting to setting, even when focused on the same object, calls into question the notion of a single panopticon with an all-encompassing master view, providing instead for "partially overlapped, asymmetrical, multi-layered accountability."

The articles by Christian Heath and Jon Hindmarsh and by Aug Nishizaka both focus on how what is to be seen in a scene (in both cases scenes that rely heavily on electronic documents and images) is structured by a range of interactively organized, embodied conversational practices that reflexively draw upon and elaborate the activities and settings in which they are embedded. The primary analytic focus of the Heath and Hindmarsh article is the way in which objects, and other material phenomena in the surround, are dynamically attended to and constituted in a relevant way through sequences of interaction. The setting they examine is the control room that monitors the operations and platform activity of one London Underground line. Through subtle analysis of a collaborative search for a specific train in the array of electronic documents visible in the room, they demonstrate how the object being attended to is reflexively constituted in a particular fashion through the sequential tasks that generated the search, embodied displays, and the material resources of the environment. In the final section of the article, they use the analytic resources developed in the first part of the article to demonstrate how "media spaces" created by linking remote locations through television and so on can systematically fail to provide the situated resources necessary to accomplish reference through acts such as pointing. Nishizaka uses a situation in which several participants are attempting to program a sequence of action that will become visible on a computer screen to challenge traditional notions of visual perception. He demonstrated how what is to be seen in a scene is organized through a range of discursive embodied practices that provide for the reflexive, interactive elaboration of task, emotion, setting, and encompassing activities. By virtue of this organization, participants are able to see not only the scene actually in front of their eyes, but also what is not there: the absence of relevant events at specific moments in time.

Michael Lynch and Kathleen Jordan examine a range of quite different kinds of representations used in a variety of activities to depict, make visible, and make claims about genetic structure. The representations examined are quite diverse, ranging from pictures and maps (some of them alive) to rationally prolix patent language, to images and metaphors in advertisements for laboratory equipment, to variations in laboratory instructions, to newspaper diagrams illustrating genetic processes for a lay audience. The article covers a range of crucial issues central to the use of representations in scientific practice, arguing that rather than incidentally conveying preexisting information, representational practices both help constitute the entities being studied and mediate crucial relations between different kinds of social actors.

In the final article, Geoffrey C. Bowker and Susan Leigh Star propose a framework for investigating the invisible but ubiquitous systems of classification (containers for holding and segmenting events) and standards (procedures for how to do things) that constitute an infrastructure for almost all forms of socially organized action, from writing a letter or an E-mail message, to the segmentation and tabulation of disease for both reimbursement and statistical study, to the segregation of people by skin color in Apartheid. Despite the way in which such processes seem both invisible and the technical concerns of someone else, they have enormous political, social, and ethical consequences and require detailed investigation.

This issue presents a range of analytic resources for the study of how human vision, as historically structured, interactively organized, temporally unfolding discursive practice mediated by artifacts of many different kinds, plays a crucial role in the ongoing constitution of the events that make up the lived social world in which work, the relations between different kinds of actors, and public knowledge are accomplished.

Charles Goodwin

REFERENCES

Engeström, Y., & Middleton, D. (1996). *Cognition and Communication at Work*. Cambridge, MA: Cambridge University Press.

Hutchins, E. (1996). *Cognition in the Wild*. Cambridge, MA: MIT Press.

Lynch, M., & Woolgar, S. (1988). *Representation in Scientific Practice*. Cambridge, MA: MIT Press.

Rogoff, B., & Lave, J. (1984). *Studying Working Intelligence*. Cambridge, MA: Harvard University Press.

MIND, CULTURE, AND ACTIVITY, 7(1&2), 4–18

ARTICLES

Embodied Practices of Engineering Work

Lucy Suchman

Department of Sociology
Lancaster University

This article explores relationships between activity theoretic and ethnomethodological studies of work and its objects, with specific reference to the case of design practices in civil engineering. My starting point is the shared interest of activity theory and ethnomethodology in the place of artifacts in everyday working practice. I review briefly some basic premises of first ethnomethodological, then activity theoretic studies of artifacts-in-use. I then offer a preliminary account of computer-aided and paper-based design work in civil engineering, informed by both perspectives. My account emphasizes the multiplicity of media and associated objects involved in the work of engineering on the one hand, and their integration in practice into a coherent field of action on the other. The article concludes by returning to the question of relationships between ethnomethodology and activity theory, focusing on differences in their respective stances toward theory itself.

Interest within the social sciences in the relationship between working practices and their associated objects has given rise to a collection of alternate research programs in the area of work and technology studies. This journal has been founded on one of those programs, that of activity theory, which offers a generative framework for the analysis of mind, culture, and activity as dialectically developing, sociomaterial relationships.[1] My own work has been deeply informed by the program outlined by Harold Garfinkel and his colleagues under the rubric of ethnomethodological studies of work.[2] Here I take this special issue of *Mind, Culture, and Activity* as the occasion to reflect on relationships between ethnomethodological and activity-theoretic projects for the study of work and its objects. In doing so I am interested in points of affinity and the difference between an anthropologically informed, ethnomethodological stance and certain aspects of activity theory's central tenets and preoccupations. My aim is not to compare these two programs in general, but to consider their respective orientations to work and its objects with reference to a particular case of

---

Requests for reprints should be sent to Lucy Suchman, 55 Bordon Street, Toronto, ON, M5S 2M8 Canada.

[1]My understanding of activity theory, although cursory, relies most directly on the writings of Bødker, 1991; Cole & Engeström, 1993; Engeström, 1990; and the articles collected in Nardi, 1996b.

[2]See, for example, Garfinkel, 1986, 1996; Livingston, 1987; Lynch, 1993. For a useful overview see Heritage, 1984.

working practice. More specifically, my reflections draw from a project concerned with the object-centered work of civil engineering.[3]

The work of civil engineering comprises activities done always in a particular place and time, but with meanings inflected by collectively remembered histories and imagined futures. While in progress, moreover, engineering projects are positioned within multiple spatial and temporal networks that must be simultaneously elaborated, managed, and contained. Coordination within and across these networks implies the accomplishment of alignment across multiple shop floors and social worlds, each with their own identities, contingencies, and concerns.[4] Given the extent and complexity of civil engineering as a practice, a few words of clarification on the limits of the discussion offered here are in order. I am concerned in particular that the boundaries that I draw around the field for my purposes might be taken as principled limits on the extent of what I take to be relevant and important to the study of civil engineering work overall. To be clear, then, I assume that a fuller treatment of the work of civil engineering would include, inter alia,

- A cultural-historical account of civil engineering and its tools.
- Location of the site studied here with respect to its particular histories, including relevant details of the political and economic circumstances of the project at hand.
- An account of the extended actor networks that make up the project, including members' own orientation to demands of engagement in time and across space.
- An account of the project's work organization and divisions of labor.
- An account of my own circumstances, as a researcher, in engaging with the project.

With that said, the limited focus of this article is on that aspect of engineering work that comprises the production of exhibits and plans and the place of computer-aided design tools and paper-based drawings as mediators of that form of engineering practice.[5] A common orientation to material artifacts as mediators of human activity is, to my reading, the strongest element that aligns ethnomethodology with activity theory. In the remainder of this article I review briefly some basic premises of, first, ethnomethodological then activity theoretic studies of artifacts-in-use. I then offer an account of engineering design work informed by both perspectives. Finally, I turn back to the question of relationships between ethnomethodology and activity theory, focusing on differences in their respective stances toward theory itself.

---

[3]My colleagues on this project were Jeanette Blomberg, Randy Trigg, and David Levy. Our study of the working practices of civil engineers went hand in hand with the design of a prototype technology for online document filing and access in collaboration with members of the study site. For a discussion of our approach to work-oriented, cooperative design, which is not the focus of this article, see Blomberg, Suchman, & Trigg, 1996; Suchman, Trigg, & Blomberg, 1998; and Trigg, Blomberg, & Suchman, 1999.

[4]See Suchman, in press.

[5]Alder (1998) provided a compelling history of the rise of projective engineering drawings in mid-18th century France. For an insightful account of relations of paper and digital media in contemporary practices of mechanical engineering, see Henderson, 1999; for another view onto the work of civil engineering discussed here and its associated disciplines of testing see Sims, 1999.

PHENOMENAL FIELD PROPERTIES

Ethnomethodological studies of work are concerned with what Garfinkel (1996), following Gurwitsch (1964), has named the "phenomenal field properties" of particular work sites and their practices.[6] Emphasis is on the irreducible relations of mutually constitutive details, through which isolable actions, objects, artifacts, and the like take on their specific, practical significance. Meanings on this view inhere neither in individual elements or properties, nor in some underlying structure that stands behind appearances, but only in relations of "mutual reference" across a field of observable phenomena (Lynch, 1993, p. 127). Ethnomethodology adds to this field the necessary presence of the embodied subject, through whose history and present engagement phenomenal relations are enlivened and made relevant to some ongoing activity. Moreover, the phenomenal field of action does not simply preexist and take its meaning from activity, but is reflexively generated through the same activity that it organizes, as found objects are appropriated and mobilized and new objects created (see also Ueno, this issue).

The mutually constitutive relation of actions and their environments includes the fact that accounts of activity are themselves crafted from the juxtaposition of observable features of embodied actions with phenomena selected from the scene in progress (Goodwin, in press). This applies equally to accounts that are internal to a given activity, as to those created about it in advance or afterwards. For ethnomethodology, then, the relationship between social practices and accounts of those practices is deeply and unavoidably a reflexive one, for participants and observers alike (Button & Sharrock, 1998; Lynch, 1993, p. 1; Ueno, this issue). And like material artifacts, formulations of action—whether done as part of an activity or as accounts of it by participants or others—are specifically situated in the occasions of their production and use. Together talk and other culturally formulated, socially and materially constituted artifacts comprise the phenomenal field of embodied practice.

MEDIATIONS

Activity theory has a rich history and many interpreters, to which I cannot begin to do justice here. Recognizing the multiplicity of researches that go on under activity theory's rubric, a central premise, as articulated by Cole and Engeström (1993), is that to grasp an activity fully one needs to understand how cultural-historically constituted artifacts both mediate activity and are in turn enlivened, given their functionality and significance, in and through it. At the same time that tools and symbol systems mediate between individual and purpose, or subject and object, artifacts are continually shaped in and through their use.[7] Most important for the analysis that follows, artifacts shift from being themselves the objects of our activity to working as transparent media through which we act with and on other objects. As Bødker (1996) put it,

> Artifacts are there for us when we are introduced to a certain activity, but they are also a product of our activity and as such are constantly changed through the activity. Artifacts thus have a double character:

---

[6]See also Lynch, 1993; Goodwin, in press.

[7]A similar perspective is developed in social studies of technology, specifically actor-network theory; see, for example, Akrich, 1992.

they are objects in the world around us that we can reflect on, and they mediate our interaction with the world, in which case they are not themselves objects of our activity in use. (p. 149)

With particular reference to computational artifacts, Bødker proposes an analysis of the use of computer applications in terms of the relation of an application to its object, "object" here having the double sense of the material thing to which our activity is oriented and its purpose or aim. She identifies three possible relations:

1. The object of activity is present only in the application.
2. The object exists as a physical object but is only present in the use activity as the rendition provided by the computer application.
3. The object is physically co-present outside the application.

My analysis of engineering design work builds on Bødker's analysis, showing the dynamic inter-relation of these logical distinctions in actual practice. The dominant relations in the case of civil engineering design work are a hybrid of Relations 1 and 2, as new roads and bridges are imaged in and imagined through the conventional graphics and symbol systems of engineering and in re-lation to a distant physical landscape and infrastructure, located some 30 miles from the district headquarters in which the design work is done. I am interested both in how we as analysts can see engineers shift among these objects in the course of their work and also in the ways in which the objects for them are effectively joined, in and through their practice, into a unified phenomenal field.

DESIGNING A BRIDGE

Historian of engineering Henry Petroski (1995) wrote that for a civil engineer, the design of a bridge is the stuff that dreams are made of. He emphasized as well the significance of the codevelopment of modern engineering practice and the artifacts of inscription and persuasion that have become as much its stock in trade as concrete and steel:

> In the association [in the mid-19th century] of bridge building with drawing and calculation and written argument before any construction was started, a new era was begun. From then on, the grandest dreams could be articulated and tested on paper, and thereby communicated to those who would have to ap-prove, support, finance, and assist in designing a project that could eventually take years, if not de-cades, of planning and construction. (p. 12)

The building of bridges is rare compared with the building of roadways and other surface struc-tures, insofar as bridges are costly projects that last on the order of thirty to in some cases hundreds of years. In the area where our study is located, six toll bridges have already been built and no addi-tional bridges are planned. At the same time, the area is threatened with earthquakes. In response to the critical problems experienced in the last major earthquake, the state government has set aside substantial funds for "seismic retrofitting" of the existing toll bridges.[8] One of the area's toll

---

[8] For additional background on these initiatives see Sims, 1999.

bridges is actually a pair of old trestle bridges that connect the north and south shores of a relatively narrow strait. Charged with ensuring the safety of these bridges, engineers at the state Department of Transportation (DOT) have argued that whereas one of the bridges can indeed be retrofitted, the other is sufficiently old—dating from 1927—and that it is both unsafe and uneconomical to try to reinforce it. Instead, they have proposed "replacement as a retrofit strategy." In this way they are able to direct funds for retrofitting to a new bridge building project.

At the same time, it is a bit misleading to say that the engineers are engaged in designing a bridge if what we imagine by that is the design of the structure itself. In this case, in fact, the bridge design is outsourced to a specialist design firm, with DOT engineers responsible for oversight. But it also turns out that the bridge itself represents a small fraction of the entire project relative to the highway approaches and interchanges that tie the bridge into the landmasses that it connects. So although the design of the bridge is contracted out, DOT engineers maintain responsibility for the bridge alignments and all connecting roadways. These make up the focus of their design work.

WORKING IN COMPUTER-AIDED DESIGN (CAD)

My analysis of engineering design work is based on a set of tutorials provided by Andrea, a lead engineer on the bridge replacement project team.[9] The first of these took place in front of her CAD workstation, where she took us on a tour of some of her recent work. The object of her activity on this occasion was the earth—in Bodker's (1996) terms an object physically existing, but present to Andrea only as the rendering of it provided by the computer system. More specifically, Andrea was engaged in figuring the volumes of dirt that would need to be displaced to construct the highway interchange on the bridge's south side. Andrea's purpose at hand was to calculate, as she put it, "how much dirt we're going to dig up—literally, not just as a figure of speech!"

The interface that mediates Andrea's access to her work's objects is actually composed of two software applications running together. An engineering application is layered on top of, or nested within, the functionality of a second, graphics application. The engineering application, in Andrea's words "uses the [graphics application] to let you see the results of actual engineering calculations." The layered space[10] of the CAD environment includes as well a collection of menus arranged as a kind of frame around the periphery of the CAD workspace. Some of these menus serve as views onto the directory structure of Andrea's hard disk and provide the means by which files are located and opened; others provide "tool boxes" of available actions to be taken on graphical objects within those files, whereas a third controls the layered space of the CAD display itself. When focus shifts to these menus as objects, they become a top layer, superimposed on the objects they are used to manipulate (see Figure 1).

Latour (1990) pointed out that representational conventions in engineering are aimed at maintaining an "optical consistency" between three-dimensional objects and the flattened renditions

---

[9]The tutorial was provided to me and my colleague Jeanette Blomberg, who interviewed Andrea as I recorded the session on video.

[10]Star's (1989) notion of *layered representations* applies here as well, insofar as the working up of drawings is almost always a matter not of beginning from scratch, but of reusing and adapting available renditions. Regarding multilayered inscriptions, see also Ueno, this issue.

FIGURE 1   CAD interface with toolbars menus.

that comprise sketches, plans, and the like (pp. 52–54).[11] These conventions include highly elabo-rated lexicons of line types, perspectives, geometries, and symbols. In the case of mechanical engineering, Henderson (1991) observed that "[t]he lexicon allows the schematic drawings to remain flexible enough that engineers can read the coded functions in the layout and understand the interrelations of the various functional components of the whole project" (p. 459). Fundamental to civil engineering in this regard is the *plan view* or *horizontal alignment,* which flattens engineering objects into something akin to a bird's-eye perspective.[12] In roadway work, the plan view relies on a geometric object called the point of intersection (PI). The PI in turn references a virtual grid laid over the mapped physical environment, establishing a series of points in space that mark the place where, as Andrea describes it, "a straight line meets a straight line." A second focal object is the *control point,* which she describes as a place of maximum constraint that consequently controls much of the design (see Figure 2).

Andrea explains it this way:

And then, you always have some control points. We have a major control point on Vista [an existing surface street], which is right here [pointing to indicate curving street to left of ramp] where it goes underneath that ramp, that controls really so much of the entire design on the new road ... We have to have clearance for trucks to go under it, and while they're building this new ramp they have something called false work-up. Which has its own depth, it might be three feet it might be six feet deep. And then there's the depth of the structure. So we know what the elevation is on the ramp, right at this point [leaning in to

[11]See also Alder, 1998; Henderson, 1991.

[12]Alder (1998) discussed the distinction between perspectival drawings, developed in the Renaissance to convey a sense of realism, and projective drawings, designed in the mid-18th century in the engineering schools of Enlightenment France to correct for the distortions of scale on which the realism of perspectival drawings relies. Such correction was seen to require shifting the viewer's stance from one positioned in relation to the scene or objects depicted to the bird's-eye view or "view from nowhere" (pp. 513–514).

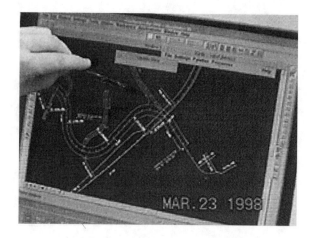

FIGURE 2   Andrea indicates control point.

show] actually its control point turns out to be right here. But we have to then add that there's a depth to that structure, then there's gonna be some false work, so we have to go way under it.

Andrea's account of the problem makes clear that highways and bridges are not self-standing objects but structural elements that are laid over and must be effectively incorporated into existing landscapes. In the case of civil engineering, moreover, the spatial field of objects is complicated by the element of time. Andrea's calculations must take into account not only the plans for the new ramp, but also the temporary structures, or false work, required for its construction. All of this in turn must be placed in relation to existing landscapes, made up not only of natural features such as geological formations, waterways, and the like, but of strata of built environments laid down over a period that may comprise hundreds of years. The pace of this latter building is accelerating, moreover, in such a way that each new project confronts an increasingly dense infrastructural archeology, including prior structures, utilities, waste disposal sites, and even areas protected for recovery from previous interventions.

All of these features must be accurately mapped for the soundness of a design to be ensured. The graphical renderings of the plan view can be interrelated with a Digital Terrain Map, which renders the 3-D contours of the physical environment in which the objects of design will actually be built and into which they need to fit. Maps are created from survey points, assembled together through the use of conventional symbols that render the topography of the original ground. Like the ground, the Digital Terrain Map appears as a kind of bottom layer that sits beneath the design objects themselves. As with the engineering and graphics applications, however, the layers are not simply superimposed but dynamically cross-referential. Specifically, once the horizontal alignment or plan view has been created, engineers need to generate a *profile,* a rendering that makes visible the relationhip between the proposed new roadways and the existing terrain. By drawing *cuts* through a particular section of the plan view of the site, Andrea is able effectively to instruct the engineering application to create a series of cross-sections for each of those cuts showing where the existing surface is, using the map as a reference (see Figure 3).

Andrea's workspace, in sum, is made up of an assemblage of computational, metrological, geometric, cartographic, and graphical tools. Together these comprise the interface through which she sees and manipulates the physical objects of her work. With reference to Bødker's (1991) framework, Andrea works *with* the elements of the layered interface that the CAD system provides and *through* the interface to the objects that those various renderings mediate: in this case, the earth, the existing and projected roadways, and her team's interests in them. Ethnomethodologically, our interest is in how these multiple elements and objects together comprise the phenomenal field properties of Andrea's embodied practice. Having enumerated the distinctions among heterogeneous elements, in other words, the question becomes how in practice does Andrea bring them together?

In our tutorial Andrea took us through her previous day's work in a way that made not only the heterogeneity but the integrity of her workspace clear. For example, she pointed out to us one of what she called the "major control points" for her design, a physical location on an existing roadway named Vista del Rio. As she explained it, a defining constraint of the design problem at hand is that one of the on-ramps to the highway must be built to run over Vista del Rio, an existing surface street. To provide enough clearance for the ramp, Vista must be effectively lowered below the current surface level by removing earth at the point where the street crosses under the ramp. As Andrea guided us through a profile of the site, she explained further:

> And you can see that at the top of Vista we're pretty much following the existing ground. And as we go down, we get *way* below it, this is about 10 meters of dirt that we're taking out. And then I think the point that we're crossing under is right on this [pointing with pencil] little flat here.

Andrea's demonstration takes the profile as a locus of what Goodwin (1994, 1995) has named "professional vision," a site from which we can "see" the contours of a roadway far removed from the place where we sit in front of her workstation and assess its relevance for the imagined future

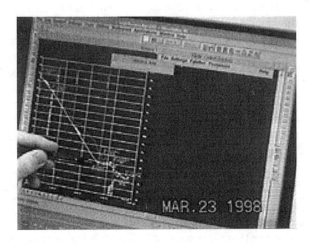

FIGURE 3 Profile view.

activity of constructing a new road.[13] In this way, the display acts as a surrogate for the physical place of engineering interest. Andrea's narrative positioned us figuratively on the physical site "at the top of Vista," from which we could "follow the existing ground." But "as we go down" this virtual roadway we enjoy the ability to continue our travels below the existing surface, removing 10 m of virtual dirt to reach the projected future crossing below. The latter is indicated by a geometric point in space, positioned figuratively under the new ramp and more literally on the flat line of the CAD display. Bringing together narrative form and imagination, metrology and geometry, Andrea is able to "see" under the existing ground, to project a newly excavated roadway that does not yet exist. In doing this work she moves fluidly between pictures and things and across time, as the artifacts and objects of her work are read through each other to achieve a rendition that aligns what is there now with its desired transformation. At the same time Andrea's small gesture, the point of her pencil, reminded us that it is with the engineer's body that this work of virtual travel and assembly gets done.

THE MEDIATING BODY

That engineering objects mediate embodied practices of engineering is clear. By looking more closely, we can see as well how bodies mediate engineering objects. So in the course of her tutorial Andrea made continuous use of various forms of what Goodwin (1994) has named *highlighting for perception,* instructing us on where and how to look with the gestures of her pencil. At other times, the performative aspects of her reading served to animate the static CAD image that we saw. So, for example, once she had used the system to create a series of cross-sections of a roadway, say every 5 or 20 m, she could then effectively "travel" along the roadway by scrolling through the sections displayed on her screen. At still other times her body itself became a reference, adding a kind of third dimension to the CAD screen as when, for example, she used the angle from her hand to her elbow to demonstrate the slope of a road.[14]

As CAD has become an increasingly central aspect of engineering practice, a perspicuous site for seeing these bodily mediations is in the relations and differences between working at the CAD station and on paper. Another way of understanding these differences is in terms of the relatively greater scale and expanse of paper. Another engineer described this to us vividly, as she enacted with gesture the difference between sitting in front of the CAD station, elbows close in to the sides of her body, hands constrained within the narrow terrain of the keyboard, eyes glued to the screen on which she zoomed in and out and traveled across the virtual space with mouse clicks, and sitting or standing over a large sheet of paper, arms outstretched or hands and arms engaged in a variety of actions of drawing, measuring, turning the paper to get another angle, moving it slightly on the table, and so on.

---

[13] Although we are concerned here with how it is that engineering artifacts mediate imagined future activities, Goodwin's (1994, 1995) analyses take up the question as well of how the mediating artifacts of professional vision can reconstitute past events, ranging from archaeologically available traces of human habitation and police actions in Los Angeles, 1994, to flows of the Amazon into the world's oceans, 1995.

[14] For an extensive discussion of the place of gestures, specifically pointing, in constituting a relevant phenomenal field see Goodwin (1994). For a discussion of the scientists' body as defined by the materials on which it depends, see Mialet, 1999.

At the same time, it is also the case that Andrea identified a great benefit of CAD as the effectively unbounded (other than by the size of files) virtual space that CAD's zooming and scrolling functions provide. Andrea is able to create an extended workspace, a kind of spatially arrayed library or storehouse of her work, made up of shrunken images that she can browse, select from, and expand. In this way all of Andrea's cumulative productions—what would comprise a bulky collection of plan drawings each at the scale of 24 in. by 36 in.—can be surveyed on a single screen simply by saying "show me everything that's in this file at once."

Another difference between paper- and CAD-based work practices could be that older engineers choose the former, whereas younger engineers more familiar with digital media choose the latter. Indeed, Andrea explained to us that in the previous week she had prepared a set of paper plans to bring a problem for consultation to one of her more senior colleagues who works only on paper. At the same time, she herself also frequently turns to paper in the course of her work. A week after our tutorial I noticed her working at her drawing table with an array of paper documents spread out around her and asked her to tell me about them. She explained that she and two of her colleagues had sat down several days before to, as she put it, "nail down" the design of the highway interchange on the bridge's south side. The primary documents were a set of three plan views taped together (see Figure 4).[15]

In this case, Andrea explained that whereas she could have done her design work with a smaller image, she wanted as she put it a "meaty" scale: "So I could really have a good picture of what's going on. When you're doing the design a tiny postcard of it is not that helpful. This is the whole interchange area."

The assembled plan view, although still a minute fraction of the size of the physical area that it renders, extends what would be available within the limits of the CAD screen to something that becomes a space for joint work. Through it the object of Andrea's work is both viewable as a whole and still within arms' reach. Andrea described the annotations evident on the paper plans as the residue of engineers' "thinking with a pencil in their hand."[16] In addition to the annotated plans, I asked Andrea about a pad of graph paper sitting on top of the other sheets. She explained that she uses the pad for her calculations:

> What I'm trying to do on the pad is something that seems like an extra step, but personally I think that it's pretty important. I'm just trying to record the calculations that I'm doing, to determine clearances and to determine actual elevations. [explains specific problem] So I could just do the whole thing with my calculator, and that's what a lot of people do. I'd come up with the number and then I would write down the number and start working. But we're at the point where we need to check it. That's why I'm

---

[15] Kathryn Henderson (1991, 1999) described the use of sketches in mechanical engineering work, comparing the flexibility of paper media with CAD. The uses of paper that she observed included (a) conscription (i.e., the enrollment of others in joint work, consultations and the like); (b) "thinking with eyes and hands" (borrowing a phrase from Latour, 1990); and (c) making things visible and intelligible to others (e.g., through exhibits that make use of color highlighting). She summed up these observations with the statement that engineering is a "visual culture," characterized by Latour as "how a culture sees the world and makes it visible," by defining both "what it is to see" and "what there is to see" (1991, p. 469, Footnote 1; see also Goodwin, 1995).

[16] Alder (1998) described free hand sketches as "a quasi-private language, used as an extension of the creative process, or as a kind of private notation to oneself or one's immediate colleagues" (p. 512). It was against the idiosyncrasies of such sketches that the principles of descriptive geometry were developed by Bachelier and his colleagues in the mid-18th century. At the same time, it becomes clear from studies of contemporary engineering practice that freehand and projective drawing comprises less a developmental sequence than a repertoire of complementary and dialogic elements.

FIGURE 4 Paper plan views.

trying to be a bit more meticulous.... The way that I see it is that the big advantage of working it out on paper is that you're leaving a bit of a trail as to how you got to the thing that's the final answer. We also save previous iterations electronically, but they're not well documented. There's not an easy way to go back and say, did anyone ever try putting a 2 percent grade on this? I think it's nice to see on paper: Oh, look, she tried 2, 2.1, 2.2, 2.3 and 2.5, look, it goes right through the point that she needed to hit, and it works.

The object of Andrea's activity in this respect was not only to find the requisite grade for the roadway, but to produce a residual trace of her actions as a visible rendering of the calculative work that she had done. Another particularity of paper, then, is that work "black-boxed" by the machinery of the electronic calculator can be made visible, and in relation to the objects that it references. The engineers' pad serves not only as a space for calculation but as a technology of accountability that makes the course of her work retrospectively visible to her colleagues (see Ueno, this issue).

In elaborating the benefits of paper as a medium, Andrea explained that 6 months ago she tried to do more with CAD, but now has realized that paper is just better for some things. Andrea's tutorial instructed us that rather than a simple progression from paper to CAD, the maturing of electronically based engineering practice may emerge as the informed, selective use of both paper and digital media, based on a deepening understanding of their particularities and of their effective interrelation. CAD might be seen, moreover, as the logical extension, the embedding into a computational instrument, of what the early progenitors of the rules of engineering drawing took to be the benefits of descriptive geometry and other conventions, that is, their force as a corrective to the artisans "ignorant and prejudiced" imagination (Bachelier, 1768, quoted in Alder, 1998, p. 512). It becomes clear from our observations of the actual use of CAD as an aspect of Andrea's practice that the calculative powers of the machinery to "make things the same" (Alder, 1998) are effective only insofar as they are enlivened by her readings of the objects rendered, in and through the interface of her workstation, as the highly differentiated, more and less obdurate materials of a fully embodied, natural–artifactual world.

CONCLUSION: SOME REFLECTIONS ON THEORY

In this account of Andrea's tutorials, I have tried to convey a sense for the close interrelations of working practices and associated artifacts as together constituting the embodied practices of engineering work. My interest is to respecify the work of engineering from general formulations to specific occasions of professional practice at the screen and on paper. In focusing on the work's objects, I have emphasized some potential lines of connection between activity theoretic concerns with mediation and an ethnomethodological interest in phenomenal field properties of distinctive forms of professionalized practice. My discussion so far would seem to suggest little difference between these two programs. In this closing section, however, I wish to turn to at least one, potentially fundamental, difference between ethnomethodology and activity theory. This difference turns on their relations to the project of theorizing itself.

Speaking on behalf of activity theory, particularly with respect to its relevance for understanding work at the screen, Nardi (1996b) proposed that "[t]here is a fundamental need for a theory of practice in human-computer interaction studies" (p. xi), including a generic lexicon or common vocabulary. She continued:

> The development of a common vocabulary is crucial for HCI. As we move toward ethnographic and participatory design methods to discover and describe real everyday activity, we run into the problem that has bedeviled anthropology for so long: every account is an ad hoc description cast in situationally specific terms. Abstraction, generalization and comparison become problematic. An ethnographic description ... remains a narrative account structured according to the author's own personal vocabulary, largely unconstrained and arbitrary. (pp. 10–11)

Setting aside for the moment the question of whether this characterization does justice to the comparative research tradition that comprises anthropology,[17] what I am interested in are the basic premises that (a) the ad hoc, specifically situated character of accounts is a special problem for the social sciences that renders comparison impossible in the absence of a unifying theory and that (b) left to themselves, individuals construct accounts according to a "personal" vocabulary that is "unconstrained and arbitrary." This premise at once obscures what I think is in fact some of the common ground between activity theory and ethnomethodology and points to what are some important differences. The common ground that seems obscured here turns on the extent to which practitioners of activity theory and ethnomethodology alike view the terms of any account as culturally and historically constituted. Rather than rendering transcendent, eternal descriptions of generic human behavior, both produce narrative accounts that are themselves embodied and embedded in particular cultural and historical circumstances. Whatever their generality, lexicons, classification schemes, models, and the like are reflexively constituted as descriptive of particular occasions of

---

[17]For a recent discussion within anthropology of the status of ethnography as a comparative program, see, for example, Clifford and Marcus (1986), Marcus and Fischer (1986), and Gupta and Ferguson (1997).

everyday activity through, and only through, the cultural–historical practices of their production and use.

Taken as a theory-building project in the sense that Nardi (1996b) proposed, however, activity theory stands in profound tension with ethnomethodology. This tension is not, as Nardi suggested, a matter of systematic versus ad hoc analyses, but rather a matter of how we understand the relationship between the two and the project of theory-building more generally. In an article titled "Silence in Context: Ethnomethodology at the Margin of Social Theory," Michael Lynch (1997) took up the question of ethnomethodology's somewhat puzzling failure to engage in traditional practices of theory-building. Lynch recast this "failure" as a studied action and offered to fill the silence with an account of "ethnomethodology's distinctive stance toward theorising" (p. 2). As those with an orientation to the cultural–historical grounds of human activity should appreciate, ethnomethodology's stance toward theorizing does not arise out of nowhere, but rather is embedded within and responsive to the particular histories of traditional sociology. As Lynch put it,

> ethnomethodology depends upon classic sociology for its research motives and themes; and thus, one needs to be thoroughly acquainted with established research traditions in sociology to appreciate why and how ethnomethodology disturbs them. (p. 6)

It is in this sense that ethnomethodology's silence is contextual, a meaningful one and not simply an absence. Lynch's argument is that ethnomethodology is not so much atheoretical as deliberately marginal, in a way that makes the margins of social theory instructive. The margins that ethnomethodology inhabits are not, he pointed out, about some kind of empiricist alternative to theorizing that posits a purely inductive process of "just seeing" what's "really" going on. Although acknowledging the use by ethnomethodologists of phrases like "naturally occurring," "actual," and the like, Lynch argued that these are specifically contextual injunctions not for empiricism but against the perpetuation of sociology as a literary, rather than an empirical, endeavor. Empiricism and empirical study are two quite different matters. Moreover, as Lynch put it: "Ethnomethodology does not simply offer an alternative theory or method … it provides an alternative sociological *practice*" (p. 6).

That practice, among other things, resists taking up the rules of sociological method, in particular the various procedures that turn lived experience and embodied practice into general lexicons and associated models. Rendered as a literary enterprise in this sense, social theory-building becomes a conversation that provides its own materials, self-referentially. Empirical studies then, not empiricism, are lost.

Some in activity theory have drawn attention as well to the problematic aspects of a view of activity theory as a theory of activity-in-general. As Kuutti (1996) put it,

> both parts of the term activity theory … are slightly misleading, because the tradition is neither interested in activities in general, nor is it a theory, that is, a fixed body of accurately defined statements. (p. 25)

It must be the case, moreover, that practitioners of activity theory themselves actually develop the meanings and extensions of the terms of the theory, in any actual instance, in a way that is necessarily contingent and even, forgive the expression, ad hoc. Any instance of the use of activity theory's canonical triangle, for example, involves a mapping of its generic terms to some aspects of the activity in question, selected to characterize it for the practical purposes of mapping it. That such mappings are—must be—ad hoc makes them no less purposeful and systematic. Rather it is falsely dichotomous to oppose the two.

Theory-building and theories-in-use are themselves specifically situated activities. The terms of the activity theoretic triangle—subjects, objects, rules, divisions of labor—are what Garfinkel (1996) called "Durkheimian things," that is, aspects of the ordinary society continually reproduced in and only in the details of lived experience and everyday activity. Like its objects, the work of the theory is accomplished not by the general lexicon but always in situ and specifically by those engaged in activities of theorizing. In Kuutti's (1996) words,

> it is impossible to make a general classification of what an activity is, what an action is, and so forth because the definition is totally dependent on what the subject or object in a particular real situation is. (p. 32)

Garfinkel (1996) argued that however much procedures of formal analysis replace the specific details of practical action with general constructs, they nonetheless thoroughly rely on those specifics both for their own activities of theory-building and for the intelligibility of their products. Nor, in Garfinkel's view, should the goal of social studies be to find a remedy to this fact, taken as a "problem." It is in this sense that ethnomethodology refuses the call to engage in theory-building, not because of some claim to be without presuppositions but out of "an uneasiness about the summons" (Lynch, 1997, p. 19). The summons to theory that is rejected is the demand that we treat the specific concreteness of practical activity, like the practices of engineering work considered here, as a problem to be solved. Instead, the proposal is that we take practical activity—including its unruliness, its "ad hocery" and its endless detail—as just the fundamental phenomenon that we as students of human activity are out to recover.

ACKNOWLEDGMENTS

My thanks in the writing of this article go first to Andrea for her dedication and gifts as an engineer, her humor and eloquence in speaking about her work, and her generosity in taking the time to help us make sense of it all. I'm indebted as well to the rest of the members of the engineering project team and to my colleagues Jeanette Blomberg and Randy Trigg, with whom this research has been a thoroughgoing collaboration. Finally, thanks to Chuck Goodwin, Aug Nishizaka, and Naoki Ueno for their helpful comments on an earlier draft.

REFERENCES

Akrich, M. (1992). The de-scription of technical objects. In W. Bijker & J. Law (Eds.), *Shaping technology/building society* (pp. 205–224). Cambridge, MA: MIT Press.

Alder, K. (1998). Making things the same: Representation, tolerance and the end of the *Ancient Regime* in France. *Social Studies of Science, 28,* 499–545.

Blomberg, J., Suchman, L., & Trigg, R. (1996). Reflections on a work-oriented design project. *Human–Computer Interaction, 11,* 237–265.

Bødker, S. (1991). *Through the interface: A human activity approach to user interface design.* Hillsdale, NJ: Lawrence Erlbaum Associates, Inc.

Bødker, S. (1996). Applying activity theory to video analysis: How to make sense of video data in human–computer interaction. In B. Nardi (Ed.), *Context and consciousness* (pp. 147–174). Cambridge, MA: MIT Press.

Button, G., & Sharrock, W. (1998). The organizational accountability of technological work. *Social Studies of Science, 28,* 73–102.

Clifford, J., & Marcus, G. (Eds.). (1986). *Writing culture: The poetics and politics of ethnography.* Berkeley: University of California Press.

Cole, M., & Engeström, Y. (1993). A cultural–historical approach to distributed cognition. In G. Salomon (Ed.), *Distributed cognition: Psychological and educational considerations* (pp. 1–47). Cambridge, England: Cambridge University Press.

Engeström, Y. (1990). *Learning, working and imagining: Twelve studies in activity theory.* Helsinki, Finland: Orienta-Konsultit.

Garfinkel, H. (Ed.). (1986). *Ethnomethodological studies of work.* London: Routledge & Kegan Paul.

Garfinkel, H. (1996). Ethnomethodology's program. *Social Psychology Quarterly, 59,* 5–21.

Goodwin, C. (1994). Professional vision. *American Anthropologist, 96,* 606–633.

Goodwin, C. (1995). Seeing in depth. *Social Studies of Science, 25,* 237–274.

Goodwin, C. (in press). *Pointing as situated practice.* Manuscript in preparation.

Gupta, A., & Ferguson. J. (Eds.). (1997). *Anthropological locations: Boundaries and grounds of a field science.* Berkeley: University of California Press.

Gurwitsch, A. (1964). *The field of consciousness.* Pittsburgh, PA: Duquesne University Press.

Henderson, K. (1991). Flexible sketches and inflexible data bases: Visual communication, conscription devices, and boundary objects in design engineering. *Science, Technology & Human Values, 16,* 448–473.

Henderson, K. (1999). *On line and on paper: Visual representations, visual culture, and computer graphics in design engineering.* Cambridge, MA: MIT Press.

Heritage, J. (1984). *Garfinkel and ethnomethodology.* Cambridge, England: Polity.

Kuutti, K. (1996). Activity theory as a potential framework for human–computer interaction research. In B. Nardi (Ed.), *Context and consciousness* (pp. 17–44). Cambridge, MA: MIT Press.

Latour, B. (1990). Drawing things together. In M. Lynch & S. Woolgar (Eds.), *Representation in scientific practice* (pp. 19–68). Cambridge, MA: MIT Press.

Livingston, E. (1987). *Making sense of ethnomethodology.* London: Routledge & Kegan Paul.

Lynch, M. (1993). *Scientific practice and ordinary action: Ethnomethodology and social studies of science.* Cambridge, England: Cambridge University Press.

Lynch, M. (1997, August). *Silence in context: Ethnomethodology at the margins of social theory.* Paper presented at the Ethnomethodology East and West Conference, Tokyo, Japan.

Marcus, G., & Fischer, M. (1986). *Anthropology as cultural critique.* Chicago: University of Chicago Press.

Mialet, H. (1999). Do angels have bodies? Two stories about subjectivity in science: The cases of William X and Mister H. *Social Studies of Science, 29,* 551–582.

Nardi, B. (1996a) Activity theory and human–computer interaction. In B. Nardi (Ed.), *Context and consciousness* (pp. 7–16). Cambridge, MA: MIT Press.

Nardi, B. (1996b). Preface. In B. Nardi (Ed.), *Context and consciousness.* (pp. xi–xii). Cambridge, MA: MIT Press.

Petroski, H. (1995). *Engineers of dreams: Great bridge builders and the spanning of America.* New York: Random House.

Sims, B. (1999). Concrete practices: Testing in an earthquake-engineering laboratory. *Social Studies of Science, 29,* 483–518.

Star, S. L. (1989). Layered space, formal representations and long-distance control. *Fundamena Scientiae, 10,* 125–155.

Suchman, L. (2000). Organizing alignment: The case of bridge-building. *Organization, 7,* 311–327.

Suchman, L., Trigg, R., & Blomberg, J. (1998, August). Working artifacts: Ethnomethods of the prototype. Paper presented at the annual meeting of the American Sociological Association, San Francisco.

Trigg, R., Blomberg, J., & Suchman, L. (1999). Moving document collections online: The evolution of a shared repository. In *Proceedings of the European Conference on Computer- Supported Cooperative Work (ECSCW'99)* (pp. 331–350). Dordrecht, The Netherlands: Kluwer.

MIND, CULTURE, AND ACTIVITY, 7(1&2), 19–36

Practices of Color Classification

Charles Goodwin

Applied Linguistics
University of California–Los Angeles

Color categories sit at the intersection of 2 central topics in the study of human cognition: (a) the analysis of vision, and (b) the study of semantic categories, or more generally processes of classification. Using as data videotape of archaeologists filling out a coding sheet that requires them to systematically describe the color of the dirt they have excavated, this article describes the practices required to competently classify color within the work life of their profession. The task of color classification is embedded within a situated activity system, which includes not only several different ways of identifying the same color (each designed for alternative uses), but also cognitive artifacts, such as a Munsell color chart and specific embodied practices. The chart creates a historically constituted architecture for perception, a heterotopia that juxtaposes in a single visual field 2 very different kinds of space. As multiple parties fill out the coding sheet together, the full resources of the organization of talk-in-interaction are brought to bear on the contingent tasks they are charged with accomplishing. This investigation of a situated activity system encompassing not only semantic categories, but also physical tools and embodied practices, contrasts with most previous research on color categories, which has focused almost exclusively on mental phenomena, and not on how people perform color classification to pursue a relevant course of action in the consequential settings that make up their lifeworld.

One of the most enduring topics in the study of cognition is the analysis of categories. This article uses videotapes of archaeologists in the field classifying color to investigate how categories are socially organized as situated practices.

At times categorization has constituted the major agenda of entire fields, such as cognitive anthropology. The classic work of Berlin and Kay (1967, 1969) on color categories provides an excellent example of one major approach to the study of human cognition. Different languages classify the color spectrum in different ways. This has been argued to provide evidence for the Sapir–Whorf hypothesis that language structures perception of the world (Bruner, Oliver, & Greenfield, 1966; Greenfield & Bruner, 1966). However, Berlin and Kay (1969) demonstrated that the diversity of human color systems was built on a universal infrastructure, one almost certainly linked to structures in the brain. To show this, Berlin and Kay first located a basic set of color terms in a number of different languages. Then they had speakers of those languages show which color patches on a Munsell color chart fell within the boundaries of each basic color term. The Munsell chart, consisting of carefully prepared samples of precisely defined colors arranged in a grid, is the accepted reference standard for color description. When Berlin and Kay compared

---

Requests for reprints should be sent to Charles Goodwin, Applied Linguistics, UCLA, Los Angeles, CA 90095–1531. E-mail: cgoodwin@humnet.ucla.edu

the Munsell maps for different languages, they found that all languages locate the foci of their basic color labels at roughly the same place in the color spectrum and, moreover, that a universal pattern exists for adding basic color terms to a language. If a language has only two color names, they will be black and white; if it has three, the third will be red; the fourth will be either green or yellow; blue will be added next, and so on. This work remains one of the central accomplishments of cognitive anthropology.

The theories and methods used to analyze how human beings build and use categories are themselves shaped by deep assumptions about what counts as human cognition, where it is located, and what constitutes an interesting and important finding. Clearly visible in the work of Berlin and Kay (1967, 1969) are a number of quite pervasive assumptions about the underlying organization of both language and cognition. First, the structures that provide universal mechanisms for human cognition reside in two interrelated places: the human brain and a linguistic system. Cognition is a psychological process, and its crucial machinery is found within the human skull. Second, meaning is defined in terms of reference, for example, the range of color patches that a speaker of a particular language identifies as falling within the scope of a specific color term. Third, the basic units being sampled are human languages such as English, Japanese, and Tezeltal. The color systems of different languages are systematically compared with each other. Fourth, this vision of where the crucial phenomena relevant to the organization of cognition were to be found had important methodological consequences. Berlin and Kay never looked at how people use color categories to pursue a relevant course of action in the consequential scenes that make up their lifeworld. Instead, all of their informants were performing exactly the same experimental task, and, with the exception of the Tzeltal speakers, all of the speakers resided in the San Francisco Bay area. The notion of a community of competent practitioners was completely irrelevant to Berlin and Kay's analysis; indeed for many languages, only a single speaker was used.

It is, however, possible to conceptualize human cognition in ways that challenge these assumptions. Thus, with respect to the second assumption in which meaning is analyzed in terms of reference, Wittgenstein (1958; see also Baker & Hacker, 1980) argued that the meaning of a term is not its bearer, the entities it refers to (e.g., shades of color). Instead, the study of meaning should focus on description of the practices required to use a term appropriately within a relevant language game. By looking at how participants deploy categories as constitutive features of the endogenous activities that make up their lifeworld, Sacks and his colleagues (e.g., Sacks, 1992; Schegloff, 1972) developed a thoroughly social perspective on human category use, and cognition more generally. The social organization of scientific practice has been insightfully probed by scholars from a number of disciplines (Latour, 1987; Lynch, 1993; Lynch & Woolgar, 1988; Pickering, 1992; Shapin & Schaffer, 1985; and much other most interesting work). The work of Vygotsky (1962; see also Cole, 1985; Wertsch, 1985) initiated another approach to cognition, one that stressed not only the social activities of multiple participants, but also the importance of tools and other artifacts (Hutchins, 1995; Kawatoko, 1995; Ueno, 1995).

We begin by looking at how archaeologists classify color as one component of the work of competently excavating a site. Rather than being lodged entirely in the world of mental representations, the perceptual task of assessing color as an archaeologist requires systematic use of specific tools, indeed the very tool used by Berlin and Kay (1969): a Munsell color chart. As a coding framework, the chart both mediates perceptual access to the dirt being classified and provides a color reference standard. This tool does not stand alone as a self-explicating artifact; instead, its proper use is embedded within a set of systematic work practices. Moreover, these practices vary from community to community. Though the chart is used by both archaeologists and linguistic anthropologists (as well as other professions concerned with color), each discipline situates the chart within different sets of work procedures. In brief, we suggest that an appropriate unit for the cognitive processes involved in color discrimination is not the brain in isolation, or the categories provided by semantic systems of languages as self-contained entities, but instead the *situated activity systems* used by endogenous work groups to properly constitute the categories that are relevant to the work they are engaged in.[1] Rather than sustaining an opposition between the "mental" and the "material," such activity systems seamlessly link phenomena such as the embodied actions of participants, physical tools, language use, work relevant writing practices, and so on into the patterns of coordinated action that make up the lifeworld of a work group.

Central to the cognitive processes that constitute science are writing practices quite unlike those typically studied by social scientists investigating literacy. To generate a data set—collections of observations that can be compared with each other—scientists use coding schemes to transform the world that they scrutinize into the categories and events that are relevant to the work of their profession (Cicourel, 1964, 1968) When disparate events are viewed through a single coding scheme, equivalent observations become possible. The process of systematically making relevant observations about the color of the materials being examined, and then writing them on a coding form, locates a small activity system. Within it the categorization of color is mediated by both material artifacts and specific work-relevant practices. Moreover, the vision required to see color in this activity has strong temporal, historical, and spatial dimensions as well; to competently perform the task, the technician(s) coding the data must use a tool to look at a specific space at a particular point in the process.

The medium that archaeologists work in is dirt. In the sequence that is examined, a pair of archaeology students is faced with the task of describing the dirt that they have just excavated. They are faced with the task because they have been given a coding form that has to be filled out (see Figure 1). The form contains slots for describing the color, consistency, and texture of the dirt being examined. Those filling in the form are faced with the task of systematically examining the dirt and making appropriate entries in each slot.

The use of coding forms such as this to organize the perception of nature, events, or people within the discourse of a profession carries with it an array of perceptual and cognitive operations that have far-reaching impact. First, by using such a system, a worker views the world from the perspective it establishes. Of all the possible ways that the earth could be looked at, the perceptual work of students using this form is focused on determining the exact color of a minute sample of dirt. They engage in active cognitive work, but the parameters of that work have been established by the system that is organizing their perception. Insofar as the coding scheme establishes an orientation toward the world, it constitutes a structure of intentionality whose proper locus is not the isolated, Cartesian mind, but a much larger organizational system, one that is characteristically mediated through mundane bureaucratic documents such as forms. Coding schemes distributed on forms allow a senior investigator to inscribe his or her perceptual distinctions into the work practices of the technicians who code the data. Smith (1990) noted that

---

[1] See Goodwin (1994, 1996), Goodwin and Goodwin (1996), Heath (1986), Heath and Luff (1992), Nishizaka (this volume), Suchman (1992), and Whalen (1995) for other relevant analysis of how seeing is lodged within situated courses of action.

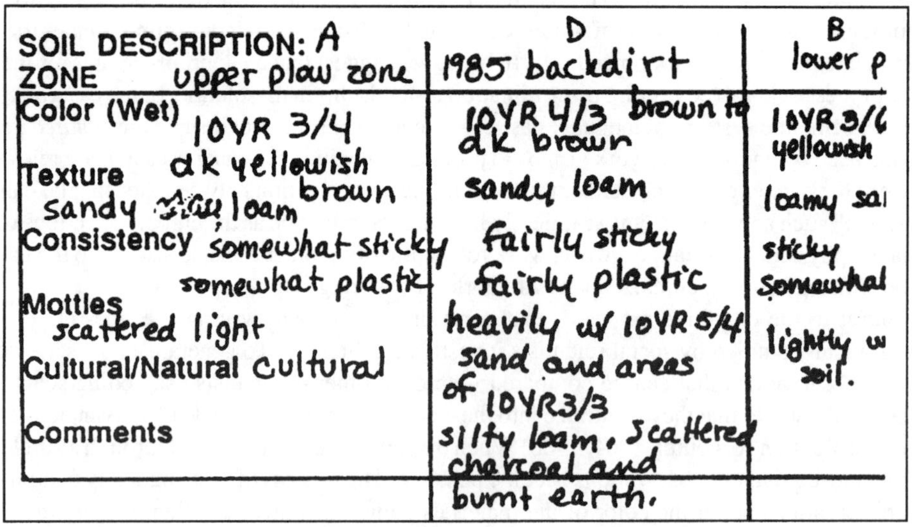

SOIL DESCRIPTION: A ZONE upper plow zone	D 1985 backdirt	B lower p
Color (Wet) 10YR 3/4	10YR 4/3 brown to dk brown	10YR 3/6 yellowish
Texture dk yellowish sandy clay loam brown	sandy loam	loamy sa
Consistency somewhat sticky somewhat plastic	fairly sticky fairly plastic	sticky somewhat
Mottles scattered light	heavily w/ 10YR 5/4 sand and areas	lightly w soil.
Cultural/Natural cultural	of 10YR3/3	
Comments	silty loam. Scattered charcoal and burnt earth.	

FIGURE 1   Coding form for excavated dirt.

the investigation of texts as constituents of social relations offers access to the ontological ground of institutional processes which organize, govern and regulate the kind of society in which we live, for these are to a significant degree forms of social action mediated by texts. (pp. 121–122)

Under the influence of Bakhtin (1981), considerable attention has been paid to multivocality. However, most of that work has focused on literary genres or oral narrative. Moreover, with the notable exception of work in conversation analysis, dialogic phenomena have been most frequently investigated within the scope of utterances spoken by a single speaker, albeit one reporting the speech of another. A quite different kind of multivocality, one organized by the craft requirements of a work task rather than the genres of the literary academy, can be found in mundane, bureaucratic forms. Such documents bring together on a single surface texts authored by different individuals situated at different positions within a work organization. This multiple authorship is frequently shown quite vividly in the contrast between printed text that remains invariant across many settings (e.g., the category labels such as "color" and "texture" in the document reproduced above) and the handwritten entries of the different parties who actually code the data (or in some work settings highlight and annotate a common form to adapt it to the needs of locally situated users). Such systems provide an example of how distributed cognition is organized through the writing practices that coordinate action across space and time within an organization.

Rather than standing alone as self-explicating textual objects, forms are embedded within webs of socially organized, situated practices. To make an entry in the slot provided for color, an archaeologist must make use of another tool, the set of standard color samples provided by a Munsell chart. This chart incorporates into a portable physical object the results of a long history of scientific investigation of the properties of color. The version of this chart that archaeologists bring into the field has been tailored to the distinctive requirements of their work situation. First, the color samples are organized as pages that fit into a small, loose-leaf book that can be easily carried to the field. Second, because dirt typically contains only a limited range of color, only a subset of the color samples that would be found in a complete chart (approximately one fifth of the total) are necessary for the work that archaeologists do.[2] Issues of cost also figure into this calculation. Even the reduced sample book costs $80. Although this is inexpensive enough to risk taking into harsh field conditions, it is still considered a costly, valuable tool to be carefully protected. By being adapted to the specific requirements of their work, the Munsell book used by archaeologists is as small, portable, and inexpensive as possible. Third, circular holes are cut next to each color patch. The archaeologist holds a sample of the dirt being coded on a trowel under the page. The trowel is moved from hole to hole until the best fit between the color of the dirt on the trowel and an adjacent patch on the chart is found.

Foucault (1970, 1986) used the term *heterotopia* to mark "a relatively segregated place in which several spatial settings coexist, each being both concrete and symbolically loaded" (Ophir & Shapin, 1991, p. 13). With elegant simplicity, the Munsell page with its holes for viewing the sample of dirt on the trowel juxtaposes in a single visual field two quite different kinds of spaces: (a) Actual dirt from the site at the archaeologists' feet is framed by (b) a theoretical space for the rigorous, replicable, classification of color. The latter is a conceptual space, the product of considerable research into properties of color, and an actual physical space instantiated in the orderly modification of variables arranged in a grid on the Munsell page. Ophir and Shapin (1991) proposed that in the modern West the sites where science is done are fundamentally heterotopic spaces (p. 13). This notion is applicable not only to tools such as the Munsell book, but also to the excavation site itself, with its specialized personnel making visible the phenomena that define their discipline in limited, carefully organized places, such as the pits they systematically dig. Though segregated from the everyday world just outside its borders, the site and its tools are systematically linked to the work and activities of other archaeologists. Thus the Munsell book encapsulates in a material object theory and solutions developed by earlier workers at other sites faced with the task of color classification. The pages juxtaposing color patches and viewing holes that allow the dirt to be seen right next to the color sample provide a historically constituted architecture for perception.[3]

The Munsell system organizes color description by using three variables: Hue, Chroma, and Value. Each page in the book is organized as a grid of Chroma and Value samples for a single Hue. In addition to the samples and viewing holes, each Munsell page also contains several different kinds of written text: (a) numbers; (b) labels for the two axes, with Value from bottom to top and

---

[2]Indeed, archaeologists have adapted their version of the book from that used by soil scientists and published by the Department of Agriculture. However, once this tool is placed in the context of their work, new uses can be found for it. For example, rather than being applied only to the description of soil, some archaeologists are now using it to describe the colors of pottery fragments and other artifacts. This requires a wider range of color samples. New pages, irrelevant to the work of scientists who focus exclusively on soils, have to be purchased. The design of this book as a loose-leaf notebook, rather than a bound volume, makes this possible (for interesting analysis of the importance of loose-leaf books to the development of documents capable of coordinating distributed work, such as nineteenth-century train schedules, see Yates, 1989). For a description of the Munsell chart by another group of scientists, biologists working the Amazon forest, see Latour (1995). See Lynch (1988) for more general analysis of how the practices, tools, and documents used by scientists to make the phenomena that are the focus of their work visible constitute in effect an "externalized retina" built through public discursive practices (see Figure 2).

[3]A most relevant and insightful analysis of similar organization in navigational tools can be found in Hutchins (1995). See Goodwin (1995) for analysis of the articulation of multiple heterotopic spaces in the work practices of oceanographers.

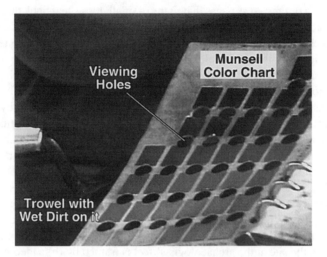

FIGURE 2   Using the Munsell chart.

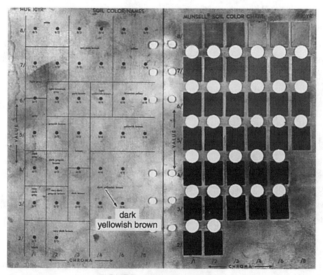

FIGURE 3   Munsell pages.

Chroma from left to right; and (c) standard color names, such as "dark yellowish brown," which are found on the facing page to the left of the actual sample page (because of the reduced size and degradation of the small print on the original page, I've rewritten the bottom right color name in larger type; see Figure 3).

The page thus provides not one, but three complementary systems for identifying a reference color: (a) the actual color patch; (b) numeric coordinates specifying its position in the grid (e.g.,

"3/4"); and (c) color names. Moreover, these systems are not precisely equivalent to each other. For example, a single color name may include several different color patches and grid descriptions. Thus, on the page reproduced previously, the color name "dark yellowish brown" in the bottom right quadrant of the grid refers to four patches or sets of coordinates: 4/4, 4/6, 3/4, and 3/6. Similarly "yellow brown" just above it includes 5/4/, 5/6, and 5/8.

Why does the Munsell page contain multiple, overlapping representations of what is apparently the same entity (e.g., a particular choice within a larger set of color categories)? The answer seems to lie in the way that each representation makes possible alternative operations and actions and thus fits into different kinds of activities. Both the names and numbered grid coordinates can be written and thus easily transported from the actual excavation to the other work sites, such as laboratories and journals, that constitute archaeology as a profession. Unlike the names, the numbers can be used in statistical analysis (the patches are carefully constructed to represent equal intervals). Moreover, as noted in the preface to the Munsell soil color book that archaeologists use, numbers are "especially useful for international correlation, since no translation of color names is needed" (Munsell Color, 1990, p. ii). However, despite its greater precision, the number system has its own distinct liabilities. To grasp the color being referred to as "10 YR 3/4," a reader needs access to a Munsell book. Color names, such "dark yellowish brown," are thus more appropriate than the numbers for general journal publication, because they can be recognized and compared, roughly but adequately for the purposes of the moment, by any speaker of the language. The outcome of the activity of color classification initiated by the empty square on the coding form is thus a set of portable linguistic objects that can easily be incorporated into the unfolding chains of inscription that lead step by step from the dirt at the site to reports in the archaeological literature (see also Hutchins, 1995). However, as arbitrary linguistic signs produced in a medium that does not actually make visible color, neither the color names nor the numbers allow direct visual comparison between a sample of dirt and a reference color. This is precisely what the color patches and viewing holes make possible. Moreover, as discrete, bounded places on the surface of the page, they can be identified not only through language, but also by pointing. In brief, rather than simply specifying unique points in a larger color space, the Munsell chart is used in multiple overlapping activities (comparing a reference color and a patch of dirt as part of the work of classification, transporting those results back to the lab, comparing samples, publishing reports, etc.) and thus represents the "same" entity, a particular color, in multiple ways, each of which makes possible different kinds of operations because of the unique properties of each representational system.

Social scientists sometimes characterize heterotopias as the epitome of disorder (Kahn, 1995). Thus heterotopias are described as spaces "with a multitude of localities containing things so different that it is impossible to find a common logic for them, a space in which everything is somehow out of place" (Ralph, 1991, p. 104). For Foucault (1970)[4] heterotopias can be disturbing "because they destroy 'syntax'" (p. xviii). Quite to the contrary, the heterotopic space brought into existence by the juxtaposition of the Munsell page and the dirt being scrutinized creates a new, highly ordered syntax, and moreover one that sheds considerable light on unique features of human cognition. Unlike most other animals, human beings have the ability to secrete cognitive or-

---

[4]Foucault's (1970) discussion of hetertopias is complex, insightful, and metaphorical. His comments about lack of syntax follow a discussion of Borges' fanciful classification of animals into incommensurate classes. I'm using the term *heterotopia* in a more literal sense, to describe the juxtaposition of unlike spaces. Some of what he opposes to Borges, such as his description of a tabula, would be quite consistent with my use of the term.

ganization into the world they inhabit in ways that create new forms of both knowledge and action, while transforming the environment within which relevant activities are accomplished. The Munsell page is a quintessential cognitive artifact. It is simultaneously a material object and a conceptual tool. It relies upon the specific properties of material media to build cognitive structure that could not exist within the confines of the skull, for example the arrangement of possibilities for color classification into an ordered grid that can be repeatedly scanned, the production of actual reference samples that can be visually compared both with each other and with the material being classified, the preservation of the reference samples across time and space, and so on. All of these operations depend upon the properties of specific physical objects. However, such objects do not exist, and could not exist, in a purely "natural" world, for example, a domain not structured by human practices. By juxtaposing unlike spaces, but ones relevant to the accomplishment of a specific cognitive task, the chart creates a new, distinctively human, kind of space. Moreover, with its view holes for scrutinizing samples, the page is not simply a perspicuous representation of current scientific knowledge about the organization of color, but a space designed for the ongoing production of particular kinds of action.

The spatial arrangement of entities on the chart also informs the syntax for use of some of the linguistic entities it contains. Both Chroma on the x-axis of the grid and Value on the y-axis are described through use of the same numbers (e.g., "4"). A convention has been adopted in which these numbers are to be produced in a particular order: The first number represents the Value and the second the Chroma. This convention is stated explicitly in the instructions at the beginning of the book and is represented on each page in the way that the numbers identifying rows and columns are presented: Value numbers on the y-axis are always followed by a slash (e.g., "4/"), whereas Chroma numbers for columns along the x-axis are preceded by a slash (e.g., "/4").

The chart does not stand alone as an isolated tool; instead, its proper, appropriate use is situated within a larger set of work-relevant practices. First, a place for taking a sample of dirt from the site has to be chosen. In its original location in the ground itself, the dirt to be sampled is embedded within a dense, complex visual environment. A trowel is used to lift the sample from this dense perceptual field so that it can be scrutinized in isolation. A figure constituted as the object of current work-relevant attention, the dirt on the tip of the trowel, is quite literally extracted from an amorphous ground. This process of positioning for perception is one particular type of highlighting (Goodwin, 1994), one of the most general practices used to reshape phenomena in the domain being scrutinized by a work group so that just those events that are relevant to the tasks they are engaged in are made salient.[5]

Archaeologists know from experience that the apparent color of a bit of dirt can be modified by many factors. After the dirt has been placed on the trowel, it is sprayed with water. By squirting all samples with water, some of the variables relevant to the perception of its color can be controlled by creating a consistent environment for viewing. The moment where the archaeologist gazes at the dirt through the Munsell chart is thus but one stage within a larger sequence of temporally unfolding practices.

Mundane, routine work with the Munsell chart seems quite distant from the abstract world of archaeological theory and the debates that are currently animating the discipline. However, the encounter between coding scheme and the world that occurs as the archaeologist in the field holds a sample of dirt under the Munsell page is one example of a key locus for scientific practice. This

---

[5]See Goodwin (1997) for description of quite similar practices used by chemists to extract fibers whose color must be evaluated from the dark solution where they are being processed.

is the place where the multifaceted complexity of "nature" is transformed into the phenomenal categories that make up the work environment of a scientific discipline. It is precisely here that nature is transformed into culture.

Despite the rigorous way in which the combination of a tool such as the Munsell color chart and the practices developed by archaeologists for its relevant and appropriate use, structure perception of the dirt being scrutinized—finding the correct category for the classification of a bit of dirt—is not an automatic or even easy task. According to the instructions at the beginning of the Munsell book,

> Rarely will the color of the sample be perfectly matched by any color in the chart. The probability of having a perfect matching of the sample color is less than one in one hundred. (Munsell Color, 1990, p. iv)

Rather than automatic matching, the person doing the coding is charged with making a competent judgment, deciding which of the chart's colors the sample falls between and which reference color provides the closest, but by no means exact, match. Moreover, the very way in which the Munsell chart provides a context-free reference standard creates problems of its own. The color patches on the chart are glossy, whereas dirt never is, so that the chart color and the sample color never look exactly the same. In the following example (see Figure 4A & 4B), two students at the field school looking at exactly the same dirt and reference colors disagree as to how it should be classified.[6]

In this sequence, the task of color classification is organized within a situated activity system that links a range of apparently disparate phenomena, including talk, the bodies of the participants, the dirt they are examining, and the tools being used to scrutinize that dirt, into a coherent course of action. It is useful to begin with consideration of the participation framework visible in the orientation of their bodies. For Goffman (1961), "focused interaction occurs when people effectively agree to sustain for a time a single focus of cognitive and visual attention" (p. 7). Orientation to such a common focus organizes the bodies of participants in an encounter into visible patterns of mutual orientation that frame the talk and other interaction that occurs within them (Kendon, 1990). Goodwin (1981) demonstrated the central importance of mutual gaze between speakers and hearers in the organization of turns-at-talk in conversation. However, here the parties are gazing not at each other, but instead at the Munsell page with the dirt sample beneath it. This chart with its viewing holes organizes not only the color spectrum represented on its surface, but also the embodied actions of those who use it. Its proper use proposes a particular orientation of the body and focus of attention. The participation framework necessary for the analysis of what is happening here thus includes not only the bodies of the participants, but also the tools they are using. Color classification could be done, indeed characteristically is done, by a single archaeologist peering through the Munsell book alone. In light of this, it is possible to see the defining feature noted in Goffman's definition, a focus of cognitive and visual attention, as applying not only

---

[6]Talk is transcribed using a slightly modified version of the system developed by Gail Jefferson (see Sacks et al., 1974). Talk receiving some form of emphasis (e.g., talk that would be underlined in a typewritten transcript using the Jefferson system) is marked with bold italics. Punctuation is used to transcribe intonation: A period indicates falling pitch, a question mark rising pitch, and a comma falling contour, as would be found for example after a nonterminal item in a list. A colon indicates lengthening of the current sound. Comments (e.g., descriptions of relevant nonvocal behavior) are printed in italics within double parentheses. Numbers within single parentheses mark silences in seconds and tenths of a second. A degree sign (°) indicates that the talk that follows is being spoken with low volume. Left brackets connecting talk by different speakers marks the point where overlap begins (see Figures 4A and 4B).

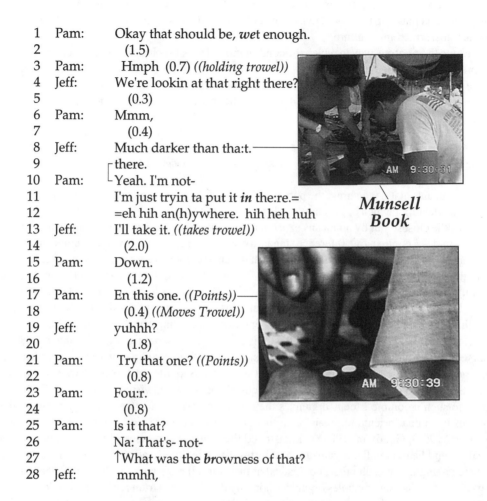

1	Pam:	Okay that should be, *wet* enough.
2		(1.5)
3	Pam:	Hmph (0.7) ((holding trowel))
4	Jeff:	We're lookin at that right there?
5		(0.3)
6	Pam:	Mmm,
7		(0.4)
8	Jeff:	Much darker than tha:t.
9		⌐there.
10	Pam:	⌐Yeah. I'm not-
11		I'm just tryin ta put it *in* the:re.=
12		=eh hih an(h)ywhere. hih heh huh
13	Jeff:	I'll take it. ((takes trowel))
14		(2.0)
15	Pam:	Down.
16		(1.2)
17	Pam:	En this one. ((Points))
18		(0.4) ((Moves Trowel))
19	Jeff:	yuhhh?
20		(1.8)
21	Pam:	Try that one? ((Points))
22		(0.8)
23	Pam:	Fou:r.
24		(0.8)
25	Pam:	Is it that?
26		Na: That's- not-
27		↑What was the *brow*ness of that?
28	Jeff:	mmhh,

Munsell Book

FIGURE 4A   Classifying color as situated practice (1).

to focused multiparty interaction, but also the engagement of a single party with a relevant tool that organizes a visible focus of attention[7] (though quite properly this situation would fall outside the scope of Goffman's focus on multiparty interaction). In brief, rather than drawing an analytic bubble that ends at the actors' bodies, it is useful to extend the notion of participation framework to encompass as well the tools that participants are working with.

Let us now look more closely at how action is organized within this framework. Use of the Munsell chart structures the activity of color classification in a quite specific way. To locate the proper color category, the sample is moved from color patch to color patch under the or-

---

[7]See also Streeck and LeBaron (1995).

dered grid provided by the page until the best match is found. Through use of the chart, the process of color classification has been reorganized as a spatial task. Consider for a moment some of the issues posed in the analysis of action that includes an intrinsic spatial component. A goal in American football occurs when a player carrying a ball crosses a particular line drawn on the field where the game is played. The action can be neither defined nor analyzed by looking at the body of the running player alone. Instead, the playing field, as a visible arrangement in space that carries specific kinds of meaning as defined by the rules of the game, makes possible forms of action (balls going out of bounds, touchdowns, etc.) that could not exist without it. The Munsell chart, the place where the archaeologists performing this classification are looking so intently, provides a similar arena for the constitution of meaningful ac-

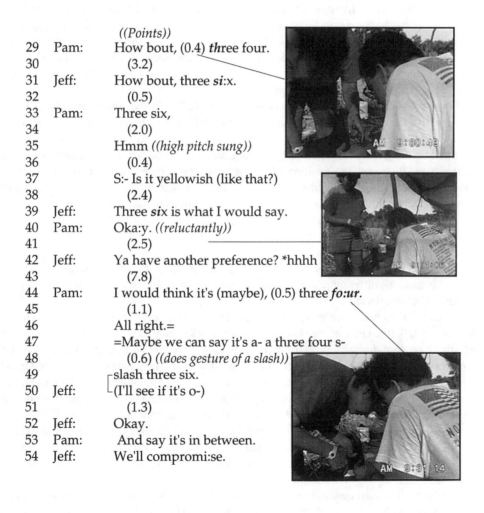

		((Points))
29	Pam:	How bout, (0.4) *three* four.
30		(3.2)
31	Jeff:	How bout, three *si:*x.
32		(0.5)
33	Pam:	Three six,
34		(2.0)
35		Hmm ((high pitch sung))
36		(0.4)
37		S:- Is it yellowish (like that?)
38		(2.4)
39	Jeff:	Three *six* is what I would say.
40	Pam:	Oka:y. ((reluctantly))
41		(2.5)
42	Jeff:	Ya have another preference? *hhhh
43		(7.8)
44	Pam:	I would think it's (maybe), (0.5) three *fo:ur*.
45		(1.1)
46		All right.=
47		=Maybe we can say it's a- a three four s-
48		(0.6) ((does gesture of a slash))
49		⌐slash three six.
50	Jeff:	⌊(I'll see if it's o-)
51		(1.3)
52	Jeff:	Okay.
53	Pam:	And say it's in between.
54	Jeff:	We'll compromi:se.

FIGURE 4B   Classifying color as situated practice (2).

tion.[8] At line 17, Pam moves her hand to the space above the page and points at a particular color patch while saying "En this one." Within the field of action created by the activity in progress this is not simply an indexical gesture, but a proposal that the indicated color might be the one they are searching for. It creates a new context in which a reply from Jeff is the expected next action.

In Line 19, Jeff rejects the proposed color. His move occurs after a noticeable silence in Line 18. Dispreferred actions in conversation, such as this rejection, are frequently preceded by gaps (Pomerantz, 1984). However, when the tape is examined, something else seems to be going on. The silence is not an empty space, but a place occupied by its own relevant activity (Goodwin, 1980). Before a competent answer to Pam's proposal in Line 17 can be made, the dirt being evaluated has to be placed under the viewing hole next to the color sample she indicated, so that the two can be compared. During Line 18 Jeff moves the trowel to this position. Because of the spatial organization of this activity, specific actions have to be performed before a relevant task, a color comparison, can be competently performed. In brief, in this activity the spatial organization of the tools being worked with and the sequential organization of talk-in-interaction interact with each other in the production of relevant action (e.g., getting to a place where one can make an expected answer requires rearrangement of the visual field being scrutinized so that the judgment being requested can be competently performed).

This has a number of additional consequences. First, Pam's own ability to evaluate the appropriateness of the color she proposed changes when Jeff moves the sample to the correct viewing hole. Only then is she in a position to rigorously compare the dirt with the Munsell color. Pam's action of pointing to a particular color patch at Line 17 could be heard as a request to perform this action, to put them both in a position where that patch might be evaluated, rather than a definitive judgment that is subsequently disagreed with. Indeed, a moment later, in Line 23, Pam suggests another possible color. However, when the trowel is moved to the appropriate viewing hole, she herself rejects the match, saying in Lines 25 to 26, "Is it that? Na: That's- not-".

This process of color classification involves a sequence of movements through space and time. What can be seen and evaluated changes at each step in this process. The relevant unit for analyzing the problematic status of a specific proposal is not primarily the mental state of a particular actor, but instead the different possibilities for seeing relevant phenomena that alternative positions in this sequence provide.

Second, it is sometimes argued that abstract, context-free language is not only superior to context-bound talk (the latter argued to constitute a restricted linguistic code), but a defining characteristic of rational discourse in institutions such as science (see, e.g., Bernstein, 1964). Here we see people who are actually doing scientific classification making extensive use of indexical language ("this one," Line 17; "that one," Line 21, etc.) tied to pointing gestures. Moreover, the very instrument they are looking at and pointing to contains both (relatively) context-free numbers for describing these entities and a set of color names that their community has explicitly agreed to treat as a common standard. However, there are very good reasons for use of indexical language here. First, the task posed at this point in the process is visual comparison of the reference color with the sample of dirt. Locating the scientific name or number for that sample requires an extra

---

[8]See Goodwin (in press) for comparison of use of the Munsell chart described here with the way in which young girls at play use the hopscotch grid they are jumping through as a framework for the constitution of meaning and action. For analysis of how larger social spaces are relevant to the organization of talk in interaction, see Duranti (1992).

step, a look away from the color of the sample to the borders of the chart or even the facing page. By way of contrast, pointing right at the sample heightens focus on its relevant visual properties, which is precisely the task of the moment. Reading off the correct name from the chart can be done later, after a particular patch has been located as the best match. Second, this gesture is lodged within multiple spatial frameworks that are relevant to the organization of the activity in progress. In addition to the way that the pointing finger locates a particular patch within the larger array, which we can gloss as the reference space, the hand carrying the gesture also constitutes a relevant action within the participation space being sustained through the orientation of the participants' bodies toward the materials (chart and dirt sample) that are the focus of their attention; Pam's hand moves right into Jeff's line of sight as he gazes toward the chart. Rather than telling him what color to look at, she shows him. Third, as noted previously, Pam's proposal constitutes a request that he move the sample to the viewing hole for this patch. By pointing at the patch, she makes a relevant move within the local action space by showing him where to position the sample next. In brief, the proposed advantages of apparently abstract, context-free descriptions, such as the standard names or coordinates, pertain to use of the Munsell system in a quite different domain, such as publishing findings in journal articles (which is of course contextually organized in its own right). Within the activity of color classification that is occurring here, Pam's gestures are not only appropriate, but rich, multifunctional actions.

Indeed the data suggest that there might be a systematic ordering of representations throughout this sequence, with pointing being the first choice and numerical coordinates the second. At Line 29 Pam starts to move her extended index finger to a particular color patch. What she says while making this movement, "How bout," explicitly classifies what her hand is doing as a next proposal. She then delays the onward progression of her talk until her moving finger actually lands on the appropriate patch. Her action of proposing a particular color category as the best match is done through the integrated coordination of talk, body movement, and the representational field provided by the Munsell chart. Only as her finger is leaving the chart does she state vocally the grid coordinates that name this patch "three four." In a very real sense, the syntactic construction initiated by "How bout" has two complements: first a visible reference color specified by the pointing finger, and second a verbal name for that color, spoken as the gesturing finger departs.[9] Pam's finger on the patch, in addition to showing Jeff the color she wants him to evaluate, might also help her read the coordinates. Her raised finger provides a prominent, fixed reference point as she moves her eyes to each of the chart's borders to find the correct numbers. The third representational system provided by the chart, the standard set of color names, is never used in this sequence. These color names do not uniquely identify reference colors, and they are written on the page facing the color samples. This page is being held in a position that makes it difficult to see.

Jeff never points to a color patch. He can't, because one of his hands is holding the Munsell book and the other the trowel with the dirt sample. However, he does perform an action that is structurally similar to Pam's points by moving the dirt sample to specific viewing holes.

At Line 31 Jeff uses the resources provided by the organization of talk-in-interaction to make visible explicit disagreement with Pam's position. Rather than simply proposing a new color, he reuses the structure of her utterance, the "How bout" frame, but replaces her proposal with his own, giving "si:x," the syllable that marks the difference, enhanced contrastive stress (see Figure 5).

---

[9]For other quite relevant analysis of how deictic structure in talk and properties of a scientific inscription interact with each other, see Ochs, Gonzales, and Jacoby (1996).

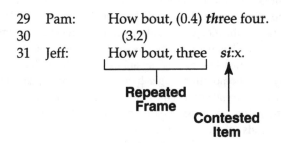

FIGURE 5   Disagreement.

Through such format tying (Goodwin, 1990; Goodwin & Goodwin, 1987; Jefferson, 1987), which attends to not only the reference colors being debated, but also the particulars of what Pam has just said, Jeff explicitly marks his proposal as a rejection of hers. It was noted previously that the process of comparison required to locate the proper category relies on the visual properties of one of the representational systems on the chart, the color patches. The disagreement made visible here makes use of the distinctive characteristics of an alternative system, the numbers naming the grid coordinates, which, unlike the color patches, can be spoken and thus displayed as particular kinds of objects (e.g., disagreements) through use of the full syntactic and intonational resources of spoken language.

Recently renewed attention has been focused on the body and the nature of embodied experience by scholars in a number of different disciplines. The situated activity system of doing color classification, with its tools and distinctive tasks, creates a framework within which the bodies of the participants are seen to be doing specific things. This visible meaningfulness arises not from the body in isolation, but rather from the way actors are can be seen to be using particular tools to perform relevant tasks. The conclusion to this sequence provides one example. Pam does not acquiesce to Jeff's "Three six" (see Lines 33 to 37) but finally agrees reluctantly to let it stand. As she says "Oka:y" at Line 40, she stands up so that she is no longer gazing intently at the Munsell chart with its dirt sample (see the picture in the transcript). The end of the classification activity is thus marked by the removal of her body from a position required to perform that task.

However, recognizing her reluctance, Jeff re-opens the task, asking at Line 42 if she has "another preference." A quite long silence ensues before she offers "three fo:ur" as an alternative to his "three six." Research in conversation analysis (Pomerantz, 1984; Sacks, 1987 [1973]; Sacks, 1995 [1992]) demonstrated that, as part of a structural preference for agreement, disagreements are frequently preceded by long silences (which can do a number of different jobs, such as giving the party whose talk is being disagreed with an opportunity to revise it before overt disagreement becomes explicit). Although upcoming disagreement is certainly relevant, the silence here is occupied by Pam visibly putting herself in a position to produce a careful, competent answer. Just after Jeff asks if she has another preference, Pam walks around to the side of the Munsell book, leans down and grasps it her hands while putting her head as close to its surface as Jeff's is (see the picture attached to Line 44 in the transcript), and then stares intently at the page with the dirt sample under it for several seconds before offering her alternative category. People are sometimes described as producing a "thoughtful" answer. Here, through a display of her body intensely scrutinizing the materials required for a competent judgment, Pam visibly demonstrates that the answer she eventually produces is the product of the systematic practices required to make such a judgment in this activity. Linguists have noted the importance of structures within a linguistic system that allow speakers to display their epistemic stance (Chafe & Nichols, 1986; Ochs, 1992) toward the propositions offered in their talk, their certainty or doubtfulness, how they know about what they are talking about, and so on. Here we find a related, though quite distinct phenomenon, organized through the processes of embodied participation that frame strips of talk.

Finally, the visible structure of the Munsell chart interacts with talk in more subtle ways as well. In an article investigating how intricate pun-like processes organize some aspects of talk, Sacks (1973) described how the selection of words and images by a speaker can be influenced by quite diverse properties of the talk that preceded it, for example, not only its explicit, topic-relevant semantic structure, but also its sound structure, the scenes it represents, and so on. In this data, when offering the compromise that ends the activity, Pam uses both the word "slash" ("we ca say it's a- a three four s- slash three six") and a gesture depicting a slash. To determine the grid coordinates of her proposed category, she has just been looking at the borders of the chart where row and column labels are written as numbers next to slashes ("3/" or "/4"). The graphic organization of the Munsell page shapes not only her task of color classification, but also her talk in many complex ways.

With respect to the scope of the disagreement that occurs here, it should be noted that the 3/4 and 3/6 color patches on the 10YR page are extremely similar to each other. I can barely tell the difference between them. Both fall within the boundaries of a single color name "dark yellowish brown." For all practical purposes, including subsequent analysis of the data being coded here, whether the color of the dirt is a 3/4 or a 3/6 will not matter at all. The carefulness of the students here, and their unwillingness to acquiesce to an answer that one does not think is quite right, in no way undermines the scientific work being done. Instead, the trustworthy, objective character of the descriptions they enter on the coding sheet emerges precisely from their detailed attention to the systematic practices used to constitute the categories of their profession and their recognition of the real difficulties involved in unambiguously classifying complex continuous phenomena into discrete categories.

The definitiveness provided by a coding scheme typically erases from subsequent documentation the cognitive and perceptual uncertainties that these students are grappling with, as well as the work practices within which they are embedded, leading to what Shapin (1989) called "the invisible technician."

This article has not attempted to challenge the findings of Berlin and Kay (1969; e.g., to propose a different sequence of color universals, or even to suggest that theirs is wrong), but instead to explore the possibilities provided by an alternative geography of cognition, one in which the crucial phenomena relevant to color classification are not located exclusively in the human brain, but instead in the situated activity systems that make up the lifeworld of a work group. Within such systems, human cognition is embedded not only in biology and linguistic structure, but also history, culture, and the details of local, situated interaction. By using historically constituted tools, new archaeologists, such as the students examined here, are able to build on the work of their ancestors in not only archaeology but also other fields faced with the task of systematically describing color. The solutions these predecessors have found, and built into material artifacts such as the Munsell color chart, shape in fine detail the processes of cognition implicated in work-relevant classification of color. However, these tools cannot be analyzed as self-contained objects in themselves. They only become meaningful when used to accomplish relevant tasks within local activity systems.

As a particular kind of heterotopia that juxtaposes in a single visual field the world being classified and an artfully crafted system of classification (one that contains multiple representations of the same category, each suited to alternative tasks), the Munsell page provides an example of a historically shaped, locally constituted architecture for perception. The analytic unit required for describing how a competent member of this social group, an archaeologist, understands an expression such as "dark yellowish brown" when used in the context of her work is not the English language as a homogeneous, autonomous structural system, but instead a situated activity system that includes not only semantic categories, but also specific tools, such as the Munsell book, and the practices required to use these tools appropriately. When multiple parties work on this task together, the full resources provided by the organization of talk-in-interaction for shaping intersubjectivity within process of coordinated action are mobilized. The objectivity of the work of coding is provided for by the in-situ articulation of a dense web of local, accountable practice, built through the actual spatio-temporal arrangement of talk, gestures, and relevant tools. The products of this process are trustworthy classifications that can be transported as written inscriptions to the other work sites (excavations, offices, journals, etc.) that constitute the field of archaeology. The outcome of the activity of color classification initiated by the empty space on the coding form is a fully realized world of space, cognition, and lived action embedded within the worklife of a particular scientific discipline.

ACKNOWLEDGMENTS

I am deeply indebted to Dr. Gail Wagner and the students at her archaeological field school for allowing us to videotape their work, and to Candy Goodwin, Aug Nishizaka, and Naoki Ueno for insightful comments on this analysis.

An earlier version of this paper was published as Goodwin, Charles (1996) Practices of color classification, Ninchi Kagaku, Cognitive Studies: Bulletin of the Japanese Cognitive Science Society, 3, 62–82.

An analysis comparing the use of the Munsell chart described here with the use of a hopscotch grid by girls at play can be found in Goodwin, Charles (2000). Action and embodiment within situated human interaction. Journal of Pragmatics, 32.

REFERENCES

Baker, G. P., & Hacker, P. M. S. (1980). Wittgenstein: Understanding and meaning. Chicago: University of Chicago Press.
Bakhtin, M. (1981). In M. Holquist (Ed.), The dialogic imagination: Four essays (C. Emerson & M. Holquist, Trans.). Austin: University of Texas Press.
Berlin, B., & Kay, P. (1967). Universality and evolution of basic color terms (Working Paper No. 1). Berkeley, CA: Laboratory for Language Behavior Research.
Berlin, B., & Kay, P. (1969). Basic color terms: Their universality and evolution. Berkeley: University of California Press.
Bernstein, B. (1964). Elaborated and restricted codes: Their social origins and some consequences. In J. Gumperz & D. Hymes (Eds.), The ethnography of communication, American Anthropologist, 66, Part II, 55–69.

Bruner, J., Oliver, R. R., & Greenfield, P. M. (1966). *Studies in cognitive growth.* New York: Wiley.

Chafe, W., & Nichols, J. (Eds.). (1986). *Evidentiality: The linguistic coding of epistemology.* Norwood, NJ: Ablex.

Cicourel, A. V. (1964). *Method and measurement in sociology.* New York: Free Press.

Cicourel, A. V. (1968). *The social organization of juvenile justice.* New York: Wiley.

Cole, M. (1985). The zone of proximal development: Where culture and cognition create each other. In J. Wertsch (Ed.), *Culture, communication, and cognition: Vygotskian perspectives* (pp. 146–161). Cambridge, England: Cambridge University Press.

Duranti, A. (1992). Language and bodies in social space: Samoan ceremonial greetings. *American Anthropologist, 94,* 657–691.

Foucault, M. (1970). *The order of things: An archaeology of human sciences.* New York: Random House.

Foucault, M. (1986). Of other spaces. *Diacritics, 16,* 22–27.

Goffman, E. (1961). *Encounters: Two studies in the sociology of interaction.* Indianapolis, IN: Bobbs-Merrill.

Goodwin, C. (1981). *Conversational organization: Interaction between speakers and hearers.* New York: Academic.

Goodwin, C. (1994). Professional vision. *American Anthropologist, 96,* 606–633.

Goodwin, C. (1995). Seeing in depth. *Social studies of science, 25,* 237–274.

Goodwin, C. (1996). Transparent vision. In E. Ochs, E. A. Schegloff, & S. Thompson (Eds.), *Interaction and grammar* (pp. 370–404). Cambridge, England: Cambridge University Press.

Goodwin, C. (1997). The blackness of black: Color categories as situated practice. In L. B. Resnick, R. Säljö, C. Pontecorvo, & B. Burge (Eds.), *Discourse, tools and reasoning: Essays on situated cognition* (pp. 111–140). Berlin: Springer.

Goodwin, C. (2000). Action and embodiment within situated human interaction. *Journal of Pragmatics, 32.*

Goodwin, C., & Goodwin, M. H. (1996). Seeing as a situated activity: Formulating planes. In Y. Engeström & D. Middleton (Eds.), *Cognition and communication at work* (pp. 61–95). Cambridge, England: Cambridge University Press.

Goodwin, M. H. (1980). Processes of mutual monitoring implicated in the production of description sequences. *Sociological Inquiry, 50,* 303–317.

Goodwin, M. H. (1990). *He-said-she-said: Talk as social organization among black children.* Bloomington: Indiana University Press.

Goodwin, M. H., & Goodwin, C. (1987). Children's arguing. In S. Philips, S. Steele, & C. Tanz (Eds.), *Language, gender, and sex in comparative perspective* (pp. 200–248). Cambridge, England: Cambridge University Press.

Greenfield, P. M., & Bruner, J. S. (1966). Culture and cognitive growth. *International Journal of Psychology, 1,* 89–107.

Heath, C. (1986). *Body movement and speech in medical interaction.* Cambridge, England: Cambridge University Press.

Heath, C. C., & Luff, P. K. (1992). Crisis and control: Collaborative work in London underground control rooms. *Journal of Computer Supported Cooperative Work, 1,* 24–48.

Hutchins, E. (1995). *Cognition in the wild.* Cambridge, MA: MIT Press.

Jefferson, G. (1987). Exposed and embedded corrections. In G. Button & J. R. E. Lee (Eds.), *Talk and social organisation* (pp. 86–100). Clevedon, England: Multilingual Matters.

Kahn, M. (1995). Heterotopic dissonance in the museum representation of Pacific Island cultures. *American Anthropologist, 97,* 324–338.

Kawatoko, Y. (1995). Social rules in practice: "Legal" literacy practice in Nepalese agricultural village communities. *Mind, Culture, and Activity, 2,* 258–276.

Kendon, A. (1990). *Conducting interaction: Patterns of behavior in focused encounters.* Cambridge, England: Cambridge University Press.

Latour, B. (1987). *Science in action: How to follow scientists and engineers through society.* Cambridge, MA: Harvard University Press.

Latour, B. (1995). The "Pedofil" of Boa Vista: A photo-philosophical montage. *Common Knowledge, 4,* 144–187.

Lynch, M. (1988). The externalized retina: Selection and mathematization in the visual documentation of objects in the life sciences. *Human Studies, 11,* 201–234.

Lynch, M. (1993). *Scientific practice and ordinary action: Ethnomethodology and social studies of science.* Cambridge, England: Cambridge University Press.

Lynch, M., & Woolgar, E. (Eds.). (1988). *Representation in scientific practice.* Cambridge, MA: MIT Press.

Munsell Color. (1990). *Munsell soil color charts.* Baltimore, MD: Author.

Ochs, E. (1992). Indexing gender. In A. Duranti & C. Goodwin (Eds.), *Rethinking context* (pp. 335–358). Cambridge, England: Cambridge University Press.

Ochs, E., Gonzales, P., & Jacoby, S. (1996). "When I come down, I'm in a domain state": Grammar and graphic representation in the interpretive activity of physicists. In E. Ochs, E. A. Schegloff, & S. Thompson (Eds.), *Interaction and grammar* (pp. 328–369). Cambridge, England: Cambridge University Press.

Ophir, A., & Shapin, S. (1991). The place of knowledge: A methodological survey. *Science in Context, 4,* 3–21.

Pickering, A. (Ed.). (1992). *Science as practice and culture.* Chicago: University of Chicago Press.

Pomerantz, A. (1984). Agreeing and disagreeing with assessments: Some features of preferred/dispreferred turn shapes. In J. M. Adkinson & J. Heritage (Eds.), *Structures of social action: Studies in conversation analysis* (pp. 57–101). Cambridge, England: Cambridge University Press.

Ralph, E. (1991). Post-modern geography. *Canadian Geographer, 35,* 98–105.

Sacks, H. (1987 [1973]). On some puns with some intimations. In R. W. Shuy (Ed.), *Report of the twenty-third annual round table meeting on linguistics and language studies* (pp. 135–144). Washington, DC: Georgetown University Press.

Sacks, H. (1973). On the preferences for agreement and contiguity in sequences in conversation. In G. Button & J. R. E. Lee (Eds.), *Talk and social organisation* (pp. 54–69). Clevedon, England: Multilingual Matters.

Sacks, H. (1992). *Lectures on conversation: Volume I* (G. Jefferson, Ed.). Oxford, England: Basil Blackwell.

Sacks, H. (1995[1992]). *Lectures on conversation: Volumes I and II* (G. Jefferson, Ed.). Oxford, England: Basil Blackwell.

Sacks, H., Schegloff, E. A., & Jefferson, G. (1974). A simplest systematics for the organization of turn-taking for conversation. *Language, 50,* 696–735.

Schegloff, E. A. (1972). Notes on a conversational practice: Formulating place. In D. Sudnow (Ed.), *Studies in social interaction* (pp. 75–119). New York: Free Press.

Shapin, S. (1989). The invisible technician. *American Scientist, 77,* 554–563.

Shapin, S., & Schaffer, S. (1985). *Leviathan and the air pump: Hobbes, Boyle and the experimental life.* Princeton, NJ: Princeton University Press.

Smith, D. E. (1990). *Texts, facts and femininity.* London: Routledge & Kegan Paul.

Streeck, J., & LeBaron, C. D. (1995, July). *Experiential roots of gestures: From instrumental to symbolic action.* Paper presented at "Gestures Compared Cross-Linguistically" at the Linguistic Institute, University of New Mexico.

Suchman, L. (1992). Technologies of accountability: Of lizards and airplanes. In G. Button (Ed.), *Technology in working order: Studies of work, interaction and technology* (pp. 113–126). London: Routledge & Kegan Paul.

Ueno, N. (1995). Reification of artifacts in ideological practice. *Mind, Culture, and Activity, 2,* 230–239.

Vygotsky, L. S. (1962). *Thought and language* (E. Hanfmann & G. Vaker, Trans.). Cambridge MA: MIT Press.

Wertsch, J. V. (1985). *Vygotsky and the social formation of mind.* Cambridge MA: Harvard University Press.

Whalen, J. (1995). A technology of order production: Computer-aided dispatch in public safety communications. In P. ten Have & G. Psathas (Eds.), *Situated order: Studies in the social organization of talk and embodied action* (pp. 187–230). Washington, DC: University Press of America.

Wittgenstein, L. (1958). *Philosophical investigations* (2nd ed., G. E. M. Anscombe & R. Rhees, Eds., G. E. M. Anscombe, Trans.). Oxford, England: Basil Blackwell.

Yates, J. (1989). *Control through communication: The rise of system in American management.* Baltimore: Johns Hopkins University Press.

MIND, CULTURE, AND ACTIVITY, 7(1&2), 37–58

Organizing Multiple Vision

Yasuko Kawatoko

Daito Bunka University

In a factory that produces large quantities of precision metal parts through the use of computer-controlled lathes, workers from different divisions of labor such as lathe operators, inspectors, and managers organize multiple vision to make cutting processes and the quality of products visible. The first part of this article investigates how the lathe operators juxtapose a range of different kinds of documents and artifacts to both program their lathes and build a perceptual field where relevant events in the process become visible. In the second part of the article, particular attention is paid to a *standard plan* as a boundary object. A common standard plan is used in different ways in different sections of the plant to accomplish its practice. A standard plan organizes multiple, perspectival vision of the "same" events in different sections while simultaneously becoming a tool for coordinating different divisions of labor.

INTRODUCTION

In the manufacture of precision metal parts with computer numerical controlled (CNC) auto lathes, every task engages the lathe operator's situatedly organized vision. Two initial tasks, programming the layout for the tool movements and calibration in the phase of *presetting,* are prominent examples of locally managed and situated practice. In both cases, lathe operators must organize a perceptual field to make the invisible movements of the cutting tools visible.

In my effort to understand the organization of knowledge and learning in a machine shop, the importance of vision as a shared social accomplishment has been forced on my analysis. By the dictates of the behaviors of skilled lathe operators, I have been persuaded that vision is neither picking up information from the environment nor translating it into code. *Vision* is the practice whereby people make objects or events visible within the organization of their perceptual fields. They do this by reconstructing the environment with the aid of various artifacts, or by adding something to the environment. When people make objects or events visible within the organization of perceptual fields, they do it not only for themselves, but for other participants as well. The practices whereby people make objects or events visible are identical to their procedures for making objects or events intelligible to each other. In working together, participants must collaboratively organize a division of labor by making each object, event, and their relations mutually visible; simultaneously, each organizes his or her own activity. For instance, each participant in a practice socially constitutes his or her vision or viewpoint by making each other's vision mutually visible.

Requests for reprints should be sent to Yasuko Kawatoko, Daito Bunka University, 3-20-15-302 Toyotamaminami, Nerimaku, Tokyo 176–0014, JAPAN. E-mail: kawato@ic.daito.ac.jp

In the first half of this article, I describe how lathe operators construct a program for cutting metal parts as a sequence of movements made by different tools in the lathe. The design of this program is shaped by both physical and economic constraints. I also provide detailed descriptions of lathe operators' interactive and reciprocating actions in the presetting process. They repeatedly produce a trial piece, measure it, and calibrate its program until they are satisfied with the measured value of the trial piece. Initially it might appear that the lathe operators are simply measuring the sample part. In reality they are measuring not only the part, but the current state of the machine, the cutting tools, and the program controlling the tools. Programming is never a self-contained process, and a measured value and its meaning are reflexively shaped in the projective course of action. By attending to the work, lathe operators make a course of action visible and useable to sensing capabilities of the machine, the operators, and other persons involved.

In the latter half of this article, I focus on a standard plan as a boundary object. I describe how the standard plan is used to coordinate action and seeing at different work sites, whereas making it possible for workers at each site to see something different as they tailor their vision to the specific demands of their work. Further, through analyzing the distinctive way in which the standard plan is both embedded within and reorganizes work, I reformulate the concept of a "boundary object" (Star & Griesemer, 1989).

A standard plan is the most important resource for all the work sections in the factory in this study in organizing their practice. A *standard plan* is composed of a drawing, some notes for processing sent by a customer, and many other items such as the type of machine allocated to the processing, the filing number of the previous program, the quality of the material, the content of post-processing, and so on. A standard plan is originally made up by a managers' section, and a copy of it is delivered to a lathe operators' section and an inspectors' section, respectively. In each section, a copy of the original standard plan is altered by putting additional notes and matters to be attended to in ways relevant to that specific division. One standard plan is reconstructed into specific versions for each section. Through these practices in a single factory, multilayered visibility for the cutting process and the quality of products is organized with a standard plan in each division of labor. Simultaneously, a standard plan becomes a tool for organizing the relations between divisions of labor.

A standard plan is regarded as an artifact for reciprocally organizing multiple contexts or divisions of labor, rather than specifications with a set of simple, Tayloristic, canonical steps. A standard plan is the artifact that organizes multiple contexts and various divisions of labor through making production and the quality of products multiply visible, while simultaneously it is structured as a boundary object through organizing multiple contexts or various divisions of labor in the projective course of action. From this observation, I argue that boundary objects are not given from the beginning. In other words, they do not "sit in the middle of a group of actors" (Star, 1989, p. 46). According to my view, a boundary object and a group of actors or a division of labor are mutually constituted by each other. Depending on the kind of artifact, it becomes possible for each participant to organize his or her own viewpoint in relation to other work contexts or other divisions of labor.

Research Site

The Shibue Precision Metal Parts Manufacturing Company (Shibue Company) is located in the industrial area in Suwa city where many small and medium-sized plants manufacture metal parts.

The Shibue Company manufactures precision metal parts, such as electrical connector pins, small motor shafts, and printer heads whose average diameters are 3 to 16 mm, with CNC auto lathes and cam-following machines. The materials used to make products are brass, phosphor bronze, free-cutting steel, stainless steel, and so on. The CNC auto lathes run 24 hr a day. They also manufacture very small metal parts whose minimum diameter is 0.5 mm, using extra fine wire materials.

The production process starts when the company gets a provisional order from a customer. A works manager reads a drawing of a workpiece sent from the customer and roughly estimates for processing the products, considering various factors such as how many cutting processes will be needed for producing one piece; which type of a lathe should be used for the processing (a CNC auto lathe or a cam-following machine); how long it will take to produce the ordered number of products; and which machine they can allocate to the processing. After giving an estimate and negotiating the cost with the customer, the factory receives a real order from the customer.

The lathe operator processing the ordered workpiece reads a drawing by drawing a layout and making a program, performs the presetting, and checks the output during a regular run. In the following sections, I describe how lathe operators manage these procedures to manufacture precision metal parts with CNC auto lathes.

READING A DRAWING AS ENVISIONING THE CUTTING TOOLS' MOVEMENT

The way in which lathe operators read a drawing of a part is embedded within the task of programming. In looking at the drawing, they must determine how they should move cutting tools for shaping a part and how they should actualize it in the form of a numerical program. As they read a drawing, they consider how many cutting tools can fit on a machine and how they should move cutting tools for the processing. In a drawing, the length and diameter of each portion of a part is usually specified at the level of a micron, as seen in Figure 1, but there are no instructions about the tool's movement for shaping it. Under these conditions, how do lathe operators envision the cutting tools' movement?

Constituting a Perceptual Field for Making the Tools' Movement Visible

To accomplish this task, lathe operators organize their perceptual fields so as to make the cutting tools' movement visible. Before further exploring this topic, I show how cutting tools and a piece of material are set in position in a CNC auto lathe. In a standard type of a CNC auto lathe, there are five to six pieces of *bite* and three pieces of *drill* provided for shaping and drilling. Bites move vertically toward the core of material to cut and shape it. Drills move horizontally toward the core of material to make holes in it (see Figure 2). A piece of material that is about 2.5 m long rotates at high speed and moves horizontally according to the cutting program.

Lathe operators call the direction of the bites' movement the x-axis and the direction of the drills' movement and material's movement the z-axis. Cutting tools such as bites and drills and a piece of material move on the x- and z-axes to shape a workpiece. When lathe operators read a drawing, they place the part in a drawing on imaginary x- and z-axes for making the cutting tools' movement visible, as seen in Figure 3. In other words, they constitute a perceptual field with x- and z-axes to make

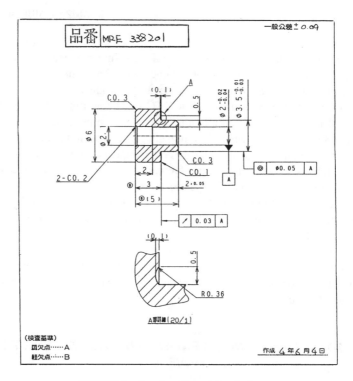

FIGURE 1　Drawing of a part (bearing).

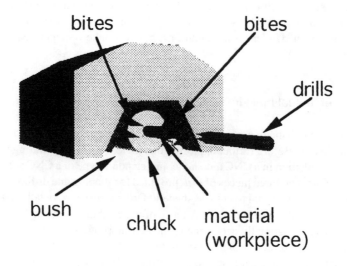

FIGURE 2　Mechanical setting in a lathe.

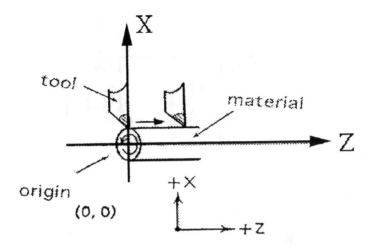

FIGURE 3   Material on x- and z-axes.

the tools' movement visible. This is similar to biologists' ways of studying lizards' territory described by Lynch (1990). In their studies, biologists transformed a natural ground into a mathematical field for objectively reckoning the positions and movements of the lizards by means of driving an array of stakes into a relatively flat plot of ground to form a grid at 20-yd intervals.

Reading a Set of Possible Actions in a Drawing

To make the cutting tools' movement visible, lathe operators also use diagrams that are composed of points and lines with arrows. We examine a case in which the edges of a groove must be smoothed (see Figure 4). In this case, the diagrams of the tools' movement could be differentiated, depending on whether they use two bites or one bite, as shown in Figures 4-1 and 4-2. Figure 4-1 shows that one bite smooths down the left edge of the groove and then draws up, whereas the other bite smooths down the right edge and then draws up. On the other hand, Figure 4-2 shows that one bite smooths down the left edge, moves a little toward the direction of the z-axis, and rounds off the right edge on the way to drawing up.

Let us look at another case in which the lathe operators must shape a right-angled form and smooth down the edge (see Figure 5). This case also has two possible ways of cutting. In the case of using two bites, one bite shapes the right-angled form, whereas the other bite rounds off the edge, as shown in Figure 5-1. In the case of using one bite, the bite first rounds off the edge and then it shapes the right-angled form as shown in Figure 5-2.

As seen in these cases, each cutting tool cuts or shapes a specific part of a workpiece through a particular movement. Each cutting tool's movement represented by a diagram makes units of processing visible. The entire processing of one workpiece can be represented in the form of accumulation of units of action by diagrams. As explained in detail in the following section, a unit of processing indicates a unit of layout and a unit of programming. Therefore, the units of processing represented by diagrams define the lathe operator's actions. Lathe operators read a set of possible

"Pat Spindle"

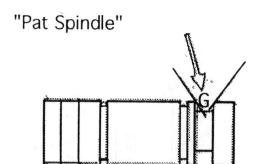

FIGURE 4   Round off edges, G.

FIGURE 4–1   Two bites = two units.

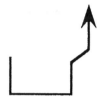

FIGURE 4–2   One bite = one unit.

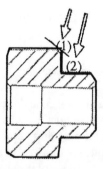

FIGURE 5   Shape and round off an edge.

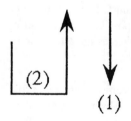

FIGURE 5–1   Two bites = two units.

FIGURE 5–2   One bite = one unit.

actions in a drawing, reorganizing the perceptual field for it with x- and z-axes, diagrams, and units of processing in the projective course of layout and programming.

SITUATED PROGRAMMING

CNC Auto Lathe Division

In a large building of the factory, three divisions of production, such as a CNC auto lathe division, a cam-following machine division, and an ecomatic auto lathe division share the floor, which also contains a quality checkroom and a small workshop for programming. In the CNC auto lathe division, 16 lathes work for 24 hr a day, fully automated outside normal working hours.

Work in the CNC auto lathe division is performed by three technicians, one of whom is called a chief lathe operator of the CNC. He has about 10 years of experience working with CNC auto lathes. When he gets a new order, he prepares for presetting in a small workshop located in the corner of the CNC division. In this plant, about 90% of the ordered parts are similar to the ones that have been manufactured previously or that have been ordered at regular intervals. So he usually looks for a plan similar to the newly ordered parts among the previous standard plans kept in a file in the lathe operators' section. Each standard plan containing the layout that was designed previously by the other lathe operator is written down. He pays attention to the previously handwritten layout as an important resource for programming. He also finds the previous program, which has been preserved on disks or papertapes. A standard plan with a handwritten layout and the previous program are juxtaposed on a desk, as shown in Figure 6, while he makes a program for the present processing. When he gets an order of a new part, he makes his original layout and its program and writes the layout into a new standard plan.

One of the other lathe operators, who has about 4 years of experience with CNC auto lathes, also makes programs for the parts whose manufacturing processes are rather simple, composed of three or four units of processing. Another operator, who is a novice, does not make programs but assists the chief lathe operator. A works manager, who is an experienced lathe operator, often gives advice to these three lathe operators or consults the cause of trouble with them.

Situated Programming Under Physical and Economical Constraints

Before describing the details of drawing a layout and making a program for processing, I briefly explain the mechanical setting for cutting metal. As shown in Figure 2, each metal material of column shape is grasped tightly by the chuck of a lathe machine and guided and supported by a bush. In this type of machine, five pieces of bite and three pieces of drill are enabled to set to a machine. A piece of material is slightly shaved down with a bite or drilled while it is rotated at high speed. This piece of material goes forward in the direction of the z-axis according to a cutting program (see Figure 3). When the whole process is completed, a workpiece is cut down from a piece of material. This whole process from the start of shaping to the cutdown from a piece of material is called *cycle time*. Whenever the lathe operators design a processing layout, they aim for the shortest cycle time to save money.

previous program

```
N3 G69
G0 X10.0 Z2.4 T2
G1 X9.0 F300
U-7.0 F35
G4 U0.2
X9.0 F300
G4
Z42.0 F700 T10
G4
U-7.5 F35
G4 U0.2
X9.0 F300
G0 X20.0
T1400
```

standard plan

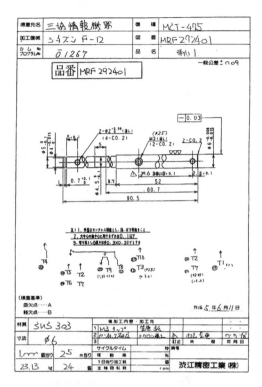

FIGURE 6   Juxtaposition of a standard plan and a previous program.

In drawing a layout and making a program, the lathe operators organize production processes as a sequence of units of cutting tools' movement, taking into account various physical, mechanical, and economical constraints. The constraints arise in various ways owing to the shape of the parts, the type of machine, the number of cutting tools they can set on a machine, the quality of the material, the size of the parts, the precision level of the parts, and time constraints, among other things. Let us see how they draw a layout under these constraints, taking the example of a bearing that is a small part of a recorder (see Figure 1).

First of all, the lathe operators place the figure of the bearing on imaginary x–z coordinates, as A or B shown in Figure 7, to decide from which direction the processing should be started. In this case, after consideration of several constraints made visible by a drawing, B is chosen. One of the constraints arises from the existence of two holes with different sizes in the figure of the bearing. The larger hole L should be drilled prior to the smaller hole S, because the larger one leads a micro drill used for the smaller one to create the right core. Besides, it is better to drill holes prior to any shaping with bites. The reason is that drilling should be done at the closer point to a chuck to avoid the risk of fluctuation of the center of a workpiece. Especially in the drilling process, the possibility of the center of a workpiece fluctuating increases as a workpiece goes away from a chuck.

Considering physical and economical constraints, the whole processing of the bearing could be drawn as follows (see Figure 8). The first three units, T1, T2, and T3, are for the drilling processes: T1 is to put a dot at the center of the hole with a center drill, and its diagram is represented as an arrow to the left. T2 is to drill the larger hole, whose diameter is 2.1 mm, with an ordinary drill, and its diagram is the same as T1. T3 is to drill the smaller 2.0 mm hole with a tolerance level between 0.02 and 0.04 with a micro drill, and its diagram is the same as T1 and T2. Up to this point, there are four key constraints that affect the decision of these layouts. The process of centering must always be before drilling; otherwise, the point of the drill could slip off. The order of drilling depends on the size of the holes, as already explained. What kind of cutting tools to be used depends

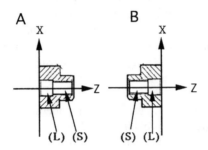

FIGURE 7   Placement of a part on the x- and z-axes.

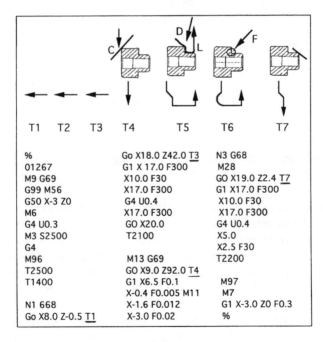

T1	T2	T3	T4	T5	T6	T7

%	Go X18.0 Z42.0 T3	N3 G68
01267	G1 X 17.0 F300	M28
M9 G69	X10.0 F30	GO X19.0 Z2.4 T7
G99 M56	X17.0 F300	G1 X17.0 F300
G50 X-3 Z0	G4 U0.4	X10.0 F30
M6	X17.0 F300	X17.0 F300
G4 U0.3	GO X20.0	G4 U0.4
M3 S2500	T2100	X5.0
G4		X2.5 F30
M96	M13 G69	T2200
T2500	GO X9.0 Z92.0 T4	
T1400	G1 X6.5 F0.1	M97
	X-0.4 F0.005 M11	M7
N1 668	X-1.6 F0.012	G1 X-3.0 Z0 F0.3
Go X8.0 Z-0.5 T1	X-3.0 F0.02	%

FIGURE 8 Layout of "bearing" and its program.

on the degree of precision specified in a drawing. In this case, T2 and T3 can be processed at the same time, using a special type of drill, if they prefer to shorten the cycle time. This special type of drill is costly, however.

The next processing step is the pressing down of the edge of C vertically (T4). In this processing, the special type of bite that has a 45° cutting edge should be used so as not to produce debris at the cut end. The diagram of T4 is an upside down arrow. T5 is to shape the portion L and smooth down the edge of D. There are two possible ways of processing here. If operators use one bite for shaping L and cutting down the D edge, the processing is one unit, and its diagram is as shown in Figure 8. If they use two different bites, the processing becomes two units, whose diagrams are exactly as Figure 5-1. The former one-unit processing shortens the cycle time, but it is rough cutting. The latter two units processing is clear-cutting. In all likelihood, the lathe operators will choose the one-unit processing, considering physical and economical constraints indicated in the drawing. The drawing says that the interior corner has to be rounded. This means that two cutting processes have to be done in this part at any rate. Then the rough cutting will be enough for the first processing, because putting on a finish can be done during the following processing in which the interior corner is rounded. Moreover, the lathe operators are expected to shorten the cycle time whenever possible for economic reasons.

The next unit, T6, is to make the interior corner rounded and to put a finish on the metal surface in the portion of L. Here a special type of bite should be used to cut the interior corner in a shape of an arc. The diagram of this unit is as shown in Figure 8. The final unit, T7, is to smooth down the edge of F and to cut down the processed piece with a regular bite. Its diagram is also seen in Figure 8.

The programming that is composed of drawing a layout and making a program is situatedly done by local decisions that are made from enlarged perspectives. There could be various physical and socioeconomic constraints such as the customer's requirements, productivity, the technical level of post-processing plants, and all sorts of concrete factors as mentioned previously in the case of the bearing. Lathe operators situatedly organize their vision for cutting processes under consideration of all those constraints. Their decision is never made beforehand. The situated procedures of drawing a layout and making a program cannot be described by a post hoc standardized flowchart, exactly as Orr (1990) showed in repair technicians' practice.

A Layout and a Program as Resources for Making Processing Publicly Visible

The program for processing parts is composed of a sequence of *blocks*. These are formed from the diagram units in a layout. Figure 8 juxtaposes a program and the diagram units it is based on. Each unit is represented in one block in numerical form in a program. Both units and blocks make the boundaries of processing visible, while simultaneously these boundaries make visible both the process of cutting and its program. The layout and the program of processing look so dissimilar, and yet these different representations mutually elaborate each other.

Lathe operators always compare the drawing, the handwritten layout, notes in a standard plan, and the previous program with each other. By juxtaposing these documents with each other, the lathe operator is able to choose the appropriate procedures under various physical and economic constraints as described previously. These documents become useful to lathe operators only because they see them with a professional eye; that is, they can envision the cutting tools' movement and read the meaning of units and boundaries represented in the documents.

In the process of making a layout, the systematic method with which the lathe operator visualizes the cutting tools' movement makes processing visible not only to the lathe operator himself, but to the other members who participate in the practice of cutting metal. The method of visualizing the cutting tools' movement makes both the tools' movement and the lathe operator's methods of processing publicly visible. The activity of organizing the cutting tools' movement and making it visible can be regarded as a methodic and skillful practice whereby lathe operators establish the order of objects, events, and relevant actions and make them mutually intelligible with various resources. It can be said that the activities whereby lathe operators organize and manage metal processing are identical to their procedures for making the activities "accountable" (Garfinkel, 1984).

SITUATED MEASUREMENT

Calibration as Situated Measurement in the Phase of Presetting

Before running a lathe machine for manufacturing products, lathe operators must adjust the grasp of a chuck and a bush of a lathe machine by passing a piece of processing material through them, attach appropriate cutting tools to the machine, and adjust the movement of cutting tools, shafts, and pipes of cooling-off oil. They then input a program, produce a trial processing piece, measure it, input calibration numbers to the program, and produce another trial piece. These reciprocating actions of calibration and trial processing continue until they get the desired measurements in a trial piece. As mentioned previously, this entire process is called *presetting* by the lathe technicians.

The most characteristic feature in the phase of presetting is the lathe operators' interactive and reciprocating actions of calibration, in which they repeatedly measure each trial piece with a micrometer, a microscope, a projector, or with the eye, comparing it with a drawing, a handwritten layout and some notes in a standard plan, and a program on a monitor screen. As seen in Figure 9,

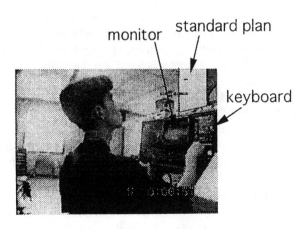

FIGURE 9   Juxtaposition of a standard plan, monitor, and keyboard.

a standard plan, a monitor screen, and a keyboard are put side by side on a CNC auto lathe so that they can input calibration numbers while measuring a trial piece, looking into a standard plan, and examining deviations.

One of the purposes of calibration in the phase of presetting is to arrive at the correct size and balance of a workpiece. For example, it sometimes happens that when a bite is taken off a machine for grinding and then reset, the origin (or starting point) of the processing shifts 0.01 to 0.02 mm from the original point specified in the program. Unless the numbers for the new origin are input into the computer, the length of a trial piece will become shorter than expected, and the balance between grooves will be broken. Therefore, the lathe operators must check the initial length.

Let us see how lathe operators actually do calibration in the presetting phase, taking the example of processing edges of the pat spindle shown in Figure 4. A lathe operator visually examined whether both edges of groove G in a trial piece were clearly cut down or not. After that, he looked at the drawing again. Then he became aware of the note that says no debris should be produced. As he measured the trial piece again with a microscope, he found tiny pieces of debris produced on one of the edges. He examined the point of the bite, but he found nothing wrong. Then he decided to change the layout of this part of the processing from two units to one unit, as shown in Figures 4-1 and 4-2. He compared the trial piece with a projector to calculate the numerical values of the x- and z-axes. He revised the program a little, input the calibration numbers, and then produced a new trial piece. He measured the new trial piece and did not find any debris on the edges. Further, he had to calibrate the balance between other portions because he changed the program. He input calibration numbers to make another new trial piece. This cycle of producing a new trial piece and calibrating was repeated six or seven times. This case shows that a lathe operator examines not only a trial-processing piece, but also its program through measuring it.

In the next example, the lathe operators examined the conditions of the machine, as they measured a trial piece. The pat spindle (see Figure 4) should be processed in at least in seven portions. However, only five pieces of bite were available because of the constraints of the machine allocated to the processing. The lathe operator decided to use one special type of bite and to make it cut three grooves together. He chose one bite whose point was thinner than the smallest groove. He calculated the movement of the bite, input the numerical values into a computer, and produced a trial piece. He measured it with a microscope, calculated calibration numbers with a projector that shows numerical numbers of length in the y-axis, and input the numerical numbers to produce another trial piece. He repeated this calibration process five times until he was able to balance the three grooves. Later, he explained that it took time to balance the space of three grooves with each other because the CNC machine he was working with did not always work as expected. It may be that some sort of resistance is generated between the cutting tool and the core of the machine.

As shown in these examples, lathe operators measure the setting conditions of cutting tools, the programming, and the conditions of the machine through measuring a trial-processing piece. In other words, measuring a trial-processing piece makes the movement of cutting tools, the method of layout and programming, and the nature of the machine visible. In this process, the trial piece, the whole mechanical setting, a program, and measurement tools are reflexively measured with each other. Thus when a trial piece is measured by a micrometer, these values simultaneously measure some mechanical setting. Numerical values in a program measure the movement of cutting tools, whereas the numerical values in a program are measured in relation to a processed piece. The adequacy of a program is measured by a processed piece. Further, a specific numerical value measured by a specific measurement tool marks the current state of the calibration process (Ueno, 1997). Here we can see the actuality of how "members" conduct measuring activities by producing local judgments on the practical adequacy, accuracy, and appropriate correspondence between measuring devices and measured phenomena (Lynch, 1991). As noted by Lynch, this is far from the classic view of measurement.

Formulating "Trouble"

As the CNC lathes are fully automated from 5:00 p.m. to 8:00 a.m., the lathe operators check processed pieces every morning when they come to work. At the time of these regular checks, they sometimes find inferior processed pieces such as ones with irregular length, diameter, and balance; a rough-grained cut end; a rounded-off corner; or a navel (a small protuberance in the center of the surface). Occasionally they hear unusual sounds from a machine. Inferior pieces and trouble provide the resources for making the conditions of the machine, presetting, and the program visible. The distribution of measured values of the inferior pieces gives the lathe operator clues in searching for the cause of trouble. The results of measurement provide a context for examining the setting conditions of cutting tools, the possibility that the quality of the raw materials has changed, and the propriety of the program for mass production. Depending on the measured values obtained, lathe operators examine a variety of factors.

For instance, if they find inferior processed pieces with irregular length or diameter, they look for either dirt in the motor, which can cause weakening of cutting power, or imbalance in the raw materials. Alternatively, if they find debris at cut ends, they examine wear and tear in the shape of cutting tools, a malfunction of setting angles of cutting tools, looseness of bolts, or misalignment with the center in a chuck. If they are unable to find a problem with these parts, they reexamine the program in light of its fitness for mass production. If the debris vanishes after a change, then the program is identified as the cause of the trouble. There are some cases where a program turns out to be inadequate for mass production or sustained operation, although it seemed to be adequate in processing trial pieces in the presetting phase.

Let us take a look at another example of how lathe operators formulate trouble. One morning, during the regular check, a novice lathe operator measured several processed pieces by eye and found something wrong with them. Then he measured the checkpoints of some processed pieces with a micrometer several times and noticed that their surfaces were slightly wrong. He asked an experienced lathe operator to examine what was wrong with them. The experienced lathe operator examined them with a magnifying glass and found that there was a navel on the surface. Then he checked the bite that was used for finishing processing and recognized that the point of it was worn away. The life of a bite is usually about 3 days. This worn-away bite had been used for only 1½ days. He wondered why it was worn away so soon. He looked into the standard plan and became aware that the quality of the material was different from the one that was used for the previous processing. He then concluded that the cutting program must have been inappropriate for the quality of this material. The interaction between the program and the specific material being cut made the point of the bite worn away.

Measured values or inferior pieces constitute the context for the search for the cause of trouble, whereas the examination of them shapes the context for formulating trouble or specifying the meaning of measured values. Thus, measuring processed pieces and formulating trouble elaborate each other, mutually constituting contexts.

Collaborative Formulation of Trouble

The discovery and repair of trouble are, in many cases, socially organized. When a lathe operator makes trouble visible, he makes trouble visible not only to himself, but to other members. Lathe operators collaboratively search for trouble, specify it, or repair it through looking closely at a series of deviations of shape, size, and balance in inferior pieces, while making the state of trouble visible and intelligible to each other. Let us take a look at how they jointly formulate trouble.

One morning while a lathe operator was doing a regular check, he found that one CNC auto lathe was stopped with one bite running into the stationary processing material that should have been rotating. He examined the chuck that held the material and the bush that guided and supported the material, taking them off of the machine, but he could not find any problems with them. Next he examined the setting condition of the bites, but he did not find anything wrong with it either. Because he was unable to find the cause of trouble, he explained what he had done to the senior lathe operator and asked for help. They began to search together for the cause of trouble. Two possibilities were uncovered. One was trouble on the motherboard of the computer, which they could not repair by themselves. The other was trouble on the oil pressure valve that connected the machine with the computer. They compared the movement of an oil pressure valve with another in the same type of machine and found that the movement of the valve in the troubled machine was different from that in the working one. Adjusting the valve of the problem machine alleviated the trouble. Thus, they identified the cause of trouble as the irregular working of the oil pressure valve.

Goodwin (1996) formulated this type of mutual constitution of contexts by the use of the concept called *prospective indexical*. He described the mutual constitution of contexts between the images on the screen and the talk in the operations room to search for the "problem" as follows:

> As the images visible on the screen are used to elaborate the prospective indexical it achieves a more definite sense and begins to be shaped into a more definite and coherent object, while simultaneously, what is seen in those images is structured by the talk "problem" which has generated the task of looking in the first place; i.e., a search for trouble. (p. 396)

In the case observed previously, the younger lathe operator's examination of the conditions of the machine and his explanation about the state of trouble to the senior lathe operator gave directions to the latter's search for the cause of trouble. On the other hand, the senior lathe operator's search specified the meaning of the younger one's examination and explanation more definitely. In this way, their actions became a collaborative prospective indexical to each other for formulating trouble.

A STANDARD PLAN AS A DOCUMENT OF ORGANIZING MULTIPLE VISION

Organizing Multiple Vision Through a Standard Plan as a Boundary Object

As previously seen, cutting processes and the quality of products are not directly observable. The lathe operators make cutting processes and the quality of products visible by using various artifacts and reorganizing the environment for processing workpieces, exactly as Lynch (1990) demonstrated in the case of scientific practice. He showed how scientists make the territory of lizards observable by driving stakes regularly just like the axes of coordinates in the ground, removing two or more toes for each lizard to be identified and recording the places where each one was caught on the sheet of the axes of coordinates. Visibility or observability for the cutting process and the quality of products is organized not only for the lathe operator himself, but for his colleagues, exactly as observability of the territory of lizards is not only for the researcher himself, but for the members in the same community of scientific practice.

In this factory, the observability is not organized at a single level. Observability of cutting processes and the quality of products is multiply organized. As Ueno (this issue) described in detail, in the managers' section, various kinds of documents for production and quality control are shown to customers when they make new orders or when trouble arises. For the customers, cutting processes and the quality of products become observable not only through sampled products but through those documents. As shown later, the inspectors' section also organizes a different horizon of observation for cutting processes and the quality of products.

This multilayered visibility in each section is accomplished by arranging several artifacts; some of them are section-specific and the others are common through sections. One artifact common to all the sections in this factory is a standard plan (see Figure 10). However, each section

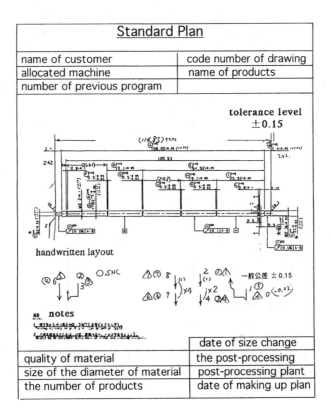

FIGURE 10   Standard plan (with a handwritten layout).

customizes the same plan to make it relevant to their specific work. Although each version of a standard plan organizes multilayered visibility in each section, it is used as a tool for communication among sections as well. In this sense, a standard plan can be regarded as a boundary object, although it does not "sit in the middle of a group of actors with divergent viewpoints" from the beginning, as I discuss later.

In the following sections, I describe how a standard plan as a boundary object organizes multilayered and local visibility in various divisions of labor and how organized multiple visibility in various divisions of labor constitutes a standard plan as a boundary object.

Remodeling of a Standard Plan in Each Division of Labor

A standard plan is composed of a drawing with some notes for processing and many other types of information, such as the type of the machine, the filing number of the previous program, the quality of the material, the number of products, and the post-processing (see Figure 10).

A standard plan is originally made up by the managers' section after managers receive a regular order and its drawing from a customer. Managers use a format sheet to make the standard plan, on which they cut and paste the drawing sent from a customer, add some notes, and fill in the previously mentioned facts in the stated sections. A copy of the standard plan is delivered to the lathe operators' section and to the inspectors' section, respectively (see Figure 11). Each copy of the

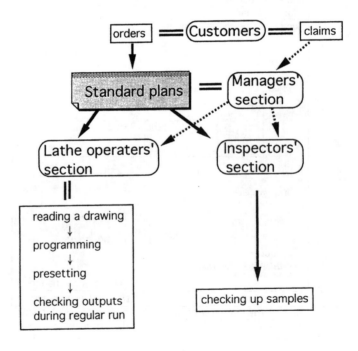

FIGURE 11   Standard plans in the flow of work.

standard plan is kept in a file in each section. The original one is kept in a file in the managers' section. As stated previously, in this factory, about 90% of the orders they receive are the same or nearly the same type of products as the ones they have processed previously, though some changes sometimes occur in size and material. Thus, one standard plan is reused repeatedly in each section.

Each section adapts a copy of the standard plan to its needs by adding notes and matters to be attended to. For instance, the lathe operator who is in charge of processing a newly ordered product usually adds a layout for processing and some additional measurements to a standard plan. After completing all the processing of the products, the standard plan is kept in a file for reusing in the lathe operators' section. Therefore, the standard plan kept in a file in the lathe operators' section always has handwritten layouts (see Figure 10). On the other hand, there are no layouts in the standard plans filed in the inspectors' section. Instead, the standard plans include marked points of measurements, checkpoints of post-processing, notes of previous trouble, and instructions to remove stains from the products.

The Use of a Standard Plan From Different Viewpoints in Different Divisions of Labor

How is a standard plan actually used by each member in each section? Let us take a look at the case where Mr. KN, a lathe operator with 10 years of experience, processes the products that have been regularly ordered by a customer. First, he checks measurements on a drawing in a standard plan, while comparing them with other descriptions already filled in. For instance, when he notices the presence of plating in a section of post-processing, he plans to cut a groove 1/100 mm wider than the central measured value, considering the thickness of plating. Then he considers what kind of cutting tools he should use in each unit of processing, while referring to a handwritten layout, some points to notice, and the tolerance level of measurements described in the standard plan. Although a previous program is used, it must be changed, to a greater or lesser extent, depending on the type of machine allocated to the processing, because each type of machine has its own cutting-tools set pattern.

For example, an SNC-type machine has a fan-shaped tool-set pattern, whereas the tool-set pattern of an RNC-type machine forms a line. When he finds an SNC-type machine allocated to the processing in a standard plan, he sets one bite, used for shaping the portion that is supposed to produce a large amount of cutting dust, to the number 5 position, the last setting position, to prevent cutting dust from sticking to the other bites. If he finds an RNC-type machine allocated in a standard plan, he makes a program in a way that each bite from the number 1 to 5 positions moves for cutting one after another to shorten the cycle time of processing. And, if he actually succeeds in shortening the cycle time in this way, he writes it into the standard plan for future reference.

The inspectors use a standard plan as they check up on samples of products before delivering them to the customer. Let us take a look at the case of Mr. OZ, an inspector with 7 years of experience. First, he looks into the tolerance level of measurements and the existence of processing a hole or a slit on a drawing; then he checks whether there is post-processing, a note on previous trouble, or a record of a claim from a customer written in the standard plan.

He selectively examines the spot on the samples where the strict tolerance level of measurements is specified on a drawing. If he finds that the central measured value of the spot slides more than

2/100 mm, he suggests that the lathe operators reexamine the setting conditions, pointing out that there is a possibility that inferior pieces outside the tolerance level could be produced hereafter.

When there is plating, he measures the external diameter of the samples, because the plating processing usually makes a processed piece thicker than an original nonplated piece. Further, he carefully examines the surface of the samples, because the plant has occasionally received complaints about surface processing. Even though this plant usually places the orders with outside plants for post-processing, this plant is responsible to the customers for the quality of all the products that it delivers.

In the managers' section, a standard plan is used for displaying the quality of products to the customers and to show how trouble is checked, recovered, and prevented.

Thus a single standard plan is locally altered and used in multifaceted ways in each work site (see Figure 12). Lathe operators seem to use a standard plan mainly in the context of organizing the activities of cutting metal. They write a layout of processing into a standard plan. They also alter a previous program based on the type of machine and the quality of the material, always referring to the handwritten layout as an important resource for making procedures of programming, mechanical setting, and cutting metal visible to themselves and to other work sections. On the

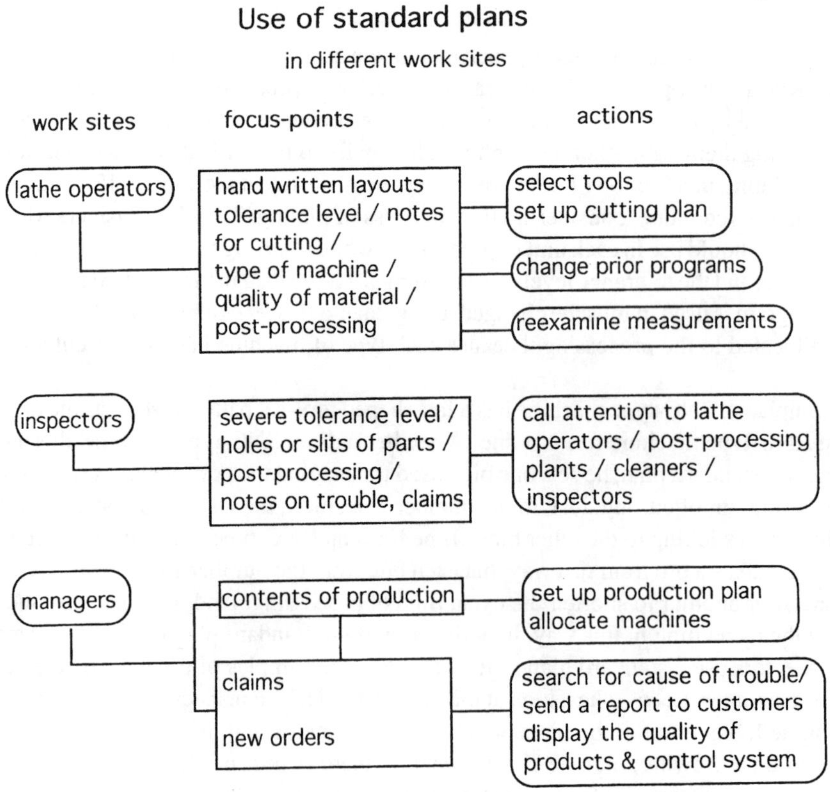

Use of standard plans

in different work sites

FIGURE 12   Use of standard plans in each section.

other hand, inspectors seem to use a standard plan mainly as a standing guarantee of the quality of goods for a customer. They examine samples at the checking points that are the descriptions on the tolerance level of measurements and on the previous claims from a customer written into a standard plan. Lastly, managers seem to use a standard plan as a medium for connecting orders from outside the factory with activities inside the factory, indicating the whole structure of manufacturing metal parts by means of a drawing and other descriptions filled in a standard plan. They also use it as a tool for showing customers their well-ordered quality control system, when they try to get new orders, or to answer customers' claims or requests.

In his study on the activity of deploying an instrument probe for measuring the physical properties of water, Goodwin (1995) noted how the same object might be viewed in different ways by parties acting on it from different situated positions. He argued,

> what is involved in this activity is not simply a division of labor, but a division of perception. There is no single participant's perspective, but instead there are multiple perspectives. Moreover, these alternative views on what is to be seen are not random, idiosyncratic or haphazard, but instead are systematic products of the organization of the endogenous activities in progress. (p. 256)

In the practice of manufacturing metal parts, one standard plan is reconstructed into each specific version in each division of labor, and multilayered visibility for the cutting process and the quality of products are organized. This multilayered visibility also organizes the boundaries of the different divisions of labor and makes them accountable.

A Standard Plan as a Mediation for Organizing Multiple Vision

In the lathe operators' section, each lathe operator makes his way of processing visible to the other lathe operators through the mediation of a standard plan. The handwritten layout and notes written into it make fellow lathe operators' ways of processing visible to the lathe operator who is newly in charge of processing the same products. Moreover, when trouble arises or the factory has claims from customers, a standard plan works as an object connecting a present lathe operator with a past one, and a novice with an experienced one.

Let us take a look at one instance. One day, a lathe operator was at a loss for what to do when he saw in a standard plan that the number 7 CNC lathe was allocated to the processing of the products whose length was 135 mm. Usually, the number 7 CNC lathe is used for processing products whose length is less than 130 mm, because the possible stroke of this machine is a length of 130 mm. He asked a senior lathe operator to help him work this out without changing the machine. They discussed it, referring to a drawing and a handwritten layout in the standard plan, and finally came up with the solution. They could create two different starting points (two origins) in one program, letting the noncutting part leap forward. Thus, the program they finally made was quite different from the one that they could have made if they had used other lathe machines.

The inspectors make their ways of maintaining the high quality of products visible to the lathe operators and the subcontract plants for post-processing, while at the same time they make their ways to guarantee the quality of products observable to the customers. They feed back the results of their checking up on samples and the claims from the customers to the lathe operators' section, or subcontract plants, through the mediation of a standard plan. Sometimes the inspectors even ask the technicians to change the ways of processing. Basically, the inspectors' activities are organized to make the process of warranting the quality of products visible to the customers.

A standard plan is also used as an artifact for sharing trouble and its repair with different sections. The Shibue factory receives 10 or more complaints about inferior products in a year. Customers send samples of inferior pieces accompanied by a document requesting that they find the cause of trouble and the best plan to cope with the situation. The managers' section is responsible for answering these claims.

For example, one day they received a claim from an assembly plant of electric parts. The workers of the assembly plant found some inferior pieces that were too short. The works manager of Shibue stopped operating the machine in question and called the lathe operators together to search for the cause of trouble. They presumed two possible causes. One was that the return-spring of the pivot of the machine might be improperly adjusted, and the other was that the fixed bush of the machine might be throttled too tightly. They presumed that the reason they could not find those inferior pieces by themselves might be in the fact that those inferior pieces occurred at irregular times. They then made a readjustment of the return-spring and the bush and resumed operation. For 2 days, they checked up on all the processed pieces, but they didn't find any inferior pieces. They finally concluded that the cause of trouble was in the imperfect adjustment of the return-spring and the bush of the machine. The works manager sent the report of these trouble-shooting procedures attached with the standard plan to the customer, and he told both the lathe operators' section and the inspectors' section to write about the trouble in their standard plans as a matter to be attended to.

In the activities of manufacturing metal parts, a standard plan becomes a tool for organizing the relations between divisions of labor. Thus, a standard plan can be regarded as a boundary object both for organizing each division of labor and for organizing the relations between divisions of labor.

Mutual Constitution of Multiple Vision, Divisions of Labor, and a Boundary Object

The practice of cutting metal is embedded in socially organized multiple vision. Cutting metal is embedded not only in the lathe operators' vision, but in the organization of the multiple vision of various divisions of labor. Multiple vision is organized by ways of using a document such as a standard plan, while simultaneously a standard plan is commonly used in various sections and becomes a boundary object connecting divisions of labor. In the practice of cutting metal, the observable and accountable multilayered network that constitutes cutting processes and the quality of products is organized through documents such as standard plans.

In this factory, the notion of standardization is quite different from that of "Taylorism which assumes that complex tasks can be successfully mapped onto a set of simple, canonical steps that can be followed without need of significant understanding or insight" (Brown & Duguit, 1991, p. 42). As already seen in the multiple ways of using a standard plan, *standardization* here implies that it provides multilayered accountable networks and loosely connects activities at different work sites.

A standard plan is regarded as an artifact for reciprocally organizing multiple contexts or divisions of labor rather than specifications with a set of simple, Tayloristic, canonical steps. A standard plan is the artifact that organizes multiple contexts and various divisions of labor by making production and the quality of products multiply visible, while simultaneously it is structured as a boundary object through organizing multiple contexts or various divisions of labor in projective courses of actions. Boundary objects are not given from the beginning; in other words, they do not "sit in the middle of a group of actors" (Star, 1989, p. 46). Rather, they are constituted along with the process of shaping divisions of labor.

In the previous sections of this article, I have described divisions of labor such as the lathe operators' section, inspectors' section, and managers' section as given entities. Actually, just as boundary objects are not given from the beginning, divisions of labor are not given beforehand either. Although each section has its own name or label, it is merely one of the resources for identifying divisions of labor. The labels of sections themselves do not guarantee the actual organization of divisions of labor. Rather, multiple visibility constituted by standard plans organizes divisions of labor and then it makes each division of labor accountable. A division of labor as well as "agency" in Actor Network Theory "exists only relationally in and through networks of action in which both humans and non-humans participate" (Suchman, 1998, p. 9). Multiple visibility and divisions of labor are mutually constituted. Further, boundary objects are mutually constituted with organizing divisions of labor and their collaboration.

Learning as Reconstruction of Multiple Visibility

This factory, for the past 15 years, has reorganized such networks of visibility for cutting processes and the quality of products along with the introduction of computers and various documents, including a standard plan (Ueno, this issue). They have reconstructed, again and again, the network system for making cutting processes and the quality of products visible to various divisions of labor in and out of the factory. This reconstructing process is precisely the learning process.

As seen previously, the lathe operators and the inspectors add whatever they find important for their practice into a standard plan. And, whenever they receive complaints about their products from customers, they write down the contents of the complaints into a standard plan as matters to be attended to. In this way, the standard plans kept in a file in each section have been renovated through practice. One standard plan pulled out of the file gives some directions to present practice, while simultaneously it may be renewed through present practice. In a sense, the contexts of past practice and present practice are reflexively organized and mutually elaborated through the mediation of a standard plan.

In this factory, the boundaries between divisions of labor, or boundaries between past practice and present practice, are always confounding. Under these circumstances, an individual member and a network of visibility or accountability mutually and reflexively organize each instance of learning. Learning is not lodged within any single individual, but is constituted within a work group that encompasses both human actors and artifacts. In line with this research, learning is regarded as the organization of multiple visibility in which members make work mutually visible to each other with various artifacts.

In relation to learning, competence is not located in the psychology of the individual brain. As already mentioned, the meaning of standardization in a standard plan is quite different from that of Taylorism. The meaning of standardization here represents a quite different view of competence from that of Taylorism as well. That is, competence resides in the network of accountability among various divisions of labor.

CONCLUSION

Every step in manufacturing precision metal parts with CNC auto lathes is accomplished by mutually organizing a visual field for lathe operators, managers, inspectors, and customers to plan, measure, cut, and evaluate products. The lathe operator's vision is socially organized by its constant interaction with the visual field available to and enforced by the machines', managers', inspectors', and customers' demands.

A lathe operator's vision is embedded in organizing multiple contexts through the juxtaposition of various artifacts. However, cutting metal is embedded not only in a lathe operator's vision, but in the organization of the multiple vision of various divisions of labor. This multiple vision is organized by ways of using a document such as a standard plan, while this multiple vision actually organizes divisions of labor and makes them accountable. A standard plan is constituted as a boundary object that organizes divisions of labor and their collaboration. A standard plan is commonly used in various sections and connects different divisions of labor as a boundary object under this dynamic constitution of multiple visibility and divisions of labor.

In short, in the practice of cutting metal, multilayered observable and accountable networks for the cutting process and quality control that are partially overlapped and mutually connected are organized with documents such as standard plans. At the same time, standard plans represent and make observable various divisions of labor or work contexts, and they are then used as tools for organizing interactions with other workplaces in and out of the plant.

REFERENCES

Brown, J. S., & Duguit, P. (1991). Organizational learning and community-of-practice: Toward a unified view of working, learning, and innovation. *Organization Science, 2,* 40–57.

Goodwin, C. (1995). Seeing in depth. *Social Studies of Science, 25,* 237–274.

Goodwin, C. (1996). Transparent vision. In E. Ochs, E. A. Schegloff, & S. Thompson (Eds.), *Interaction and grammar* (pp. 370–404). Cambridge, England: Cambridge University Press.

Garfinkel, H. (1984). *Studies in ethnomethodology.* Cambridge, England: Cambridge Polity Press.

Lynch, M. (1990). The externalized retina: Selection and mathematization in the visual documentation of objects in the life science. In M. Lynch & S. Woolgar (Eds.), *Representation in scientific practice* (pp. 153–186). Cambridge, MA: MIT Press.

Lynch, M. (1991). Method: Measurement-ordinary and scientific measurement as ethnomethodological phenomena. In G. Button (Ed.), *Ethnomethodology and the human science* (pp. 77–108). Cambridge, England: Cambridge University Press.

Orr, J. E. (1990). *Talking about machines: An ethnography of a modern job.* Cambridge, England: Cambridge University Press.

Star, S. L. (1998). The structure of ill-structured solutions: Boundary objects and heterogeneous distributed problem solving. In M. Huhns & I. Gasser (Eds.), *Distributed artificial intelligence 2* (pp. 37–54). Menlo Park, CA: Morgan Kauffmann.

Suchman, L. (1998). Human/machine reconsidered. *Cognitive Studies, 5,* 5–13.

Ueno, N. (1997, April). *Cutting metal as situated practice.* Paper presented at the meeting of Society for Social Studies of Science, Tucson, AZ.

MIND, CULTURE, AND ACTIVITY, 7(1&2), 59–80

Ecologies of Inscription: Technologies of Making the Social Organization of Work and the Mass Production of Machine Parts Visible in Collaborative Activity

Naoki Ueno

National Institute for Educational Research, Japan

This article focuses on technologies for making social organization, work, and mass production mutually visible in collaborative activity. I describe how practitioners in a manufacturing factory mutually organize accountability of their own social organization, the work, and the mass-produced products through using various inscriptions and other technologies along with concretely demonstrating these presuppositions of society and work. Among them, I focus on how multilayered accountabilities are organized and on how the multilayered accountabilities or multiply-organized activities are linked up and coordinated with inscriptions and other technologies. At linking points, mutualities of various divisions of labor are organized. In addition, at a linking point, what occurs is not the transmission of invariant information, but the transformation of the information. Imaging the relations across inscriptions as a linear chain can be viewed as one of the more popular inscriptions locally utilized by management on specific occasions.

INTRODUCTION

This article focuses on technologies for making social organization, work, and mass production mutually visible in collaborative activity. This title was given under the influence of situated approaches to learning and artifacts and technoscience studies on workplace and technologies (Latour, 1990; Lynch, 1990; Lynch & McNally, 1997; Suchman, 1993, 1995). The focus on "technologies of mutual visibility" allows for a consideration of critical issues concerning the nature of society, social organization, community, and activity.

A presupposition of this article is that society, social structure, or community is not already there. These things are not given social facts. Rather, we organize these things through making them mutually intelligible with various technologies and methods such as interactive resources, inscriptions, and other artifacts. Even though we reside in the given historical condition, the given history is not naturally visible for us without inscriptions, categories, and other artifacts. In addition, it is not possible to distinguish the given history from the inscriptions and categories that describe the history.

Requests for reprints should be sent to Naoki Ueno, National Institute for Educational Research, 5–22 Shimo-Meguro 6–Chome, Meguro-Ku, Tokyo, JAPAN. E-mail: nueno@nier.go.jp

A second presupposition is that the practice of making society visible is a mundane activity rather than an exclusive privilege of such sociologists as Garfinkel and Sacks (1970) formulated. Actually, in the workplace under analysis, people are organizing their collaborative activity along with making their social organization, work, and mass produced products observable with various inscriptions and other technologies. My interest is not to elaborate researchers' accounts of social structure, social organization, community, or activity, but to clarify practitioners' methods and technologies for accounting of social organization and work. Practitioners' accounting of social organization and work is not an independent activity from their practice, but is embedded in their practice and organizes the practice. People cannot organize their practice without making the practice visible and accountable.

In this article, I describe how practitioners in a manufacturing factory mutually organize accountability of their own social organization, the work, and the mass-produced products through using various inscriptions and other technologies along with concretely demonstrating the previously mentioned presuppositions of society and work. In particular, I focus on how multilayered accountabilities are organized and on how the multilayered accountabilities or multiply-organized activities are linked up and coordinated with inscriptions and other technologies based on the concept of "ecologies of inscription." Through ecological metaphor, I would like to emphasize that inscriptions and other technologies that make work and social organization visible are part of the environments we reside in.

USING TOOLS TO ORGANIZE THE OBSERVATION OF OBJECT, SCENE, AND SOCIETY

Using Tools to Organize the Observation of Object and Scene

Before going to workplace research, let me show some examples of using tools to organize the perception of object, scene, and society. A simple example of demonstrating observation with a tool is the use of a pencil as a gauge for organizing a visual field while trying to draw a picture. By holding a pencil between one's face and the scene under analysis, one can obtain the structured visual field of spatial relations between a mountain, a house, and a sky in the scene.

A much more elaborate example of observation with tools is demonstrated by the case of drawing the picture of linear perspective with a grid as shown in Figure 1. In this example, the grid located between an observer and a model organizes the observer' s perception of the model. The grid helps to make it possible for the observer to draw the picture with linear perspective.

A third example of organizing observation with tools is from scientific practice. According to Lynch (1990), biologists of ecology organize perceptual fields by reconstructing the natural ground by means of driving stakes regularly exactly per the Cartesian coordinates (see Figure 2). Markers for the location where lizards are captured are not previously given in the environment. It is through the use of tools that the locations where each lizard is captured at some period can be represented in the axis of coordinates and the territory mathematicized. Further, biologists cut the fingers of each lizard in different ways to discriminate individual lizards. Thus, by reconstructing the environment, the territory of lizards becomes observable and this mathematicized territory can be shared among biologists (Lynch, 1990).

FIGURE 1   Organizing linear perspective drawing by a grid. From *Representation in Scientific Practice*, M. Lynch & S. Woolgar (Eds.), 1990, Cambridge, MA: MIT Press. Copyright 1990 by MIT Press. Reprinted with permission.

FIGURE 2   Map of study area showing marked lizards.

These examples demonstrate that the perceptual field in the environment is not something given. Rather, the perceptual field is organized by adding something to the perceptual field, by marking on or reconstructing the environment with tools or inscriptions. Reconstructing the environment gives directions that lead our observations. We do not merely pick up information from the environment, but reflexively constitute the perceptual field that makes objects and the environment visible. At the same time, our observations give directions that reconstruct the environment or the perceptual field. In short, the activities of reconstructing the environment with tools and organizing a system of perception are mutually constituted. This mutual constitution was concretely demonstrated by Goodwin (1994, 1996) in his research on scientific practice as well.

Thus, perceiving can be regarded as embedded in methodic, skillful practices whereby people establish the order of objects, events, and actions and make them mutually intelligible with various resources. Perceiving cannot be separated from the activity for constituting objects, events, and the environment, or from actions for making them mutually visible.

Using Tools to Organize Observation of "Macro Society"

How about the case of observation of society, social organization, or activity? Is it similar to observation of a scene or of a territory of lizards? Partially, the answer is yes. In fact, we use various tools and inscriptions to make these things visible. For example, in Figure 1, it is possible to substitute macro social structure for a model person. It shows that we use some tools to make macro social structure observable because it is impossible to perceive it directly.

Let us take a look at an example of making macro social structure visible with kinds of grids. The example is the revolution of Seven-Eleven stores in Japan in the domain of distribution and exchange. Seven-Eleven Japan opened its first shop in 1974 in Tokyo and has established and reorganized a very systematic network for the distribution and exchange of goods and information. This system is called the point of sale system.

In the point of sale system, when a customer pays one's bill at the checkout counter after buying goods, data such as the varieties of goods, time of sale, generation, and sex of the customer are inputted into a computer at the counter. The data gathered in this way are regularly sent to the data analysis center and analyzed. The results of analysis are quickly realized as changes in the varieties of goods sent to each shop and changes in the layout of goods in the shops. For example, in the case of lunch boxes, the frequency of sales for each kind of lunch box, the time of sale, and the type of customer for each kind of lunch box are analyzed. If a tuna lunch box does not sell well in each shop, another kind of lunch box is quickly substituted. The time and the area of good sales for each product is also analyzed. Ideally, goods are distributed with appropriate timing and to the appropriate places.

For Seven-Eleven Japan, the organization of distribution and exchange is very systematic, and control of the details of the flow of objects has been attained. The network system of distribution and exchange of merchandise and information has been frequently reorganized. After Seven-Eleven, many other chain stores have imitated and followed the point of sale system.

The case of Seven-Eleven Japan shows how people can make "macro social structure" visible. To borrow a phrase from Latour (1987), the data analysis center of Seven-Eleven Japan can be regarded as a typical "center of calculation." In the center, many kinds of computer and paper documents are accumulated, transformed into various forms, and utilized for planning and reorganizing sales and networking. These documents compose a "cascade of inscriptions" (Latour, 1990). In this center, every day, attempts are made to make the behavior of consumers all over Japan—the macro structures of consumption—observable and accountable with multiple layers of inscription and other technologies. The data, tools, and so on in the center is regarded as competent by practical sociologists who can make much quicker analyses and smarter judgments than actual sociologists because of their systematic technologies for inscribing and networking distribution and exchange.

In the center, the "mass" or the "macro" is not a given entity. As shown previously, through construction of the network of distribution and exchange of merchandise and information, data gathering, inscription production, data analysis, and by arranging the spatial layout of goods in a shop, the macro is organized, represented, and made observable, accountable, and reportable for the members in the center.

Exactly like biologists, the practical sociologists in the data analysis center also add something to, mark on, and reconstruct the social environment and link up various places with various technologies and inscriptions to make macro social structure observable and accountable. Categories in the taxonomy of customers can be regarded like the stakes regularly driven on the ground in the case of the lizards' territory. In this way, the masses of customers are located in the grid of categories and spatiotemporal coordinates and given order and structure. Just as stakes regularly driven in the ground are part of the environment for biologists, the grid of categories and spatiotemporal order, which is a tool for members in the center, is not independent from the macro social structure but part of it. The macro social structure is not already there exactly as the environment for biologists is not something given.

It is not possible to distinguish social reality from tools such as a grid that formulates social reality, as Latour (1995) pointed out in the case of things and signs. Paraphrasing Latour, we never detect the rupture between social reality and technologies or inscriptions, and we never find ourselves faced with the imposition of arbitrary and discrete tools upon shapeless and continuous social reality. Social reality is a mixture or a specific configuration of ongoing events, things, people, and tools. In short, technologies or inscriptions are part of social reality, and they make social reality visible. In other words, these inscriptions will be a constituent part of the macro society they describe, and, in endless and unavoidable ways, they elaborate the macro society and are elaborated by it, as Garfinkel and Sacks (1970) pointed out in the case of organization of talk.

Regarding the micro–macro dichotomy, the example of Seven-Eleven Japan demonstrates that practice of organizing the macro, and technologies and inscriptions for organizing the macro, must be continuously analyzed instead of presupposing macro social structure as a given. I would like to emphasize that even the practice of making macro social structure visible with various inscriptions is still a local, situated practice rather than an actual acquisition of a master view for observing macro social structure. "Making macro social structure visible" does not mean that one grasps the given social structure with various tools and technologies. Rather, it should be regarded as locally organizing macro social structure with tools or inscriptions for the members who engage in the activity of data gathering and data analysis. The research on centers of coordination done by Suchman (1993, 1994) and Goodwin and Goodwin (1996) clearly demonstrated that even activities in places like centers are locally, situatedly organized. Their analysis of centers of coordination can be regarded as the alternative to the popular view of the micro–macro dichotomy as well.

Making Work and Events Visible

In their workplace project, Suchman (1993, 1994) and Goodwin and Goodwin (1996) demonstrated how personnel in the operation room of an airport, as a center of coordination, make aircraft situatedly, locally visible with various technologies and inscriptions of their collaborative activities. According to Goodwin and Goodwin, a complex sheet or flight schedule is "a grid which links destination to unique aircraft identification numbers" (p. 63). Thus, a complex sheet can be regarded as a tool for making events and aircraft visible and for locally establishing social order as shown in Figure 3.

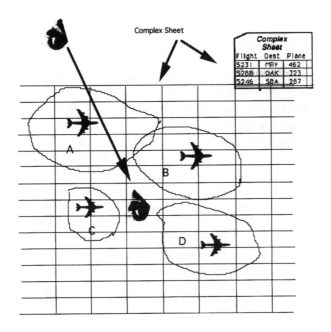

FIGURE 3   A complex sheet as territory map of aircrafts.

In this case, a complex sheet can be regarded as part of social circumstance in the activities of aircraft operation. Again, society or activity is not already there. Society or activity is organized by adding something to, marking on, or reconstructing the social environment with tools and inscriptions.

Goodwin and Goodwin (1996) emphasized that the viewpoint of personnel in an operation room is not like the bird's-eye view but embedded in a situation, as also shown in Figure 3. Personnel themselves, who locally utilize the juxtaposition of technologies and inscriptions, are also embedded in the gird of a complex sheet, instead of having a master view that makes the whole event and the movement of aircraft simultaneously observable. As Goodwin and Goodwin pointed out, the embeddedness of observers in the situation, in the case of personnel's understanding society, is one of the major differences from the case of scientists' understanding the territory map of lizards.

Observation as Mutual Accomplishment

In addition to the previously mentioned points, it should be noticed that observation of society is always mutually accomplished, as Figure 4 shows, although this mutual observation is not symmetrically accomplished. Paraphrasing McDermott's (1976) phrase, we are environments for each other with tools and objects. In other words, we make society, circumstance, or each activity mutually visible, along with utilizing inscriptions and other technologies in collaborative activities. For example, in the case of the airport operation room, pilots in the aircraft also attempt to make the activities of personnel in the operation room observable with tools and technologies, along with an accounting of their own activities. This mutuality of observation is also different from the observation of a territory of lizards. In the following sections, I focus on this mutuality of observation in addition to the multilayered organization of accountability to work and mass production in a factory.

WORKPLACE RESEARCH IN A MANUFACTURING FACTORY

In the following, I summarize our research on technologies for organizing mutual accountability among various divisions of labor in collaborative activity. The analysis focuses on inscriptions as the grids used in a factory to make objects and activities of various divisions of labor mutually visible.

Research Site

The factory we observed processes very small and fine products such as printer and computer parts, and the work is accomplished with computer numerical control (CNC) lathe machines and cam-following machines that are mechanically controlled by a combination of cams. The CNC auto lathes work 24 hr a day and are particularly useful for handling the ordinary order of production of 3,000 to 6,000 of the same pieces. The mechanically controlled cam-following machine can handle larger orders as it can produce 3,000 to 6,000 of the same pieces. As described in Ueno (1997), because the merit and demerit of each machine is different, technicians choose the type of machine depending on the order.

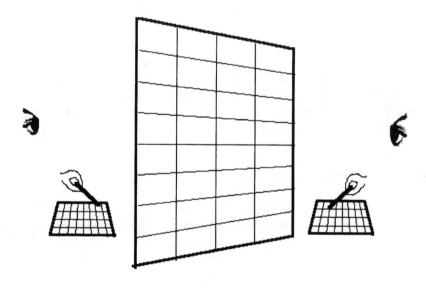

FIGURE 4   Mutual organization of observation with tools.

Making Work and Mass-Produced Products Visible in the Factory

In the factory, production control and quality control are critical tasks because of mass production and 24-hr-a-day automatic production. Quality control can be regarded as the activity for making work, social organization, and mass-produced products visible. Actually, the activity of total quality control covers not only the quality control of products, but the monitoring work of technicians and management of social organization for production.

As is the case for the observation of objects and scenes, it is impossible to observe directly the huge number of products and the whole range of work of mass production without reconstructing the environment with inscriptions and other technologies or without organizing observation with tools. Thus, members in each section of the factory use various inscriptions in addition to sampled products to make both the mass-produced products and the work process visible and accountable.

Strictly speaking, there are critical differences between the grid for lizards and the inscriptions for production control and quality control in the factory. For example, first of all, as Kawatoko (this issue) described and analyzed, in the factory, the grid is customized and utilized in various divisions of labor, and it makes the different aspects of mass-produced products and work visible according to divisions of labor. Second, in addition to multiple uses of the same inscription, in the factory, multiple layers of inscriptions are utilized as grids and also make the different aspects of mass-produced products and work visible. It is not possible for one master grid to cover all aspects of work and mass-produced products. This article focuses on the multiple layers of inscription in the factory. Third, the persons for whom the work and products are made visible are different, depending on the situation. The third point is related to the multiple uses of the same inscription and the use of multiple layers of inscriptions noted in the first and second point. Fourth, in the factory, the users of grids are often part of the objects of the same grids, and users have to make their own activities and social organization mutually visible with these grids. Later, I discuss the fourth point in relation to the issue of chain (Latour, 1995; Lynch, 1998) and coordination (Suchman, 1997).

Factory uses of inscriptions are different from the use of inscriptions by biologists' study of lizards. Factory inscriptions embody the practice of human social organization that makes social organization itself, as well as its mass-produced products, visible for all participants to see in their different ways. If so, the analysis of these points sheds new light on the issue of inscription and its use. In the following sections, I describe and analyze concrete cases of inscription use in the factory along with taking notice of the previously mentioned points.

Inscriptions in the Management Department

In the management department, the inscriptions recommended by the world standard for manufacturing, such as ISO 9000 (standardized by the International Organization for Standardization), are produced and utilized. These documents are composed of a standard plan, a chart of processes of production, a chart of quality control for each kind of product, a rule book of production control and quality control, a written format of coping with complaints, and other documents.

A chart of processes of production (see Figure 5) describes the sequential units of the whole work for production and the allocation of work units to each department such as management, processing, and inspection. A chart for quality control (a QC chart; see Figure 6) shows check-

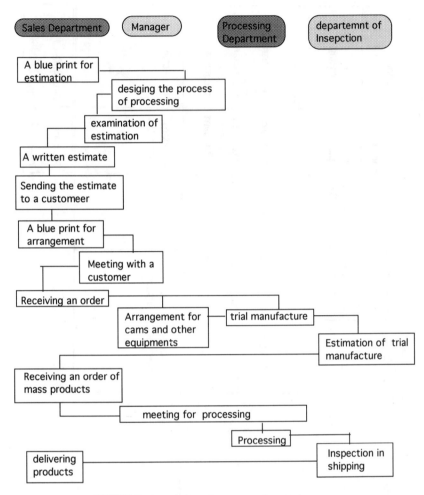

FIGURE 5   Description of processes of production.

points for measuring, tolerance, compulsory measuring instruments, and inspection standards for the complete work process from receiving materials, CNC lathe processing, and shipping. This chart is drawn up for every kind of product. The rule book is composed of a set of descriptions of normative rules for production and quality control, including CNC operation and son on. For example, the rules of quality control include the rules for making and managing a standard plan, issuing a product voucher, inspection of products, coping with a complaint from customers, and issuing the document for coping with a complaint.

After receiving an order from a customer, a standard plan is written by a member of the management department by pasting various kinds of information, such as a drawing with some notes from a customer, the destination of the type of a machine allocated to the processing, the program number, the quality of the processing material, a cycle time of the processing of one piece, the number of products, and a plan for post-processing such as plating, grinding, heating, and milling.

symbol of process	process	jig, machine	check points	specification	measuring instruments	inspection standard	relevant document	section in charge
△	receiving materials	SUS 303 ϕ 3.0	external diameter, flaw, bend	ϕ 3.0-0.02	micrometer	ϕ 3.0-0.005 -0.02	standard plan	chief of processing
◈ ○	CNC Lathe	Esco Q-2	external diameter, length	ϕ 3.0-0.02	micrometer	ϕ 3.0-0.005	standard plan	technician
				17.0±0.15	micrometer	17.0 ± 0.1	standard plan	technician
			surface radius	R 0.2	microscope	R0.2 ± 0.1	standard plan	technician
◇	shipping inspection		leftchips	removal of leftchips	visual inspection		standard inspection	inspector
⇧	shipping							

Product	Pin, Shift
Customer	CPM

FIGURE 6   Chart of quality control.

How are these inscriptions utilized? At least two types of use could be identified. The first is to use them as a kind of evidence that guarantees new customers the quality of products and the systematic organization of production in the factory. New customers often request that the management department show the documents for production and quality control when they start dealings with the factory. In negotiations, these documents covering trial manufacture are utilized for making visible the quality of products and work in the factory. To some extent, these inscriptions do tell the customers about the quality of products and work in the factory. For example, a chart of quality control for each product implies how much trouble was experienced and how these troubles were handled.

Second, inscriptions in the management departments are utilized as resources for establishing normative order of contingent events such as trouble and delay of production, exactly as Goodwin and Goodwin (1996) and Suchman (1997) formulated in the research on ground operation in an airport. According to Goodwin and Goodwin and Suchman, prescriptive, normative inscriptions, such as flight schedules (complex sheet), in the work of ground operation can be regarded as a resource that makes a contingent event and a situation visible and accountable. It helps to produce social order. For example, a contingent event and a situation in the personnel's present such as "timely" movement of an airplane, stair-pulling, and getting an airplane off the ground are interpreted and ordered by referring to normative rules that the schedule prescribes. When the flight tracker in the operation room confronted such situation, she used expressions such as the modal "should" and "hopefully." For example, "the airplane should be so. However, actually, it is not so" and "it must leave soon, hopefully." In this way, normative inscriptions are one kind of resource that produces social order and makes contingent events observable and accountable.

In the case of a manufacturing factory, documents such as a chart of the processes of production can be regarded as a normative inscription that organizes accountability for the management departments themselves and for customers. For example, in the management department, inscriptions are also utilized for finding gaps such as miscommunication between sections and for seeing where the responsibility lies when trouble or a delay in production occurs. In other words, contingent events such as troubles and delays can be made visible, accountable, and ordered by utilizing these normative inscriptions. For example, a "gap" between sections can be made visible and identified by using a chainlike description of processes of production when troubles and delay occur (see Figure 5).

Let us take a look at an example. In the summer of 1997, the factory received a complaint from a customer. There were two problems: (a) The surface of some products was rough, and (b) the external diameter of some products was 0.001 less than its tolerance. In this case, the ratio of inferior products was 10%. The cause of rough surface was identified as heating with dust and scrapped powder on the surface of products in the heat processing conducted in post-processing at a different factory. The cause of lesser diameter was also determined: The tips of materials received from the trader were less than the standard. From an organizational viewpoint, the chart of processes of production helped to locate the problem of the lesser diameter of products in the gap between the supplier of materials and the processing section in the factory. In the case of the rough surface of products, there seemed to be a gap between the factory and the factory that conducted heat treatment post-processing. The post-processing factory seemed not to care about heat treatment of products with dust and scrapped powder. As long-term measures, these gaps had to be reorganized from the viewpoint of the management department. In addition to a reorganization of the relation to suppliers and the post-processing factory, the long-term measures inside of the factory were altered. As for the rough surface of products, it became a standard procedure to wash products twice, where as previously operators had washed the products only once after cutting. They also started to expose the products to compressed air after washing. Regarding the lesser external diameter of products, they started to sample received materials and to inspect the diameter of the tip of the materials. This example shows how (problematic) mass-produced products and work are made visible with specific inscriptions and how accountable order of contingent events in production, such as troubles, are normatively, organizationally, locally established in the management department.

In addition, in the actual organization of work, the processes represented in boxes in Figure 5 are often overlapped, and the boundary between sections or the allocation of processes to sections is not always explicitly defined. For example, many processes in Figure 5 are allocated to both the management department and the sales section. The boundary of work between management and sales is often not clear. On specific occasions, accounting work for customers or finding out the cause of trouble and delay actually works from an organizational perspective to the extent that it makes contingent events visible and accountable.

Certainly, the documents produced and utilized in the management department can be regarded as a kind of tool for making work or activities visible. These documents and their use merely account for part of the work of the production and a specific aspect of the activity of quality control. These inscriptions and the use of them do not account for the detail of situated practices in the field of lathe machine technicians as described later. Organizing accountability in different parts of the division of labor often produces problems. How the different accountabilities are coordinated in the factory is described and analyzed in the last section.

Inscriptions and Their Use for Lathe Machine Technicians

As Ueno (1997) and Kawatoko (this issue) described in detail, lathe machine technicians mainly focus on the movement of cutting tools and materials while presetting and operating. Because it is naturally impossible to observe the precise movement of cutting tools directly, they use various inscriptions to make the movement of cutting tools observable.

When presetting a machine—that is, when mounting cutting tools, drills, and materials on the lathe machine—technicians repeatedly produce trial pieces and measure them. Based on these measurements of trial pieces, they adjust the setting of cutting tools and the degree of clearance of bush that is the part of the CNC lathe machine where the material is inserted and where it is supported. By measuring trial pieces, they attempt to observe the condition of presetting and the movement of cutting tools.

When measuring trial pieces, technicians often refer to a drawing and handwritten layouts of the movement of the cutting tools in a standard plan. They also refer to a computer program. The drawing is transformed into layouts that represent the outline of the movement of the cutting tools. Layouts give direction as to how the computer program should be read. In a computer program, layouts of the movement of the cutting tools are mathematicized as the movement in x–y–z three-dimensional Cartesian coordinates. A program precisely specifies the movement in layouts. The layouts give the context to read the program, and the program specifies the movement in the layouts. On the other hand, the result of measuring trial pieces is evaluated in the context of reading the layouts and the program. In this way, the gap between the ideal and actual movement becomes observable. This observable gap leads technicians to adjust the presetting of the machine or to revise the program.

After presetting, the CNC machine automatically produces products. Technicians have to monitor the operation of the machine every morning and evening. Monitoring is done by a sampling inspection of each lot. When monitoring products, they notice whether the shape of the products is irregular, whether debris is left on the products, and whether the dimensions of the products fall within the limits allowed by the standard plan. If the distribution of product size is extremely scattered, technicians search for the computer program or the mechanical setting of the machine. For example, it may imply a loose bolt in the cutting tools or a loose chuck. When one of the cutting tools is chipped, it may imply that the computer program for cutting applied too strong a force for the materials, and it made the cutting tool chip.

As shown in the case of technicians, they do not merely attempt to see the general probability of inferior products. For them, the statistical probability of inferior products is a secondary problem. Rather, they attempt to see the quality of products in the context of searching for a mechanical setting of a lathe machine and of examining a computer program. What they make observable with sampled products and inscriptions is the operation of the lathe machine and computer program for mass production, that is, the movement of cutting tools and materials. Thus, they pay attention not only to the distribution of the samples' size, but to a pattern of change of samples' diameter and length. For example, a sudden change in the size of products implies that one of the cutting tools has suddenly chipped, whereas a gradual change of the size of the products shows that a cutting tool has naturally worn away by friction in normal operation. On the other hand, personnel in the sections of inspection and management have a priority to make general characteristics of the population of mass-produced products observable for customers and themselves. Although the work of production and the mass-produced products made visible as objects partially overlap among sections, focused objects or focused aspects of objects are obviously different.

For lathe machine technicians, a standard plan with a drawing and other additional descriptions can be regarded as one of the tools that makes the movement of cutting tools visible. In addition, a standard plan and a computer program are also resources for future use by other technicians. Technicians organize observability or accountability of work not only for themselves, but for present and future colleagues.

People's Methods and Technologies and the Multiple Organization of Accountability

One of points in this article is that skilled practitioners engage in making their activities and social organization observable with various tools and communication resources in ongoing interaction, before researchers such as sociologists and anthropologists formulate social organization, activity, and work. People themselves organize their activities so their activities mutually make sense. By the same perspective, Button and Sharrock (1998) described the details of how engineers make their work organizationally accountable. They analyzed engineers' methods (members' method) and their technologies for making their work mutually intelligible for collaborative work. Similarly, I attempted to describe how practitioners themselves who reside in practices mutually locally organize accountability of work and mass-produced products instead of formulating work, social organization, and mass-produced products from an external, panoptic point of view.

However, in the workplace, organizing visibility or accountability of work and products is accomplished not only by members who share knowledge and competence of a specific activity, but by others partially connected in the division of labor exactly described by Goodwin and Goodwin (1996). For example, in the manufacturing factory, making work and the quality of products visible is done by members in various sections in various ways. Further, for whom people organize visibility or accountability is not the same in each section. For example, lathe machine technicians mainly organize visibility for cutting products for themselves and their colleague technicians. On the other hand, in the management department, the visibility of work and quality of products are mainly organized for themself and customers, although visibility for customers is partially overlapped with that for technicians.

Aspects of work, produced products, and the quality focused on are not the same across divisions of labor either. As described in the previous section, lathe machine technicians attempt to relate the quality of products to the context of cutting metals, mechanical settings, and writing a program. On the other hand, for personnel in inspection and management, making observable the general characteristics of mass-produced products are important for customers.

The focal aspect of trouble is also different across sections. For example, the management department focuses on an organizational account of trouble such as the gap between sections and processing in the entire production cycle, whereas lathe machine technicians notice, as the cause of trouble, ways of moving the cutting tools, the condition of mechanical settings, and the interaction between the mechanical settings and the work of the computer program. The meaning of causes of trouble and the inscriptions utilized for identifying the causes are different across sections, although some inscriptions are used commonly.

The management department often makes work and the mass-produced products normatively visible and accountable. In the management department, members attempt to establish a normatively accountable order of contingent events, whereas lathe machine technicians mainly attempt to maintain the mechanically, technologically accountable order.

In short, visibility or accountability of work and produced products is organized by various people with various inscriptions in various ways for various parties. The juxtaposition of methods and inscriptions for making work and mass-produced products visible is different from one section to another. In this way, accountability is not only locally organized, but multiply organized. Further, collaboration is not just accomplished based on the activity of making activity mutually observable and accountable. The activity of making work and mass-produced products visible is also collaboratively, collectively accomplished.

In the domain of engineering, it is common to distinguish standardization from customization and to discuss the conflict between them. However, as discussed in the previous section, it is not possible to make the ensemble of work, social organization, and mass-produced products visible by a monotonous, standardized, formalistic inscription. Accountability of work is organized in multilayers with various juxtapositions of method, tools, and inscriptions, locally, partially, and situatedly organized in each division of labor. Any formalistic, standardized inscriptions and technologies are customized everywhere, even in the place characterized as the management department. If not, they do not become available in actual activities. If so, the problem resides not in the conflict between standardization and customization, but in the relation between different organizations of accountability of work and products. Following the description of multilayered accountability in the previous section, at least two types of accountability can be identified: bureaucratic accountability (Lynch & McNally, 1997) and field accountability.

Activity in the management department organizes bureaucratic accountability whereas activity in the production section—even the same activity—can be regarded as organizing field accountability. As previously pointed out, in the management department, visibility and accountability for work and quality are normatively organized with inscriptions such as a chart of processes of production, a chart of quality control, and a rule book of production and quality control. Certainly, these documents can be regarded as kinds of tools for making work or activities visible. However, these accounts are simply part of the work of production and are a specific aspect of quality control. This accounting work and mass-produced products are not directly useful for technicians who attempt to explore the troubles of machines and computer programs. If lathe machine technicians literally have to follow a description of the steps of production described in the inscriptions, it would definitely make their work difficult.

Lathe machine technicians organize field accountability. Although technicians in the field also try to make the overall process visible, the context and the viewpoint are different from those of management. Although they also use formalistic inscriptions such as a standard plan, how they use it is different. Lathe machine technicians attempt to make the quality of mass-produced products technologically visible and accountable in relation to the movement of cutting tools, the mechanical setting, and the work of computer program.

Summing up, standardized, formalistic inscriptions themselves do not characterize both bureaucratic accountability and field accountability. Standardized, formalistic inscriptions are customized and locally and situatedly utilized as one kind of resource in the activities of both management and production sections. The critical difference between bureaucratic and field accountability resides not in the difference between standardization and customization, but in how formalistic inscriptions are locally, situatedly used, where they are used, for whom, and what they make visible or accountable.

Confusions of Multiple Layers of Accountability

Based on the formulation of multiple layers of accountability, it might be possible to reformulate cases that have been understood as the conflict between standardization and customization, or, alternatively stated, formalism and situatedness.

Let us take a look at some examples. Wenger (1990) pointed out that a normative, formalistic, procedure-oriented sheet of paper for claim processing in an insurance company would make a boundary between the claim processor's section and the management department as shown in the following:

> Normative structures such as the ones I have described play an essential role with respect to this reciprocal disconnectedness ... Normative structures act as a specific type of "boundary objects" (Star, 1989; Star and Griesemer, 1989) between the communities of workers and the communities of management. (p. 61)

Brown and Duguit (1991), following and summarizing Orr (1996), also contrasted the standardized, formalistic repair manual for copy machines to the situated practice of repair technicians:

> Many organizations are willing to assume that complex tasks can be successfully mapped onto a set of simple, Tayloristic, canonical steps that can be followed without need of significant understanding or

insight.... Although the documentation becomes more prescriptive and ostensibly more simple, in actuality the task becomes more improvisational and more complex.... As a result, a wedge is driven between the corporation and its reps (repair technicians): the corporation assumes the reps are untrainable, uncooperative, and unskilled; whereas the reps view the overly simplistic training programs as a reflection of the corporation's low estimation of their worth and skills. (p. 42)

These cases may not be conflicts between formalism and situatedness, or between standardization and customization. Rather, two kinds of confusion can be identified. The first is a confusion of different accountabilities. For example, a simple, Tayloristic, canonical repair manual for copy machines can be regarded as a tool for accounting for repair work by the management side. However, this organization of accountability of repair work is not the same as that of repair technicians as Orr (1996) described. When one view is forced to another side—for example, if the use of a standardized repair manual in the management side is forced on repair technicians as a tool for deskilling repair work—the repair manual will be a kind of specific artifact that constitutes disconnectedness between the communities of workers and the communities of management exactly as Wenger (1990) described. In other words, the repair manual can be understood as a "normative inscription" embedded in the organization of reciprocal disconnection between the management and technicians' side. These cases described by Wenger and Orr can be regarded as the examples of a confusion of bureaucratic accountability and field accountability. If one set of inscriptions is forced onto another side—for example, if the use of a normative inscription for the management side is forced on technicians—the inscriptions look too simple and are not useful from technicians' side. Such confusion can constitute the disconnectedness between the management side and technicians' side.

In these cases, another confusion can be identified as well. That is confusion between rule-governed accounting and rule-oriented actions or procedure-governed accounting and procedure-oriented actions. In rule-governed accounting, actions and interactions are explained by rules or procedures. Rule-governed accounting leads the normative explanation such as "they act like that because they follow the rules" or "the cause of trouble is that they did not follow the rule." On the other hand, in rule-oriented actions, rules are used merely as resources for organizing actions and interactions. For example, in the case of the copy machine repair technicians, according to Orr (1996), even a simple, Tayloristic, canonical repair manual is sometimes used as one of resources for repairing. However, use of these inscriptions is embedded in situated practice, and they are utilized as one of the resources for repair work. In this case, descriptions from the manual do not govern behaviors of technicians. Technicians are merely orienting to the descriptions of the manual as one resource. On the other hand, when the corporation utilizes similar inscriptions, these are regarded as a set of normative rules that technicians have to follow. The rule-governed accounting of the management side is also embedded in its own situated practice just as the complex sheet in ground operation and a chainlike representation of production processes in the manufacturing factory are so. It may be useful to make work visible from the viewpoint of management side, although it does not organize accountability for technicians. In other words, rule-governed accounting makes the work of management accountable, but not the technicians' work. Through this confusion between rule-oriented actions and rule-governed accounting, "a wedge might be driven between the corporation and its repair technicians" (Brown & Duguit, 1991, p. 42).

Following the previous analysis, normative, formalistic inscriptions are useful to make work and mass-produced products visible in their specificity. For example, these things are useful and necessary if they are utilized without confusion for both bureaucratic accountability and field accountability. Bureaucratic accountability gives a different viewpoint on work or activities from that in the field. Similarly, normative, formalistic inscriptions are also locally utilized and organize only a partial accountability of work. In other words, normative, formalistic inscriptions such as a chart of processes of work are tools for accounting for part of the specific work in the management department instead of accounting for all of the work from a macro viewpoint. Based on this viewpoint, boundary crossing is done not by using normative, formalistic inscriptions, but by technologies and methods for making various accountabilities visible or observable (Suchman, 1997).

In the factory we researched, as far as we know, different multilayered accountabilities were not confused, although they were not free from various troubles and from the problem of training younger technicians. In the following, I attempt to analyze the coordination and the links in the factory.

Mutuality of Observation in the Factory

Some inscriptions sit in the middle of divisions of labor, and are utilized as resources for making work and mass-produced products mutually visible, as shown in Figure 7. For example, a standard plan originally produced in the management department is used when organizing accountability for customers, management, and technicians. For customers, a standard plan is regarded as one of documents that guarantees the quality of products and the systematic production in the factory. A standard plan is part of the resources for grasping how total quality control is conducted in the factory. At the same time, it can be regarded as a tool for translating a customer order to lathe machine technicians and inspectors in the factory. In a standard plan, as Kawatoko (this issue) described in detail, a drawing with notes comes from a customer. The other descriptions in a standard plan, such as a type of a machine allocated to the processing, the computer program number, the quality of the processing material, the cycle-time of the processing of one piece, and the post-processing in the outside of the factory, are added by the management department. In this way, the drawing that came from a customer is embedded in additional descriptions, and these specify the context for reading the drawing for lathe machine technicians. For example, the description of the allocated machine type is critical for technicians. Because the numbers of cutting tools and the possible length of products processed are different from one machine type to another, the design of the layout of movement of cutting tools often has to be altered according to machine type. Similarly, the description of post-processing allocated to another factory is also important information for lathe machine technicians. If there is plating to be done, lathe machine technicians have to change the degree of cutting. The degree of cutting should be a little bit more than the sizes described in the drawing, because plating naturally increases the size of products. Thus, a standard plan produced by the management department can be regarded as a partial translation of a customer's order for technicians and other members in the factory, although it is also shown to customers if necessary.

A QC chart for every kind of product, also produced by the management department, is utilized for accounting for work and mass-produced products for customers and technicians. As described previously, in a QC chart, checkpoints of measuring of materials and products, tolerance, compulsory measuring instruments, and other factors are listed. Checkpoints in this chart are not necessarily picked up based on deductive rules. Rather, these points reflect the history of troubles in

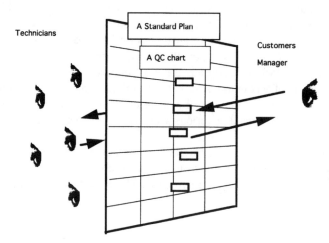

FIGURE 7   A standard plan and a QC chart as a tool organizational mutual observation.

production. For example, the sizes of materials supplied from a trader are always distributed in a range. The distribution of size of materials gives rise to a problem in some cases. If the diameter of the head portion of materials is distributed over a range, the sizes of the diameter in specific products may be distributed over tolerance. However, it is not possible to inspect all portions of all materials when receiving them from traders. Only the rich, past experiences of trouble inform the critical checkpoints of the sizes of materials for the specific product. Thus, in a QC chart, the history of troubles is accumulated and recorded. The QC chart tells the level of quality control to customers to some extent. For technicians, it shows the history of past complaints of customers and the past technicians' experience of troubles for the products.

In these cases, customers and technicians mutually observe each other with specific inscriptions. These inscriptions are resources for making work and mass-produced products mutually visible and accountable as shown in Figure 7, although what these inscriptions make visible for customers and technicians is not symmetrical.

The inscriptions that organize mutual accountability are produced by the management department. The management department links various places by producing various inscriptions. A standard plan and a QC chart reciprocally link customers with technicians and managers themselves with technicians. These inscriptions link one technician with other technicians or present technicians with past technicians as well. On the other hand, a chart of processes of the entire production cycle and a rule book for quality control and production control link the management department itself with its customers. Thus, the management department in the factory locates itself at the center of various links by producing and utilizing various inscriptions.

The management department in the factory does not unidirectionally sum up mass or macro, but bidirectionally, multidirectionally makes work and mass-produced products visible by producing and utilizing various inscriptions. Further, the work in the management department is not just to sum up mass or macro, but to transform it multiply, exactly as Henderson (1995) described in the case of engineers' various versions of drawings. For example, a standard plan is not just summing up the production. Rather, various descriptions are added into a drawing and the drawing is recontextualized by these additional descriptions. The other inscriptions of quality control and production control shown to customers are not just summing up the work of technicians and mass-produced products either. They focus on different aspects of work and mass-produced products than that on which technicians focus. The focal range in these inscriptions is different from that of technicians as well. Thus, the production of inscriptions in the management department is not simply summing up, abstracting, formalizing work and mass-produced products. If inscriptions, that is immutable and mobile (Latour, 1990), merely sum up mass and carry invariant information, they cannot link up various places. "The second order" and "third order" cascade of inscriptions are useless without dynamic recontextulization of "the original." Finally, the links between various places produced by inscriptions and interactions are not something fixed. Rather, inscriptions are often rewritten, added, recontextualized, and newly produced, and the links are organized and reorganized every day.

In the factory, multiple layers of accountability are organized according to different versions of the same inscription and according to the different juxtapositions of inscription. At the same time, some of these inscriptions link up various places by making both work and mass-produced products mutually, asymmetrically visible. Further, through the link, the viewpoint is transformed rather than maintaining invariant information. For example, the same standard plan is utilized as a resource for maintaining normative order and as a resource for processing according to divisions of labors by customizing it. Coordination among various places is embedded in this link between production activity and customization of the inscriptions. Instead of unifying the inscriptions and their use, or instead of confusing various organizations of accountability, multiple layers of accountability are coordinated and linked up to each other by day-by-day production and customization of inscriptions.

It is also possible to reinterpret boundary objects (Star & Griesemer, 1989) as a link between different organizations of accountability rather than as the object merely used by different communities. The inscriptions such as a standard plan and QC chart that represent multivoicedness, and the methods and customization of their use in each division of labor, might explain how different accountabilities are made mutually visible and linked up with each other.

Ecologies of Inscription

As a concluding remark, I outline the relation across different juxtapositions of inscriptions in the factory as an ecology of inscriptions. As analyzed, multiple accountabilities are organized with different juxtapositions of inscription and other technology. For example, a set of inscriptions utilized among customers and management organizes a bureaucratic accountability contrasted to field accountability in the section of lathe machine technicians. The juxtaposition of inscriptions among the management indicates the kind of accountability organized, although the juxtaposition does not specify the detail of inscriptions use in situated activity. Two points have dominated my description of inscriptions: (a) An inscription does not stand alone; in every case, practitioners locally and situatedly use the juxtaposition of inscriptions and other technologies to make work and products visible, and we can say that in sequence inscriptions mutually give each of the context and specificity to their uses, and (b) divisions of labor are also made visible by uses of different juxtapositions of inscriptions.

At the same time, the relations across different juxtapositions of inscription are not just parallel, but cross at the specific linking points (see Figure 8). Some inscriptions, such as the standard plan or the QC chart, are located at the linking points and have a special status. Some inscriptions become specific "actants" (Latour, 1995) in relation to other inscriptions. At linking points, mutualities of various divisions of labor are organized (see Figure 7). Actually, we are environments for each other with inscriptions and other technologies. Practitioners in the factory cannot be environments for each other without a juxtaposition of inscription. In addition, at a linking

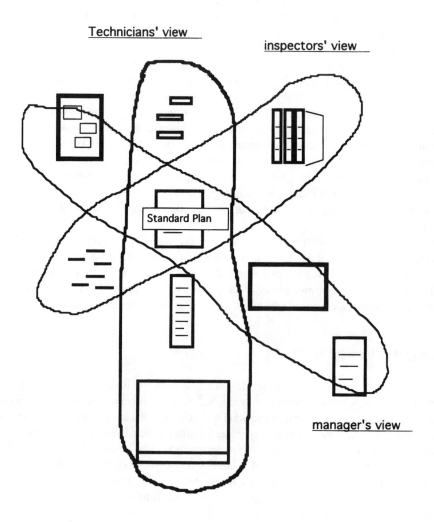

FIGURE 8   Different juxtapositions of inscriptions and the linking points.

point, what occurs is not the transmission of invariant information, but the recontextulization of the information. The recontexualization or reorganization of one accountability is accomplished by the arrangement and use of a different juxtaposition of inscription as in Figure 8. For example, descriptions in a standard plan produced by the management are recontextualized by technicians with their own juxtaposition of inscriptions and technologies. The networking of inscriptions is not like a linear chain simply summing up the invariant information step by step. In fact, imaging the relations across inscriptions as a linear chain and possible gaps among them (Latour, 1995) can be viewed as one of the more popular inscriptions locally utilized by management on specific occasions. In other words, the figure of a linear chain of inscriptions itself can be regarded as a inscription for bureaucratic accountability.

The network of inscriptions does not stand alone either. Rather, it organizes specific mutuality and collaboration across various communities while these are embedded in the specific organization of mutuality and collaboration. The network of inscriptions and a specific organization of mutuality and collaboration reciprocally constitute each other. For example, the arrangement of the multilayered juxtaposition of inscriptions and the linking across them in the factory are embedded in a specific organization of mutuality and collaboration across the divisions of labor while the arrangement organizes the specific mutuality and collaboration. The use of a claim-processing sheet in an insurance company drawn by Wenger (1990) can be understood as a boundary object or a normative inscription embedded in the organization of reciprocal disconnection between management and the claim processors; at the same time, that same reciprocal disconnection is organized and maintained by the normative and formalistic inscription. In short, the mutual creation of specific inscriptions and specific social relations or specific boundaries constitutes ecology as well.

ACKNOWLEDGMENTS

This research was financially supported by National Science Foundation, Japan 10831010. I would like to express my great appreciation to the following for their help with the survey in the factory: Yoshio Akabane, Toshiaki Shibue, and Tadashi Taguchi. I owe Ray McDermott and Mizuko Ito special thanks for commenting on this article and revising English. I deeply appreciate Chuck Goodwin and Lucy Suchman for their valuable comments on this article as well.

REFERENCES

Brown, J. S., & Duguit, P. (1991). Organizational learning and communities-of-practice: Toward a unified view of working, learning, and innovation. *Organization Science, 2,* 40–57.
Button, G., & Sharrock, W. (1998). The organizational accountability of technological work. *Social Studies of Science, 28,* 73–102.
Garfinkel, H., & Sacks, H. (1970). On formal structures of practical actions. In J. C. McKinney & E. Tiryakian (Eds.), *Theoretical sociology: Perspectives and developments* (pp. 160–193). New York: Appleton-Century-Crofts.
Goodwin, C. (1994). Professional vision. *American Anthropologist, 96,* 606–633.
Goodwin, C. (1996). Transparent vision. In E. Ochs, E. A. Schegloff, & S. Thompson (Eds.), *Interaction and grammar* (pp. 370–404). Cambridge, England: Cambridge University Press.

Goodwin, C., & Goodwin, M. H. (1996). Seeing as a situated activity: Formulating planes. In Y. Engestrom & D. Middleton (Eds.), *Cognition and communication at work* (pp. 61–95). Cambridge, England: Cambridge University Press.

Henderson, K. (1995). The visual culture of engineers. In S. L. Star (Ed.), *The culture of computing* (pp. 196–218). Cambridge, England: Basil Blackwell.

Latour, B. (1987). *Science in action.* Cambridge, MA.: Harvard University Press.

Latour, B. (1990). Drawing things together. In M. Lynch & S. Woolgar (Eds.), *Representation in scientific practice* (pp. 19–68). Cambridge, MA: MIT Press.

Latour, B. (1995). The pedofil of Boa Vista: A photo-philosophical montage. *Common Knowledge, 4,* 144–187.

Lynch, M. (1990). The externalized retina: Selection and mathematization in the visual documentation of objects in the life sciences. In M. Lynch & S. Woolgar (Eds.), *Representation in scientific practice* (pp. 153–186). Cambridge, MA: MIT Press.

Lynch, M., & McNally, R. (1997, March). Enchaining a monster: The production of representation in impure field. Paper presented at the science lecture series sponsored by the Portugese Ministry of Technology and Gulbenkian Foundation, Lisbon, Portugal .

McDermott, M. (1976). *Kid make sense: An ethnographic account of the interactional management of success and failure in one first-grade classroom.* Unpublished doctoral dissertation, Stanford University.

Orr, J. E. (1996). *Talking about machines: An ethnography of a modern job.* Ithaca, NY: Cornell University Press.

Star, S. L., & Griesemer, J. R. (1989). Institutional ecology, "Translations" and boundary objects: Amateurs and professionals in Berkeley's Museum of Vertebrate Zoology, 1907–39. *Social Studies of Science, 19,* 387–420.

Suchman, L. (1993). Technologies of accountability of lizards and aeroplanes. In G. Button (Ed.), *Technology in working order—studies of work, interaction, and technology* (pp. 113–126). New York: Routledge.

Suchman, L. (1994). Working relations of technology production and use. *Computer Supported Cooperative Work, 2,* 21–39.

Suchman, L. (1995). Making work visible. *Communication of the ACM, 38*(9), 56–64.

Suchman, L. (1997). Centers of coordination: A case and some themes. In L. B. Resnick, R. Saljo, C. Pontecorvo, & B. Burge (Eds.), *Discourse, tools, and reasoning: Essays on situated cognition* (pp. 41–62). Berlin: Springer-Verlag.

Ueno, N. (1997, October). *Cutting metal as situated practice.* Paper presented at the annual meeting of the Society for Social Studies of Science, Tucson, AZ.

Wenger, E. (1990). *Toward a theory of cultural transparency: Elements of a social discourse of the visible and the invisible.* Unpublished doctoral dissertation, University of California, Irvine.

MIND, CULTURE, AND ACTIVITY, 7(1&2), 81–104

Configuring Action in Objects:
From Mutual Space to Media Space

Christian Heath and Jon Hindmarsh

King's College London

It has long been recognized that the material environment is an essential feature of the organization of social action and interaction. It is only recently, however, that we have witnessed a burgeoning body of empirical studies, from within both the social and cognitive sciences, that has begun to delineate the ways in which objects are socially constructed and feature in social relations and activities. Despite this growing interest in the object in social life, there remains a paucity of research concerned with how objects are reflexively constituted in and through social interaction. In this article, we consider how aspects of the material environment are rendered momentarily intelligible in and through interaction and the ways in which objects provide a resource for the recognition of the actions and activities of others. We examine interaction in both conventional working environments and new experimental spaces created through advanced telecommunication and communication technologies to reveal the ways in which the sense and significance of social actions and activities are embedded in, and inseparable from, the local ecology.

In doing sociology, lay and professional, every reference to the "real world," even where the reference is to physical or biological events, is a reference to the organised activities of everyday life. (Garfinkel, 1967, p. vii)

And since the organism and environment determine each other and are mutually dependent for their existence, it follows that the life-process, to be adequately understood, must be considered in terms of their interrelations. (Mead, 1934, p. 130)

INTRODUCTION

In recent years, we have witnessed a growing body of research concerned with the object and the ways in which the material environment features in human action and perception. These developments have emerged in various disciplines and fields within the social, cognitive, and computer sciences and reflect a wide diversity of analytic commitments and substantive concerns. They have been driven by theoretical debates, conceptual innovations, and empirical findings, which powerfully expose the disembodied character of social action conventionally found in the human sci-

Requests for reprints should be sent to Christian Heath, Work, Interaction and Technology Research Group, The Management Centre, King's College, University of London, London SE1 8WA, GREAT BRITAIN. E-mail: christian.heath@kcl.ac.uk

ences (see, e.g., Callon & Latour, 1992; Clarke & Fujimura, 1992; Latour, 1988; Lynch & Woolgar, 1990; MacKenzie & Wajcman, 1985). They have also arisen in the light of the rapid development of information and communication technologies, tools, and artifacts that provide new ways of capturing, presenting, connecting, and re-embodying material realities (see, e.g., Benford, Greenhalgh, & Lloyd, 1997; Dourish & Bly, 1992; Finn, Sellen, & Wilbur, 1997; Gaver, Sellen, Heath, & Luff, 1993). Despite the richness and variety of these developments, we still have relatively little understanding of the ways in which objects, be they highly complex representations or simple artifacts, feature in social interaction, that is in the talk and bodily conduct of individuals in their dealings with each other.

In this article we wish to consider the ways in which objects and other aspects of the material environment are momentarily and reflexively constituted within social interaction. In the course of the discussion, we examine two interrelated issues that are of relevance to our understanding of the ways in which actions and activities are embodied in, and simultaneously embed in, their immediate physical environment. On the one hand, we address how individuals momentarily make reference and mutually orient to some aspect of the local environment, thereby giving some-"thing" its momentary significance and intelligibility. On the other hand, we consider how occasioned properties of the environment provide resources through which participants make sense of each other's actions and activities. In a sense, therefore, we are interested in how participants themselves constitute material realities as both "topic and resource" in the developing course of their action and interaction. In this way, we hope to reveal how the sense and significance of particular objects are inseparable from the environment in which they are located and the specific courses of action in which they figure.

The fragments discussed in the article are drawn from video recordings of social action and interaction within various environments. In the first part of the article, we discuss fragments drawn from more conventional work settings and in particular the line control rooms of London Underground. The thrust of the observations is to demonstrate ways in which participants rely on, and mutually constitute, properties of the immediate setting in the course of particular actions and activities. In the second part of the article, we consider a very different environment—an experimental "media space" in which two offices are connected through multiple cameras and monitors providing participants with access to each other, artifacts such as documents, and more broadly the offices themselves. Media spaces are cutting-edge developments concerned with providing remote participants with the ability to engage in (object-focused) collaborative work. Taking one example, we reveal the ways in which this particular media space fragments ecology and action and thereby undermines the ordinary ways in which participants configure and invoke objects and the material environment. While focusing on the details of interaction within these very different environments, we share an aim with much research on the object, that is, to demonstrate that social action and interaction are inextricably embedded within the material setting.

Before discussing a number of fragments, it is perhaps worthwhile to mention one or two additional issues that bear upon our current research and more generally studies of the material environment. In recent years, we have witnessed the emergence of a growing body of empirical research concerned with work, interaction, and technology. This corpus of research, commonly known as workplace studies, is one, among a variety of developments, that has helped place the object, in particular technical artifacts, at the heart of the analytic agenda for both sociology and cognitive science (see, e.g., Goodwin & Goodwin, 1996; Harper & Hughes, 1993; Heath & Luff, 1996, 2000; Hughes et al., 1988; Hutchins, 1995; Suchman, 1996; Whalen, 1995; Zimmerman,

1992). This body of research, primarily naturalistic studies of work in complex organizational environments, is beginning to provide the resources through which we can reconsider and respecify more traditional understandings of human–computer interaction and in particular reveal the ways in which technologies are embedded in, and dependent upon, socially organized practices and procedures. We hope that this article contributes to such studies and more generally our understanding of human–computer interaction. In particular, we wish to demonstrate the ways in which individuals rely upon socially organized practice and reasoning with which to notice, look at, consider, see, and interpret information presented on screens and electronic displays and how these "noticings" and "observations" emerge within the real-time interaction of participants.

Activity theory, as inspired by Vygotsky, also has a long-standing concern with the material aspects of social life. Studies in activity theory have been directed at an exploration of the relations between material artifacts, everyday practices, language, social systems, and cultures. Indeed, the recent application of activity theory to topics and issues in human–computer interaction and computer-supported cooperative work have focused on the use and development of new technologies while promoting their conceptualization within broader social systems of coordination and communication (e.g., Bodker, 1991; Engeström, 1993; Kuutti & Arvonen, 1992).

The observations discussed in this article also bear upon a related body of technical and social science research. The emergence of new computational and communication technologies has given rise to a range of complex systems designed to support real-time collaborative work among individuals located in different physical environments. Videotelephony and videoconferencing are the early precursors to these developments, innovations that include telepresence, media space, and collaborative virtual realities. Alongside these technical innovations, we have witnessed the emergence of a range of empirical studies in both the social and the cognitive sciences concerned with the characteristics of "interaction mediated through new technologies" (see, e.g., Finn et al., 1997). Although such studies have provided a rich body of findings concerning new and changing forms of interpersonal communication, they have not as yet explored how the dislocation of action from a common habitat can undermine the ability of interactants to produce and coordinate their conduct. This article therefore reflects on how a consideration of the ways in which individuals refer to and embed objects in action in conventional environments may provide some insights into problems that could emerge in more futuristic, virtual environments.

The analysis begins by examining how participants can encourage each other to examine the environment to look for a specific object and, on finding it, reveal its location. It then considers how actions may be entailed in objects, such that a participant responds to the environment rather than the action of the other. We go on to consider how individuals may have a coparticipant notice something they themselves have noticed and the ways in which the physical environment can provide resources for interpreting a colleague's conduct. Finally, we examine how a particular type of media space, known as Multiple Target Television, can undermine collaborative activity by fragmenting the action from its environment.

OBJECTS IN THE WORKPLACE

Because a number of the fragments are drawn from a particular setting, namely the Bakerloo Line Control Room, it might be helpful to introduce the environment and highlight some of the features that lend themselves to the study of objects in action. The Bakerloo Line Control Room is a complex multimedia environment that includes a range of technologies such as closed-circuit television (CCTV) screens, digital line displays, touch-screen telephones, and input monitors, and running the whole length of the room is a fixed line diagram showing the position of the all the trains running up and down the Bakerloo Line between Elephant and Castle in the south to Queen's Park in the north.

Therefore the objects in question are primarily textual information screens, diagrammatic displays, and CCTV images. The diagrams show, in various ways, sections of the line and the location of particular trains. They can show different sections of the line or different representations of the same section. So, for example, whereas the fixed line diagram provides an overall view of the line, the screens display more detailed diagrams of particular sections, including the actual numbers of individual trains. The CCTV screens provide views of platforms, including both passengers and trains in each station. Views are selected, and only one view of one platform can be provided at any one time. In consequence, one can look at various representations of the "same thing," such as a station. The immediate environment therefore consists of various objects, a number of which provide representations of phenomena (trains, passengers, signals, stations) that lie outside the control room.

In the course of the discussion, the data to which we refer are transcripts, diagrams, and pictures based on video recordings of work and interaction in these various settings. In each of the settings, we undertook extensive fieldwork and video recording; the material discussed here is, of course, extracted from a tiny fraction of the data we collected.

The setting involves close, ongoing collaboration between various personnel who are responsible for the day-to-day running of the line and developing a coordinated response to the problems and emergencies that inevitably arise in the operation of a rapid urban transport network. The personnel are seated at two consoles (see Figure 1). At the one console is the line controller and a colleague know as

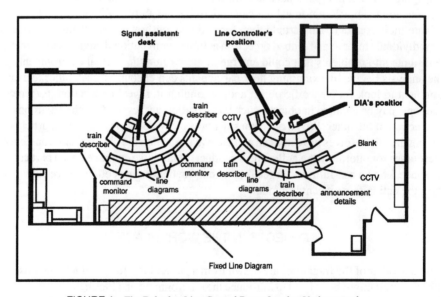

FIGURE 1   The Bakerloo Line Control Room London Underground.

the divisional information assistant (DIA), who is principally responsible for providing information for passengers. At the other, are seated the two signal assistants, who oversee the operation of the computerized signaling system and who reschedule trains and crews when the occasion demands.

These sort of work sites have some very interesting features with regard to the relation between action, objects, and the local environment, and it is perhaps worth mentioning one or two that may be relevant to the discussion. Although information that is presented on screens and diagrams vary according to the changing circumstances, particular types of information are associated with particular sources. So, for example, the CCTV screens on the line controller's console can only be used to provide images of station platforms; also, on the fixed line diagram, the position of stations in relation to each other does not vary. Moreover, it should be added that the personnel largely remains in specific locations within the control room itself and tools and information displays are seen as "belonging" to certain individuals. There is, therefore, a certain ecological stability that allows experienced participants to know where colleagues are looking and, on occasion, what they might be looking at. So, for example, it is possible to tell which station a colleague may be looking at when he or she is looking at the fixed line diagram.

Secondly, information on particular monitors, or the use of particular tools in the domain, is often associated by personnel with certain activities. For example, the input signaling monitor and keypad are routinely used to reschedule trains when the vehicles are out of timetabled order. Or, for example, although the CCTV may be used for various sorts of purposes, they are routinely referred to prior to delivery of public announcements to a station. There is, therefore, an interesting relation among certain sorts of activities and particular sources of information or tools within the domain, and this relation can be oriented to and exploited by colleagues in making sense of each other's actions. None of this is to suggest that the interpretation that participants make of each of other's conduct within the domain is independent of the developing activities in which they are engaged, but rather that they can exploit the relative stability of the environment and its relation to certain sorts of actions and activities.

In considering the ways in which participants render aspects of the local environment visible to each other in the course of their work, we consider various sorts of activities from searching for something, to pointing out mistakes, to making jokes and revealing problems. In considering these sorts of activities, we begin by examining occasions in which one participant explicitly characterizes the object to be found within the local environment and end by addressing occasions in which one participant simply encourages a colleague to notice something that he or she has noticed. In this way, we hope to provide a sense of the delicacy with which individuals who are working together are sensitive to each other's orientation to the environment of objects and its implications for action and interaction in the workplace.

SEARCHING TOGETHER

Within the control room, personnel often receive calls from remote colleagues requesting information. This information can often be provided without recourse to any visible information source. At other times, however, personnel must search through the array of technologies and documents to answer the query. The technologies and documents present images, text, numbers, diagrams, and the like—objects that themselves are "representations" of trains, crews, sections of line, and the like. On such occasions, participants explicitly orientate to particular aspects of the local environment and, in various ways, objects feature in action.

Consider the following fragment drawn from the signal desk, in which John (J) receives a phone call asking him where a train, Number 225, is currently positioned.

Fragment 1

    J: Hello there.
        (3.2)
    J: Two Two <u>Fi:</u>ve:: Let me have a look for it.
        (0.4)
    J: <u>Two</u> <u>Two</u> <u>Fi:</u>ve:::? (.) He's around here somewhere
    G: Two Two Five:s at er: (0.6) It's up there?
        (0.3)
    J: Oh he's in the <u>shed</u><he's in Queen's Park (.) *hh <u>Sou:th</u> Sheds:.
        (1.2)
    J: Indeed he is:.
        (1.2)
    J: Okay then?
        (.)
    J: Thank you:

The utterance of particular interest is John's turn, "<u>Two</u> <u>Two</u> <u>Fi:</u>ve:::? (.) He's around here somewhere. " Although the utterance is spoken into the handset, John simultaneously looks at various screens along the console. The first part of the utterance is emphasized, (hence the underling), and the word "five" is stretched (indicated by the colons) and has a rising intonation (represented by the question mark). Following a brief gap "(.)" of roughly 0.1 sec, John continues with "he's around here somewhere." During the utterance, John turns and looks at the monitor to the left of Graham (G; see Image ii), a monitor that shows the timing of the trains over the section of line for which Graham is responsible (south of Piccadilly Circus).

Fragment 1: Images i–iii

              G   J

(0.4)

i

J: <u>Two Two Fi:ve:::</u>? (.)

ii

J: He's around here somewhere

iii

As John turns toward the monitor to his left, Graham follows his gaze and they look at the screen together. So John has not only encouraged Graham to help him look for something that moments ago was not explicitly relevant, but encouraged him to look at and momentarily inspect the information on a specific screen, in a certain way. As John turns away, failing to find the train and uttering the word "around," Graham continues the search by first looking at the fixed line diagram and then at the monitor directly in front of John. Uttering "Two Two Five:s at er: (0.6) It's up there," Graham points to the image on the screen directly in front of John and at which John is now looking:

<u>Fragment 1: Image iv</u>

G   J

G: It's up there?

iv

John responds with "Oh he's in the shed<he's in Queen's Park (.) *hh Sou:th Sheds:.". So John finds the object in question, Train 225, by virtue of Graham's search and point. He informs the caller where the train is and simultaneously displays to Graham that he has both found the object and located its "exact" position.

John's original turn that elicits Graham's help in the search not only establishes how the object might, if found, be presented to John, namely revealed rather than simply informed, but also sets the very parameters of the search itself. The utterance identifies the object to be found, and the accompanying inspection of the monitor and scan of the console specifies the domains in which the object may be located. This turns out to be wrong, and in fact the train is right under John's nose, but all the same, Graham initially organizes his search with regard to John's looking. By pointing to the object and having John look at it and display he has seen it, and seen such that he can answer the question, the participants momentarily and collaboratively constitute the sense of particular feature of their local environment: the location of a particular train presented on a visual display unit.

The object itself, the details displayed on the screen, is perceived at that moment in a particular way; it gains its determinate sense or intelligibility within the activity at hand and, in particular, the search for the train in question. The caller, and the query he raises, provides resources to John with which to inspect the local milieu, and, in turn, John encourages Graham's participation. The actual location of the train on the railway, as portrayed in various ways on displays and monitors, is unknown at the beginning of the search; indeed, how the train might be portrayed, even represented, in part is dependent on the where it is actually found. John's initial turn and accompanying bodily orientation provides the resources through which Graham constitutes a range of potentially relevant features of the local milieu, ranging from the train listen monitor to his side, through to the fixed line diagram, and finally the diagrammatic monitor showing Queen's Park.

The scene is shaped, rendered intelligible, with regard to the resources provided by John and the sequentially appropriate activity, discovering and displaying the position of the train in question.

The sense of the scene, and the mutual recognition of the object in question, is momentarily established and forms the basis of subsequent action and activity. Graham's search for and discovery of the train is itself responsive to John's preceding actions—the point encourages John to look at a particular feature on the monitor and display appropriate recognition to his coparticipant. Simultaneously, its mutual discovery and constitution provides the resources to enable John to give the sequentially relevant response to the caller, that is, a description of where the train is currently located. We can, therefore, begin to see how the local environment, and a particular object momentarily, "mediates" the interaction and is itself constituted through that interaction. Successive features of the environment are made visible by virtue of the resources provided by John, and the position of the train is mutually and interactionally discovered and constituted. More generally, discovering and seeing the object, or rather constituting one aspect of the physical environment in a particular way, engenders sequentially relevant actions by both John, Graham, and presumably at some later date, by the caller himself.

The activity of responding to the query and of searching for the location of the train informs the way in which the workplace environment is discerned. In other words, the search provides for the realm of relevancies with which the two participants inspect, make sense of, and "respond to" successive features of the environment. These aspects of the environment, screen displays and diagrams, are reflexively produced and rendered intelligible in terms of the ongoing search. Although the participants confront the scene as a physical reality, which constrains where and how they look, their actions and interaction constitute that physical reality in a particular way. The object that forms the focus of the search, and which is discovered and mutually recognized, is produced and rendered intelligible within the interaction.

Furthermore, the object in question, the position of a particular train as displayed on a monitor, gains its determinate sense with regard to its location within the surrounding collection of objects and artifacts. Its sense is constituted in part through its relation to other potential sources of information. As successive features of the environment are inspected, they are in turn "ignored" until the relevant information is discovered on a particular screen. The image appearing on that screen, and its relation to other displays, informs how the query will be answered. The search involves discriminating a range of potentially relevant sources of information in the control room and, through a series of lookings, discovering the object in question: the section of a diagrammatic and textual display revealing the location of train '225.' The object provides the solution to the search and the basis for answering the caller's query. It is the answer to a puzzle, a puzzle that is part of the practicalities of dealing with traffic management on London Underground.

EMBODYING ACTION IN AN OBJECT

Within Fragment 1, the object is characterized prior to its discovery. The participants know what they are looking for—the 225—but need to find where it is within the local terrain of information. However, an object may stand in a rather different relation with regard to the actions of particular individuals. In other instances, for example, individuals encourage a coparticipant to look at an object. In doing so, they give a "flavor" of what the object is and how it might be responded to. In this way, an individual may embody an action in the object itself.

Consider the following fragment. It is drawn from a different work setting, namely the control center of a provincial police station. On the afternoon we join the action, the center is staffed by two police officers, Debi (D) and Susan (S). Debi and Susan are seated alongside each other typing. As she types, Debi notices something and bursts out laughing. "*thhhthhhhh" captures a lengthy in-breadth through the teeth, which in this case is part of her displaying but withholding her laughter. Moments later, Susan also begins to laugh, marked by "*hhhhhh."

Fragment 2

```
     Debi and Susan are typing
     :
• D:  Heh heh
      (1.2)
  S:  What you doing now::?
  D:                      *heh
      (0.3)
  D:  *thhhthhhhh
      (1.3)
  D:  *heh heh
      (0.6)
  D:  I meant to put a han::dle: *hhh
```

```
        (3.2)
 • S:  *hhhhhh
        (0.4)
 (D):  (*hhh)
        (1.2)
   S:  *hh hhhh
   D:      he heh
        (0.6)
   D:  Heh
```

As she bursts out laughing, Debi doubles up and looks at her monitor, as if overwhelmed by the joke that she has noticed on screen (see Image i). Although her outburst is not addressed to Susan, it serves to invite her colleague to find out what's made her double up in laughter. Moreover, the outburst not only gives a flavor as to what it is that Debi's noticed, namely it is funny, but also as to where the humorous thing is located, namely on the screen.

Fragment 2: Images i and ii

D   S

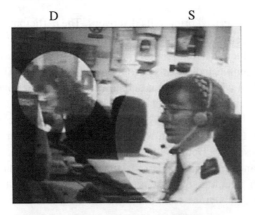

i

D: Heh heh
   (1.2)

S: What you doing now:::?

ii

The actions successfully elicit an inquiry, "What you doing now::?" and as Susan turns toward her colleague she finds Debi with her face on the screen smiling and laughing. As Susan speaks, Debi turns and looks at her monitor and then swivels it toward Susan to enable Susan to see for herself just what so tickled Debi. As Susan turns toward the swiveled monitor, Debi points to the relevant line of text and says, "I meant to put a han::dle: *hhh."

So rather than tell Susan what she has found, Debi encourages her colleague to see the joke for herself. Her original outburst, bodily conduct, and subsequent description not only give a sense of what the object is (something funny), but also pinpoint where it may found (in the text on Debi's screen). She provides the resources through which the object can be found and perceived.

It takes some time for Susan to find the object in question, and by the time she begins to laugh, Debi is almost doubled up in excitement. Susan's response is beautifully designed. She bursts out laughing and points to the object; thereby producing the sequentially appropriate response. The response displays both her discovery and her appreciation of the joke. Debi's original outburst, her "uncontrollable" laughter at the mistake that she made, not only encourages Susan to find out what has happened, but provides the resources through which she eventually discovers the source of the joke.

The fragment reveals how individuals may distinguish between describing an object from having a coparticipant experience the object for themselves. Rather than inform Susan of the mistake she made, Debi provides her colleague with resources to discover the object and to experience the joke for herself. It is as if the error in the text is intrinsically funny, an object that, in its own right, would serve to engender laughter from the participants. As we have seen, however, Debi goes to some trouble not only to encourage Susan to abandon the activity in which she is engaged and look at the materials on her screen, but to provide her with the resources with which to see (constitute) the object in the relevant way. Through the ways in which it is revealed, Susan experiences the joke and produces a sequentially appropriate response, namely laughter. The success of the joke hinges on the ability of Susan to find for herself what is funny about the object that she confronts. Indeed, she must find the joke almost independently of the ways in which it has been revealed.

The object therefore achieves a momentary visibility and significance it would not otherwise have. It gains a certain interactional relevance or sequential import. Susan laughs at the mistake that Debi has made. Debi presents her computer screen such that Susan encounters the object almost independently. The very ways in which Susan is led to perceive and experience what she sees serves to cast sequential import into a physical feature of the local environment. It is as if Susan's experience and response is engendered by the object itself rather than the ways it has been constituted by her colleague. Indeed, her laughter does not seem responsive to Debi, or even the way in which Debi has portrayed the object, but rather to the intrinsic qualities of the object itself (the mistake in the text). The object itself, or rather the error in the text, is constituted as essentially or intrinsically funny and engenders their laughter and enjoyment. The object and its perception is separated or fragmented from the very ways in which it is rendered noticeable, and thereby stands before the participants as an "objective order of social fact." They respond to the particular feature of the local milieu as if it is independent of their actions and the interaction. Yet, in doing so, they simultaneously and actively constitute that feature.

RENDERING AN OBJECT "NOTICEABLE"

In the fragments discussed so far, one participant builds a characterization of an object. The characterization may consist of a train number or something funny. The characterization informs the ways in which the environment is inspected by the coparticipant and how the particular object is discovered. It also informs how the coparticipant experiences and subsequently deals with the object. The precharacterization projects what the object may consist of, where within the local environment it may be found, and how it should be responded to or dealt with. The sense of the object and the ways in which it is constituted turns on the way in which it is introduced, invoked, and precharacterized (c.f. Goodwin, 1996, on "prospective indexicals").

Even in Fragment 2, as Debi's outburst encourages Susan to discover and experience the joke for herself, she nevertheless sets the ways in which it should be treated, namely as a joke. On some occasions, however, one participant may wish to have another notice something within the local environment without characterizing either what the object is or how it should it be perceived. One individual may simply attempt to render something "visible" without providing the coparticipant with a sense of what it is or why he or she should look at it. In rendering an object noticeable in this way, an individual invites a coparticipant to discover for him or herself why it has been drawn to his or her attention, to provide an account as to the potential relevance of the object to the here and now. It is for the coparticipant therefore to discover, retrospectively, why the object might have been brought to his or her attention. It is interesting, phenomenologically, in that an individual is encouraged to search the world for something that is unknown to him or her as he or she undertakes the search, but obvious once he or she has found (produced) it.

Having people discover an object for themselves not only allows coparticipants to experience an object "raw" or "uncontaminated," so to speak, but also provides an opportunity for someone to point something out without committing him or herself to a particular characterization, or claim to the relevance, of the object in question. It allows individuals to almost conceal that it is they who have had you notice something. So, for example, if it turns out to be unimportant or irrelevant, then they are not seen as foolish or to blame. It also, in workplace environments, allows individuals, for example, to subtly bring to the attention of their superiors things that the superiors themselves should have noticed and have been dealing with. And of course more generally, we find an example of the way in which individuals can keep an eye out on the world with regard to the interests of their fellows and delicately bring to their attention events that may be of relevance to their interests, responsibilities, and activities (cf. Sacks, 1992).

The following fragment is a long and complex piece drawn from a moment in the life of the Bakerloo Line Control Room. We join the action as one of the Underground staff (Vic [V]), who is visiting the control room is telling the controller (C), a story about the then Minister of Transport turning up to a function rather the worse for wear, or "pissed" (a colloquialism for "drunk"). In the course of the story, the DIA appears to notice a potential problem emerging at Waterloo that the controller might have to deal with, but is reluctant to interrupt the story-telling. He tries to bring the problem to the controller's attention without interrupting the tale or committing himself as to whether there is indeed a problem.

<u>Fragment 3</u>

    V: Carrying on the <u>st</u>ory wer (.) with the three p: (.) <u>th:r</u>ee
    V: (part most of the to ner), four <u>par:t</u>
•   ((Ding Dong))
        (0.8)

- V: <u>Vi</u>ctoria Line at Ri<u>ck</u>mansworth, (0.6) on Mon:day <u>nigh</u>:t^
     (0.4)
  V: an he:(r): like (.) The Minister of Transport <*Lipton (it is) turns <u>up</u>^ (0.5) at er::
     (0.4)
- V: Rickmonsworth to see the: (0.6) the Waterloo <u>Tra</u>in,
     (0.8)
  V: they've fini<u>sh</u>ed there: >then immediately go back to
     Claphham hehhhhhsss heh heh
  C: they <u>fini</u>shed on frhhom
     therheh <u>he</u> <u>h</u> heh
  V: (*heh heh)
- C: Bri<u>lliant</u>
  V: (That was)
  C: Brilliant
     (0.2)
  V: He <u>really</u> was <u>pissed</u>.
     (1.8)
- C: That Thirty <u>Three</u> at Waterloo?
     (0.6)
DIA: Yeh.=
  C: =He's (time:) >no he's tight
DIA: Fif<u>teen</u>::^
  C: Yeah

The controller is physically orientated toward Vic, who is standing to the rear of the console. The DIA is facing forwards, looking at the timetable. As Vic tells his tale, the doorbell suddenly rings and momentarily interrupts the story. The DIA looks up at the fixed line diagram, resets his CCTV monitor to Waterloo (see Image i), and as the image emerges, turns to the controller (see Image ii) and then immediately back to the monitor (see Image iii).

<u>Fragment 3: Images i–iii</u>

V   C   DIA

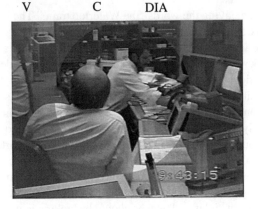

i

V: <u>Vi</u>ctoria Line a Ri<u>ck</u>mans-
workth, (0.6)

V: on Mo<u>n</u>:day ni<u>gh</u>:t^

ii

V: (0.4) an he: (r) : like (.)

iii

The selection of the image by the DIA, and his shift of gaze to the other and then the monitor, encourages the controller to look at the screen (just noticeable on Image iii). The DIA's actions appear to point to the screen and encourage his coparticipant to inspect the scene for a potentially relevant event. So, the DIA's actions momentarily render a particular feature of the local environment of potential significance to the other. The controller looks at the screen for a couple of moments, and then, either because he is unable to see anything of any importance or simply due to Vic's continuing tale, he returns his gaze to the speaker.

A little later, Vic once again pauses, delaying the words "the Waterloo train." The DIA seems to exploit the break in the story. He once again turns to the controller, then to the CCTV monitor.

The DIA's shifts in orientation once again encourage the controller to turn from Vic and look at the screen with his colleague. The break within the developing course of the story provides the DIA with the opportunity of rendering a particular object within the local milieu noticeable; the DIA's glance to the controller and then the monitor encourages his colleague to inspect the very same scene as the DIA. As Vic continues the story and utters "Waterloo train," both the controller and the DIA are looking at the same image; curiously the image on the screen is a train at Waterloo station.

It looks, therefore, as if the DIA encourages the controller to look at, and notice, a particular object within the local environment. The object in question is a CCTV picture of a platform; itself a representation of part of an environment that lies beyond the walls of the control room.

Why the image or the domain is brought to the controller's attention is not available within the ways in which it is pointed out. Indeed what "it" is and why he should be looking at it is unknown to the controller. It may be the case that there is no need at all for the controller to look at the image, and yet then, within the confines and enjoyment of a story, he finds himself orienting to an image, one image among many displayed in this highly complex environment, trying to find a reason as to why he should be looking at it.

The controller decides to exit from his conversation with Vic and find out whether difficulties are emerging at Waterloo, the scene that he has been encouraged to look at on the monitor.

His response to the story, "Brilliant Brilliant," is nicely designed to display his appreciation, while simultaneously allowing him to step out of the conversation with the visitor. As he utters his appreciation, he turns away from Vic and re-orientates bodily toward the console. As he re-orientates, he turns first to the CCTV monitor and then the fixed line diagram, looking in the area of Waterloo, and utters, "That Thirty Three at Waterloo?" The query is designed to discover more about what may happening at Waterloo and in particular which train it is that is standing at the platform.

As the controller helps bring the story to completion, therefore, he is already sensitive to the possibility of a problem in the running of the service and where that problem might be. In consequence, as he exits from the story, he initiates a sequence through which he attempts to identify the train at Waterloo and then goes on to make various changes to the running times and numbers of a series of trains. His inquiry to determine the number of the train derives from the ways in which some aspect of the immediate environment has been rendered noticeable and potentially accountable by the DIA. In making his inquires, the controller does not know what the problem is, or even whether there are definitely difficulties arising with the service, just that a colleague appears to have noticed "something" at a particular location on the Underground. Rendering something noticeable appears to make it potentially problematic and worthy of further inquiry. In a very different vein, Sacks (1972) makes a similar point:

> For Western Societies at least, being noticeable and being deviant seem intimately related. The notion that one is suspect whose appearance is such that he stands out, have the deepest foundations. Indeed, in Judeo-Christian mythology, human history proper begins with the awareness of Adam and Eve, that they are observable. The next bit of social information thereupon we learn is: to be observable is to be embarrassable. (pp. 280–282)

Whether the DIA knows what the problems is, or whether he is simply sensitive to something not being quite right at Waterloo, is unclear. However, as Vic delivers the story, the DIA exploits potentially vulnerable breaks within that story, namely an interruption and later a pause, to produce and display particular actions. Although the actions in which the DIA engages do not disrupt or interfere with the continued production of the story, they serve to display to the recipient of the tale, the controller, that something may be noticeable. In particular, in resetting the CCTV monitor, and in turn glancing at the fixed line diagram, the controller, and then to the screen, the DIA displays that he himself has noticed something happening at Waterloo and that it may be relevant to the controller. The DIA's actions render a feature within the local environment, noticeable, worthy of attention, and by re-orientating to and from the controller, displays that whatever is on the monitor may be of interest to his colleague.

The DIA's actions exploit the controller's ability to notice conduct outside the direct line of his regard. Even though the controller is oriented toward the story's teller, Vic, and is participating as a recipient of the tale in the course of its production, he is sensitive to the DIA's actions and the ways in which those actions are tailored not only to allow the DIA to look at the monitor, but are simultaneously designed to display those lookings to the controller himself. It is, of course, the display of looking, rather than simply the looking, that renders the DIA's actions and the focus of those actions relevant to the controller. Moreover, it is not simply that the controller is peripherally aware or sensitive to the movements of the DIA, but rather he is able to embed the DIA's conduct within the local environment of objects and artifacts. The DIA's looking is used as a vehicle for the controller to locate a potentially relevant object (the image on the screen) within the local environment, just as the image on the screen provides a resource for assembling the sense of the DIA's look.

Unlike some of the earlier fragments, in the case at hand, no precharacterization concerning the nature or even the locale of the object is provided. The controller is not told what he should be looking for, the reasons he should be looking for it, or even the exact feature at which he should be looking. The resources through which the controller is able to establish mutual orientation with his coparticipant consist of no more than the DIA resetting a monitor and then looking at that screen and the fixed line diagram. Sequentially they emerge within an activity in which they have little bearing. Therefore, although certain resources suggest the general domain of scrutiny, not only a solution but the problem itself has to be discovered by the controller. As he turns to look at the screen that has been brought to his attention, his looking is instructed merely by the fact that something is noticeable and of (potential) relevance to him. Indeed, as he turns, the extent to which the image might engender further action is yet to be determined. So, unlike the earlier fragments in which some next action (answering a query, appreciating a joke, etc.) is embedded in the object, in this instance, the controller himself must determine the relevance of the screen image. He has to decide what to do, having seen the screen. In this case, the sight of the screen image leads the controller to ask for further information about the identity of the train depicted on the screen. Therefore, the meanings of the image on the screen are embedded prospectively in what will turn to be relevant or not. The DIA's actions prefigure their own characterization and the activity in which they may eventually be seen to have initiated. They simply rely upon the controller's ability to notice a noticing and his interest in developing an account as to why a colleague might have noticed that object.

OBJECTS AND "VIRTUAL" ACTION

Now it is a basic axiom of any interpretation of the common world and its objects that these various co-existing systems of co-ordinates can be transformed one into the other; I take it for granted, and I assume my fellow-man does the same, that I and my fellow-man would have typically the same experiences of the common world if we changed places, thus transforming my Here into his, and his – now to me a There – into mine. (Schutz, 1962, pp. 315–316)

In various ways, we can begin to see how participants momentarily constitute particular features of the local environment and how such features can gain a certain significance within their activities. The character of these "physical" properties of the local environment is interactionally determined, then and there, in the dealings between the participants and within the developing course of their conduct. It is not simply therefore that something is looked at, but rather by rendering the object relevant, the participants give some feature of their local environment, even if it is itself a window on a milieu outside the domain, a particular significance and meaning. The production of the object, its mutual constitution, is also relevant to the participants' subsequent conduct in various implicating actions and even activities. The environment, therefore, is not simply the product of the participants' actions, but itself gives sense and relevance to their conduct and the activities in which they are engaged or are about to be engaged. There is, if you like, an embeddedness, a congruence between the environment and the action; the conduct of the participants reflexively constitute the momentary sense and significance of (some aspect of) the local environment, whereas the environment (as constituted) gives sense and significance to the participants' actions. This reflexivity between action and object is critical to production and intelligibility of the participants' conduct.

With the growing interest in developing technologies to support collaborative work among physically remote individuals, the implications of the observations discussed previously may go beyond a sociology of the object. For example, even if we consider basic videotelephony and videoconferencing, we can begin to consider how the interconnectedness of action, object, and local milieu may generate some interesting problems and issues. For instance, if one provides the participants with access to each other, is it necessary to provide access to the objects that the participants might ordinarily rely on when working together. If this type of access is provided, the question is how can you guarantee that the participants can see the object in mutually compatible ways (for the practical purposes at hand).

These sorts of issues informed a series of experiments we recently conducted at Rank Xerox Research Laboratories in Cambridge. The experiments, known as MTV I and II, were designed to provide individuals based in different physical locations with the ability to speak and see each other and to see each others' local environment. The system was designed to enhance, in an experimental setting, the sorts of access that more basic telecommunications technologies can currently provide (see Gaver et al., 1993; Heath, Luff, & Sellen, 1995; and for related studies Dourish, Adler, Bellotti, & Henderson, 1996; Dourish & Bly, 1992; Heath & Luff, 1992). It is merely one example of a burgeoning body of research being undertaken both in Europe and elsewhere concerned with "media space" (computational and video infrastructures that provide support for distributed working). Rather than merely providing a head-and-shoulders view of a remote coparticipant, numerous images of the other were made available in MTV II: a conventional head-and-shoulders view; an "in-context" view of the other in their room; and a desktop view, showing the document or model being worked on. Figure 2 provides a sense of the links and access between the two offices in which we experimented with the system.

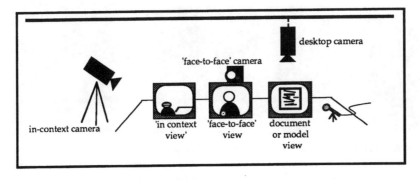

FIGURE 2   MTV II Experiment.

We organized a series "naturalistic" experiments where participants were assigned various collaborative tasks that required reference to objects located within their respective environments. It may be worth briefly considering a fragment taken from one of those experiments where two participants were asked to arrange the furniture in a model room, which was located in only one of their offices. In the extract, Kathy (K) attempts to point to the position in which David (D) should place the speakers in the model room. The model containing the furniture is located on David's desk and is visible to Kathy on both her desktop and in-context monitors.

Fragment 4

D: So: (.) the speakers need to go (0.5) s:(ome) s:<u>ome</u>where: like tha::(t)=

K: =yeah I would suggest the one on top of the fireplace actually comes down to this:::
    (0.7)

K: the corner.
    (.)

K: Actually you can't see where I'm pointing can you *hhh

To show David where he should place the speakers, Kathy points at the corner of the model room as it is shown on her desktop monitor. As she says, "suggest the one on top," her finger points at the model, dropping down to the corner of the screen as if indicating that the speaker should be removed from the fireplace and placed on the floor. She continues to point at the screen throughout the utterance, recycling the pointing emphasis in the gesture with the words "this" and "the corner." She only begins to withdraw the gesture as she begins to utter, "Actually you can't see where I'm pointing."

The coparticipant, David, can see the gesture, though he appears unable to discern where Kathy is pointing. The gesture appears on two of his monitors, and the model at which it is pointing is placed before him on his desk. For David, the difficulty is that although he can both hear and see Kathy, and knows presumably that Kathy is referring to the model, he cannot see the gesture with regard to the object at which it is directed. The best view he has of the gesture is provided on his desktop-view monitor, which shows Kathy reaching across to point. However, as Image iii shows, the target of the pointing gesture (the model room) cannot be recovered from that image:

Fragment 4: Images i–iii

 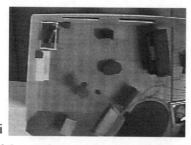 

i   ii   iii

Kathy points at one of the monitors on her desk (Image i), which depicts the model under discussion (Image ii). However, the scene available on David's "desktop-view" monitor (Image iii), depicts Kathy's pointing gesture in isolation from the image at which she is pointing.

His view of the model, as it sits before him, is not simply different from Kathy's, but rather dislocated from his view of her. In other words, David is not simply unable see the world in the way in which Kathy sees the world, but more important, cannot reassemble his view of the model with his view of Kathy and her gesture. The fragmentation of the views undermines David's ability to assemble the actions of the reference and the referent itself.

The fragment also reveals a second, perhaps more interesting, problem. Kathy is able to see David, she knows that the model is located on his desk, and she is aware of the views that he has of her. Despite this, she points to the model displayed on her monitor. She presupposes that David can see her pointing to a location in the model, a model that is actually sitting on his desk. Moreover, in the face of receiving no acknowledgement from David, she recycles the gesture, continuing to assume that it and its referent are mutually visible. It is perhaps only as she begins to describe, rather than show, where he should position the speaker, uttering "the corner," that she begins to realize that David cannot make sense of her actions. For some reason, therefore, the participants assume that if they can see it, their coparticipant can see it in the same way; they presuppose a "reciprocity of perspective" (Schutz, 1962). They design actions that presuppose that the other can see what they can see in roughly the way that they can see it. They assume not only that can they be seen, but that their coparticipant is able to use his or her visual and bodily orientation to determine the character and location of features and objects within their respective environments.

Although the system provides individuals with variable visual access to each other's domain, we found that it failed to support the sorts of mutual reference and pointing that is fundamental to many of the activities discussed earlier. In particular, it was found that though the system provided each individual with views of the other and their respective domains, the fragmentation of the images undermined the participants' ability to find what the other was pointing at and how it was relevant to the activity at hand. Indeed, the system also raised troubles for the people doing the pointing. They were unable to see whether their coparticipant was actually looking at the object at which they were pointing. The separation of the physical environment and the person across a number of screens undermined the individual's ordinary abilities to embed the action of the other within the material milieu in which it occurred. So although the experimental systems provided a relevant set of views, the fragmentation of the scenes undermined the social and interactional relation between action and environment.

In a sense, therefore, the problem derived not so much from what the other could see and could not see, but rather from the ways in which the technology undermined an individual's ability to embed action within specific features of its local material environment.

For the purposes at hand, such technological environments reveal some interesting aspects of the ways in which individuals in copresent interaction rely upon access to each other within their local physical environment. The problem with this and other forms of advanced technologies to support distributed collaborative working is that they allow individuals to assume congruent access to each other while undermining their ordinary abilities to establish mutual orientation. Indeed, they give an individual the sense of shared access to the other's local domain while simultaneously corrupting that access. In particular, by providing limited and fragmented images of the respective domains, the systems fragment the other, and the actions of the other, from the local physical environment in which those actions are embedded.

It also seems that participants find it difficult to reassemble the occasioned relation between action and the local milieu, so that the disembodied character of the participants' conduct undermines the sense and sequential import of particular actions and activities. For example, the seemingly trivial inability of participants to assess the gaze and bodily orientation of the other with regard to the other's environment, let alone one's own milieu, removes a critical element of the resources through which the participants can momentarily establish the interactional relevance of some object or artifact. And of course, more delicate ways in which a coparticipant can render aspects of his or her local environment visible in the course of, or to initiate, activity simply pass unnoticed. Curiously, however, such systems appear to mislead the users, encouraging them to assume that they have access to each other and their respective environments, only to discover in the course of interaction that their coparticipant is unable to disambiguate their conduct. A cruel media indeed.

DISCUSSION

An important influence on the growing body of research in both the social and cognitive sciences has been the emergence of new technologies and in particular the computer. In cognitive science, for example, the growing interest in distributed cognition, situated reasoning, and the like has arisen, in part, in the light of the burgeoning critique of human–computer interaction, artificial Intelligence, and its reliance on plan-based, goal-oriented models of human conduct (see, for example, Suchman, 1987). Over the past decade, we have witnessed the emergence of a wide range of research that has attempted to respecify the relations or interaction among human beings, tools, texts, and technologies, and in particular attempted to delineate the cognitive practices through which tools, ranging from the banal to the complex, provide representations of the world and a foundation to action. Although sociology has been less concerned than the "new wave" cognitive science with the indigenous use of technologies in practical situations, nonetheless, through the sociology of scientific knowledge and parallel developments in the sociology of technical systems, a growing body of research has emerged that reveals the ways in which objects and artifacts, tools and technologies, gain their significance by virtue of social organizations that delimit their meaning(s), relevance, and significance.

In one sense, this article and related workplace studies (see, e.g., Goodwin & Goodwin, 1996; Heath & Luff, 1996; Suchman, 1996; Whalen, 1995) can be seen as an attempt to interweave the growing concerns in these very different disciplines, on the one hand to place the indigenous use of objects and artifacts, tools and technologies, and the local physical environment at the forefront of the analytic agenda and on the other to delineate the ways in which their production and intelligibility are dependent on and embedded in social action and social organization.

The materials discussed here point perhaps to a more radical and distinctive sociological treatment of the relation betweem objects, including tools and technologies, the environment, and action. They suggest that in the course of particular actions and activities, participants may orientate to a range of features within the local milieu, and the arrangement and interconnection of these objects is an integral aspect of the organization of the participants' conduct. They also suggest that aspects of the immediate environment, for example information and images on computer screens, gain their sense and intelligibility in and through the ways in which they feature in interaction between the participants; interaction that is emergent, accomplished, and unavoidably in flux. The sense or intelligibility of an image on a screen or whatever is assembled by the participants at particular moments in the developing course of the interaction; its significance is bound to the moment of action in and through which it occurs. The screens of information do not provide an overarching influence on the conduct of the participants or preserve a stable sense or meaning through time and space, but rather are embedded in, and inseparable from, the action and activity in which they arise. The participants do not attribute meaning to a preexistent environment or interpret the scene at hand (although this may indeed occur); rather in the course of their action and interaction, they reflexively produce their surrounding material world.

In a number of the instances discussed in this article, the actual object constituted by the participants becomes explicitly relevant when one of the individuals initiates a course of action. For example, in Fragment 1, a signalman not only searches for a particular phenomenon, the indication of a train on one of the screens, but invites his colleague to help him find that object. In the course of the search, the participants discriminate the scene with regard to the practical problem at hand, the location of the 225, and thereby reflexively constitute the sense of various objects and images. During the course of their very looking, the participants do not simply shift the focus of their attention, but rather, in searching for the object in question, render aspects of the scene both relevant and intelligible. The object, the section of the diagram indicating the location of the 225, stands to the participants as a feature of the local milieu, as an "objective order of fact" with which there can be little debate. And yet, the discovery of the 225, its particular sense or meaning, is embedded in and inseparable from the ways in which the participants have inspected (constituted) the scene and established a mutual orientation toward a particular feature of the environment.

Furthermore, action is embedded in objects in various ways. So, for example, in Fragment 2, we can see how a participant casts sequential import into an object. She encourages her colleague not only to notice something that hitherto was unavailable, but to react to the object in a particular way, as something to be enjoyed as a joke. In this way, the coparticipant is able to experience the object as a joke firsthand, and the object itself seems to engender the appropriate response. Both the discovery of the object and the action it engenders are accomplished in and through the ways in which the line of text is pointed out to the other. The exclamation and the pointing project a relevant sequence of actions by the coparticipant: to discover the object (in a particular way) and to produce the sequentially appropriate response. In this, and many other ways, features of the local environment are rendered momentarily visible and are given a significance within the action that they would not otherwise have.

The examples also reveal how the local environment provides a resource for making sense of the actions of other individuals. So, for example, in Fragment 1, the signal man shifts his gaze across various displays. The sorts of information they embody provides a resource for his coparticipant to make sense of these actions. Both the (inferred) focus of the signalman's gaze, coupled with the order in which he inspects the environment, enables his colleague to embed the talk and recognize that he is engaged in a search. In a similar manner, in Fragment 2, seeing her colleague looking at the screen allows the police constable to recognize just what it is that the other has seen and why she might be laughing. In Fragment 3, one participant has another notice something within the local milieu and render a particular aspect of a scene, a train arriving in a station, visible. Moreover, seeing the other notice that object allows the DIA to render intelligible the controller's glances and subsequent query. Therefore, the actions of individuals are firmly embedded in, and, more crucially, made sense of, with regard to their position in the local physical environment.

In the 1950s, Schutz (1996) discussed the communicative problems that might arise with the emergence of new technologies such as the telephone and television. He argued that such media introduce limited and asymmetrical access to the vocal and visual conduct of the participants to the interaction, and in so doing may undermine their ability to establish or maintain a reciprocity of perspective, which for Schutz is central to the accomplishment of intelligible social action and interaction. In the materials at hand, we can begin to see how the issues that arise with certain forms of new technologies although they may occasion difficulties in presupposing and preserving a reciprocity of perspective, undermine social action in ways unanticipated by Schutz. They reveal in dramatic form how participants rely upon their abilities to make reference to and invoke features of their local environment, and how, as a matter of course, they presuppose and maintain a reciprocity of perspective. At its most simple, individuals are confronted with the realization that what they have seen may not necessarily be visible to others, and if it is visible, it is not necessarily visible in a mutually compatible way.

But the problem is not simply one of reference and establishing a mutual orientation toward relevant features of the local milieu. Rather, the very ways in which actions are embodied in, or related to, objects within the respective milieus are undermined by the technology so that, for example, the sense of a gesture or utterance can be misconstrued. Participants are unable to use features of the other's environment to read their actions, just they are unable to satisfactorily refer to objects within their own domain. It is the disconnection between action, object, and environment that renders media space and the like such curious and unrewarding domains in which to conduct collaborative activities.

Although all human action and interaction occurs within some surrounding physical environment, the task perhaps for sociology and cognate disciplines is to delineate the ways in which material realities feature in, and are relevant to, particular courses of action. There has been a tendency, at least in sociology to think of the immediate physical environment as a framework in which conduct occurs, and even more recent developments in cognitive science have preserved the idea that physical realities provide a preexistent "domain" that is represented and transformed through human reasoning. In this article we hoped to show how the sense and intelligibility of objects within the local milieu arises within the course of particular actions and activities, and their meaning and relevance does not remain stable through time and space; indeed the character of an object and its significance to an activity can transform within the emerging course of single action, such as a turn at talk (see also Goodwin, 1994).

In this light, it is interesting to note that for the sorts of domains addressed in this article, namely co-located workplaces, the material environment is invoked and rendered relevant and intelligible in and through interaction; it gains its sense and significance with regard to the collaborative conduct of the participants in concert with each other. As one examines such domains, it becomes increasingly clear that to separate language, bodily conduct, and interaction from the physical environment, or vice versa, for analytic purposes can be problematic, because the very production and intelligibility of social actions and activities is embedded in and simultaneously constitutes material features of the local milieu. In attempting to reconceive objects as integral features of mundane action and interaction, it may be the case that we not only begin to throw light on the reflexive properties of human conduct and its ability to produce the very realities that it confronts, but to rethink how we might understand the role of tools and technologies in work organizations. It may provide an opportunity for developing a sociology of the artifact and technology that takes human interaction seriously and begins to reveal how complex systems in the "new institutions" are dependent upon social organized practice and interaction.

ACKNOWLEDGMENTS

This research was supported by ESRC Grant number R000237136. Earlier versions of this article were presented at the Institute Paris La Defence (1995), The Social Research Methods Summer School University of Essex (1996), and Germany Sociology Meetings in Dresden (1996). We would like to thank, among others, Paul Luff, Abi Sellen, Bernard Conein, Ani Borzeix, Diedre Boden, Hubert Knoblauch, John Gumperz, David Silverman, David Greatbatch, and Kjeld Schmidt for their helpful comments on a number of the issues discussed here.

REFERENCES

Benford, S. D., Greenhalgh, C. M., & Lloyd, D. (1997). Crowded collaborative virtual environments. In *Proceedings CHI '97* (pp. 59–66). New York: ACM Press.

Bodker, S. (1991). *Through the interface: A human activity approach to user interface design.* Hillsdale, NJ: Lawrence Erlbaum Associates, Inc.

Callon, M., & Latour, B. (1992). Don't throw the baby out with the Bath school! A reply to Collins and Yearley. In A. Pickering (Ed.), *Science as practice and culture* (pp. 343–368). Chicago: Chicago University Press.

Clarke, A., & Fujimura, J. (Eds.). (1992). *The right tools for the job: At work in 20th century life sciences.* Princeton, NJ: Princeton University Press.

Dourish, P., Adler, A., Bellotti, V., & Henderson, A. (1996). Your place or mine? Learning from long-term use of audio-video communication. *Computer-Supported Co-operative Work, 5,* 33–62.

Dourish, P., & Bly, S. (1992). Portholes: Awareness in a distributed work group. In *Proceedings of CHI '92.* New York: ACM Press.

Engeström, Y. (1993). Developmental studies of work as a Testbench of Activity Theory: The case of primary care medical practice. In S. Chaiklin & J. Lave (Eds.), *Understanding practice: Perspectives on activity and context.* Cambridge, MA: Cambridge University Press.

Finn, K. E., Sellen, A. J., & Wilbur, S. E. (Eds.). (1997). *Video mediated communication.* Mahwah, NJ: Lawrence Erlbaum Associates, Inc.

Garfinkel, H. (1967). *Studies in ethnomethodology.* Englewood Cliffs, NJ: Prentice Hall.

Gaver, W. W., Sellen, A., Heath, C. C., & Luff, P. (1993). One is not enough: Multiple views in a media space. *Proceedings of INTERCHI '93* (pp. 335–341). New York: ACM Press.

Goodwin, C. (1994). Professional vision. *American Anthropologist, 96,* 606–633.

Goodwin, C. (1996). Transparent vision. In E. Ochs, E. A. Schegloff, & S. Thompson (Eds.), *Interaction and grammar* (pp. 370–404). Cambridge, England: Cambridge University Press.

Goodwin, C., & Goodwin, M. H. (1996). Seeing as a situated activity: Formulating planes. In D. Middleton & Y. Engeström (Eds.), *Cognition and communication at work: Distributed cognition in the workplace* (pp. 61–96). Cambridge, England: Cambridge University Press.

Harper, R. H. R., & Hughes, J. A. (1993). What a f-ing system! send em all to the same place and then expect us to stop 'em hitting. In G. Button (Ed.), *Technology in working order: Studies of work, interaction and technology* (pp. 127–144). London: Routledge & Kegan Paul.

Heath, C. C., & Luff, P. (1992). Media space and communicative asymmetries: Preliminary observations of video mediated interaction. *Human–Computer Interaction, 7,* 315–346.

Heath, C. C., & Luff, P. K. (1996). Convergent activities: Collaborative work and multimedia technology in London Underground Line control rooms. In D. Middleton & Y. Engeström (Eds.), *Cognition and communication at work: Distributed cognition in the workplace* (pp. 96–130). Cambridge, England: Cambridge University Press.

Heath, C. C., & Luff, P. K. (2000). *Technology in action.* Cambridge, England: Cambridge University Press.

Heath, C. C., Luff, P., & Sellen, A. (1995). Reconfiguring media space. In S. Emmot & D. Travis (Eds.), *The information superhighway: Multimedia* (pp. 161–187). London: Academic.

Hughes, J. A., Shapiro, D. Z., Sharrock, W. W., Anderson, R. A., Harper, R. R., & Gibbons, S. C. (1988). *The automation of air traffic control* (Final Report). Lancaster, England: Lancaster University, Department of Sociology.

Hutchins, E. (1995). *Cognition in the wild.* Cambridge, MA: MIT Press.

Kuutti, K., & Arvonen, T. (1992). Identifying CSCW applications by means of Activity Theory concepts: A case example. In *Proceedings of CSCW '92.* New York: ACM Press.

Latour, B. (writing as Jim Johnson). (1988). Mixing humans and non-humans together: The sociology of a door-closer. *Social Problems, 35,* 298–310.

Lynch, M., & Woolgar, S. (Eds.). (1990). *Representation in scientific practice.* Cambridge, England: Cambridge University Press.

MacKenzie, D., & Wajcman, J. (Eds.). (1985). *The social shaping of technology: How the refrigerator got its hum.* Milton Keynes, England: Open University Press.

Mead, G. H. (1934). *Mind, self, and society* (C. W. Morris, Ed.). Chicago: University of Chicago Press.

Sacks, H. (1972). Notes on the assessment of moral character. In D. Sudnow (Ed.), *Studies in social interaction* (pp. 280–293). New York: Free Press.

Sacks, H. (1992). Lecture 3, Spring 1972. In G. Jefferson, (Ed.), *Lectures on conversation: Volume II* (pp. 542–553). Oxford, England: Basil Blackwell.

Schutz, A. (1962). *The problem of social reality: Collected papers I* (M. Natanson, Ed.). New York: Academic.

Schutz, A. (1996). *Structures of the life world: Volume II* (T. Luckmann, Ed.). Portsmouth, NH: Heinemann.

Suchman, L. (1987). *Plans and situated actions: The problem of human–machine communication.* Cambridge, England: Cambridge University Press.

Suchman, L. (1996). Constituting shared workspaces. In D. Middleton & Y. Engeström (Eds.), *Cognition and communication at work: Distributed cognition in the workplace* (pp. 96–130). Cambridge, England: Cambridge University Press.

Whalen, J. (1995). A technology of order production: Computer-aided dispatch in public safety communications. In P. ten Have & G. Psathas (Eds.), *Situated order: Studies in the social organization of talk and embodied action* (pp. 187–230). Washington, DC: University Press of America.

Zimmerman, D. H. (1992). The interactional organization of calls for emergency assistance. In J. Heritage & P. Drew (Eds.), *Talk at work* (pp. 418–469). Cambridge, England: Cambridge University Press.

MIND, CULTURE, AND ACTIVITY, 7(1&2), 105-123

Seeing What One Sees:
Perception, Emotion, and Activity

Aug Nishizaka

Department of Sociology
Meiji Gakuin University

In this article, it is demonstrated (a) how seeing is organized in the spatiotemporal arrangement of bodies and conduct within which the participants display and manage their orientations to the ongoing activity, and (b) how seeing and emotion are mutually constituted in the precise coordination of conduct and how they, can constitute resources for organizing the ongoing activity. The view advanced in this article sharply contradicts the traditional conception of visual perception, according to which the verb "see" names a discrete process, event, or state hidden under the individual's skin. Seeing is rather an organizational feature of an embodied, visible activity.

INTRODUCTION

According to the typical cognitivist conception of seeing, when one sees something, first light strikes one's eyes or retinas, then the information it carries is processed in the brain so as to produce a seeing of the thing. For example, Nakayama, He, and Shimojo (1995) begin their chapter contributed to an introductory volume on visual cognition by mentioning "[o]ne of the most striking things":

> Retinal images are formed on the back of our eyeballs, upside down; they are very unstable, abruptly shifting two to four times a second according to the movements of the eyes. ... Yet, the visual scene appears to us as upright, stable, and homogeneous. Our perception is closely tied to surfaces and objects in the real world; it does not seem tightly related to our retinal images. (p. 1)

From here, they seek "a critical intermediate stage of vision poised between the earliest pickup of image information and later stages, such as object recognition." It is, they say, "the first stage of neural information processing, the results of which are available to us as conscious perceivers." I do not have anything to say about any particular hypotheses presented by either psychologists or physiologists. However, in what follows, I focus on some essentially important aspects of visual perception that are neglected by the basic conception underlying those hypotheses. The conception is that seeing is a process starting from retinal images or an event resulting from (neural or other) information processing, which occurs under the individual's skin. What I want to show in

Requests for reprints should be sent to Aug Nishizaka, Department of Sociology, Meiji Gakuin University, Minato-ku, Tokyo 108-8636, JAPAN. E-mail: augnish@soc.meijigakuin.ac.jp

this article is that, contrary to this conception, seeing belongs within the public and normative order of activity, rather than taking place under an individual's skin.

In a lecture in 1967, Harvey Sacks indicated that we can see what others think as easily as we see others "eating lunch"; people who have had some university training are specially wont to say, "You don't really know about somebody until you … etc."

> But our language is not built in such a way. Persons use psychological terms with the same freedom and "lack of knowledge of other persons" as they do any other terms. And persons perfectly well figure they know what somebody is thinking; they know why people are doing things, etc., on the same basis that they know that they are "white" or "Jewish," etc., and on the same basis that they know what they're doing. (Sacks, 1964–1972/1992, Vol. 1, p. 558)

We can tell quite easily that someone in front of us is angry and what he or she is angry at. We can tell these things "via what they are doing" (Sacks, 1964–1972/1992, Vol. 1, p. 559). In the same way, we can tell quite easily, too, that someone in front of us sees something or some state of affairs and what he or she sees. Seeing is, in this sense, a public phenomenon, rather than a genuine "mental" one that is basically inaccessible to others. We use vision not only to identify objects, for example, to navigate around rocks located in a rapidly moving stream, and so on. Seeing is also an interactional resource for coordinating actions to complete a given task in a distinct activity; the participants must and do see not only the proper thing exactly at a recognizable specific moment, but also see it in such a way that they can see what and how each other sees.

In the analysis of audio-visual recordings of distinct activities where more than one person is involved that follows, I demonstrate that—and how—seeing is jointly achieved in and through the actual course of an activity.[1] What one sees and how one sees it are interactionally organized both through the temporally unfolding course of interaction and the spatial arrangement of bodies. Then I discuss some implications of the demonstration.

Note that I do not intend to *prove* any hypotheses with empirical data, but rather elucidate, with the help of concrete examples, some aspects of the knowledge of seeing we as members of society already have. In these terms, here are chosen for analysis just those materials that seem to demonstrate well the public and normative character of seeing.

THE INTERACTIVE ACCOMPLISHMENT OF SEEING

Seeing Within an Embodied Activity

The first data to be examined in this demonstration are excerpted from an audio-visual recording of three teenagers jointly playing a computer game. The game, "AlgoBlock," was designed by educational engineers to support collaborative learning.[2] It is unique in that all the commands in the programming language used to move a submarine on a computer screen are given to the players as blocks approximately 10 cm × 10 cm × 10 cm, which are linked to the computer. Players "write"

---

[1]This viewpoint has already been developed by Charles Goodwin and Marjorie Harness Goodwin (Goodwin, 1994. 1995, 1996; Goodwin & Goodwin, 1996). See also Lynch (1988) and Lynch and MacBeth (1998) for the organization of vision in distinct activities.

[2]For the designers' own description of the system, see Suzuki and Kato (1995).

programs by laying out the blocks on a table in the order they want. Once they have done this, they press the play button connected to the blocks to see if their instructions actually produce the turns and other movements of the submarine on the computer screen as they want. While moving on the screen, the submarine produces a series of beeps; these cease momentarily each time the submarine makes one of its programmed turns. In Fragment 1, the players try to bring the submarine back to its home position through some points on the screen.

Fragment 1 starts when one of the participants presses the play button after they have finished laying out blocks in their second attempt. They have failed in their first attempt, that is, the submarine did not make a turn at the second turning point as they had expected, and, therefore, they had to program the movement of the submarine once again. Whereas on the first attempt they expected the submarine to go straight toward its home position after the second turn, they have decided to let the submarine make another turn, a third turn, to its home position by only adding another few blocks, instead of replacing the "wrong" ones:[3]

#1 (AB: 0:14:58)

Transcript 1 (The Original Transcript and its Phrase-by-Phrase Translation)

1 C: ((Presses the play button to let the submarine start))

2 A: *Yossha.   Korede   ikeru   kana?*=
   All right   this way   go well   I hope

3 B: = *Daijoobu,   daijoobu*
   okay   okay

4 C: (*Nopposan //doko*)
   ((untranslatable))

5 A: *Kokoni   sashikon   de ...*
   here   insert   and

---

[3]Symbols used in transcripts are:

// A double oblique marker indicates the point at which the next utterance starts.

(1.6) A number in parentheses indicates in seconds and tenths of a second the length of a time interval within an utterance or between utterances.

(.) A dot in parentheses indicates an untimed brief interval (more or less than a tenth of a second).

( ) Empty single parentheses indicate no hearing.

= An equal sign indicates that an item latches on the preceding one.

. A period indicates a stopping fall in tone.

::: Colons indicate that the prior sound is prolonged.

? A question mark indicates a rising intonation at the end of a phrase.

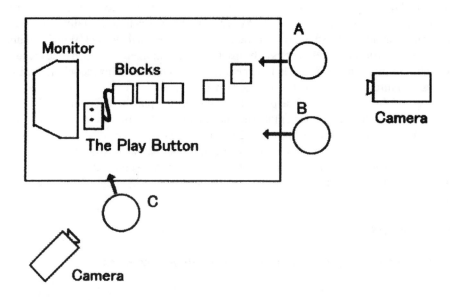

FIGURE 1   The participants, tools, and the location where the participants look at the beginning of Fragment 1, as indicated by the arrows.

Before going into the details of their interaction, it should be noted that all the three participants' bodies are arranged in such a formation that they can appreciate where each other is positioned. Sitting or standing very close to each other, they surround a table on which the items relevant to their activity are placed (see Figure 1). That is to say, they are in a position to be *mutually* oriented to each other's orientations.[4] Now, their faces (or gazes) are directed toward the computer monitor when one of them, C, who is nearest to the button, presses it (at line 1). They can see then that each other is oriented toward the monitor. In and through creating and preserving the very formation in which their mutual orientation is secured to the computer monitor, exactly what to see now (i.e., that they should now see something on the computer screen) is collaboratively made clear to the participants. A "shared" visual field is established on the computer screen in this way. Indeed, they are now running the program they have written with the blocks to see if the submarine is actually moving on the monitor screen as they had programmed.

However, as soon as the monitor is switched on, A and C look away from the computer monitor to those blocks laid out on the table, which is another visual field possibly relevant to their activity in progress (see Figures 2A & 2B):

---

[4]This kind of formation is called "F-formation" by Kendon (1990). The point here is, however, the establishment and maintenance, not just of a *common* "transactional segment" (each individual's transactional segment being "the space from which [the individual] immediately and readily reaches for whatever objects his current project may require he manipulate," that is, "the place immediately in front of him that the individual projects forward and keeps clear if he is moving" [p. 248]), but rather of a bodily arrangement where the individuals' bodies with their own transactional segments are put within each other's transactional segment. See also Goodwin's (1981) and Heath's (1986) arguments on participation.

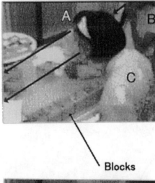

Blocks

FIGURE 2A   They look at the monitor screen.

FIGURE 2B   They look away from the monitor to the blocks.

#1 (AB: 0:14:58)

Transcript 2[5]

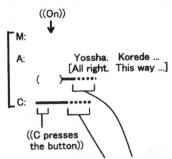

((A and C almost simultaneously look away from
the monitor and toward the blocks laid out on the table))

Certainly, all of the participants once look at the monitor just after the submarine starts (i.e., starts to emit beeps), but soon they look away again; A looks toward the blocks again, commenting on their layout, while C, this time, toward A, utters something inaudible:

---

[5]The following conventions are used in this and the following transcripts:

- All the lines advance in time simultaneously from left to right.
- At lines designated as A, B and C, the participants' utterances are written, immediately under which are their translations in parentheses.
- == at the line designated as M indicates the sound of the submarine.
- Solid lines under each line designated as A, B or C indicate that each participant's face is directed to the computer monitor during the time period corresponding to the length of the lines.

#1 (AB: 0:14:58)

Transcript 3

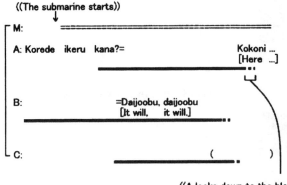

((A looks down to the blocks, pointing to one of them))

Why do they not keep their eyes on the visual field that has been established as "shared"? In what follows, I focus on one utterance in Fragment 1, that is, A's utterance made immediately after the button was pressed, "*Yossha. Korede ikeru kana?* [All right. This way everything will go well?]" (at Line 2). It brings into prominence *this* attempt as contrasted with the preceding one in which they failed, especially by starting the substantial part of her utterance with "*korede* [this way]." Immediately after this utterance of A's, B assures A that they will succeed this time, by saying "*Daijoobu* [It will]" (at Line 3). This small exchange between A and B specifies what to see, by contrasting this attempt with the preceding one. Moving her gaze down to those blocks on the table, A refers to the "program" in front of them that they have just written. What they have done this time to the program, that is, the layout of blocks, is only to add those blocks related to the third turn and the subsequent course of the submarine. They did this because their task at hand this time is to let the submarine make another turn after they failed in the preceding attempt to get it to turn toward its home position at the second turn (see Figures 3A & 3B). In view of all this, it is not simply accidental that once they looked at the monitor screen after the submarine started, it never happened that all of them returned their faces to the screen again until it came close to the third turn (although, of course, they turned their faces to the monitor separately during that time). This conduct serves to bring into prominence where what to see lies against the background of other places that are not so important for their purpose at hand.

As noted previously, while moving, the submarine emits a unique sound that stops briefly while the submarine is in the process of making a turn. Therefore, without looking at the monitor, each of the three could know approximately where the submarine was at each moment from the sound, along with the positions of the submarine on the screen they saw the previous time.[6]

---

[6] It is suggested here that not only vision but all the sensory perceptions are embedded in the current activity. I am indebted to Chuck Goodwin for his drawing my attention to this point. In a personal communication, he indicated in connection with the case being discussed here that "a full 'multi-sensory' environment" is being organized by, and being used as a resource for organizing, the actual course of action. Indeed, not only sensory perceptions but also emotion are sequentially organized within, and sequentially organizes, an activity, as we see shortly.

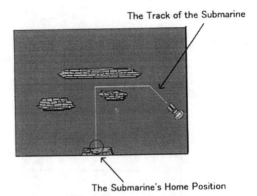

The Track of the Submarine

The Submarine's Home Position

FIGURE 3A   An image on the monitor screen. The actual track of the submarine at the first attempt.

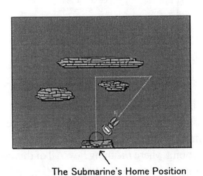

FIGURE 3B   The route they wanted at the first attempt.

The Submarine's Home Position

What to see is thus embedded in the local history of the activity in progress. It depends on what the participants have achieved so far and where they are right now in the course of the ongoing activity. However, on the other hand, it should be kept in mind that this local "history" is only activated through specifically designed talk such as A's utterance at Line 2, which in turn is just part of the activity encompassing its whole history. History and talk (and other relevant conduct, perhaps) elaborate on each other such that a distinct activity is organized as a distinct and unique one.

Now when participants returned their faces to the monitor after the second turning point, all three jointly built up the same formation as when the play button was pressed (see Transcript 2 of Fragment 2):

#2 (AB: 0:15:11)

Transcript 1

1 B: ((Coughs twice))

2 A: *EE:::::::::::: //::::::::*

3 B: *E:: chigattawa.*
        it was wrong

4 C: *AA:: //(chiga   )*

5 A: *Hora   dakara   45   do   tteitta   jan*
    look   so   degree I said you know

Transcript 2

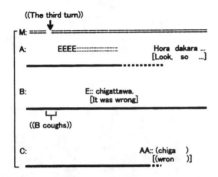

By building the formation up, the participants can display to each other their understanding that they have now come close to what to see. Moreover, by coughing at almost the same time as when the submarine makes the third turn (at Line 1), B may also possibly indicate to others that here and now is precisely the point where *the* thing lies. All of this corresponds to that exchange of utterances at Lines 2 and 3 in Fragment 1, in which what to see (i.e., the submarine's third turn and its subsequent course) is specified jointly by the participants. Now, it can be said, the fact that what they should see is exactly here and now is achieved through the spatiotemporal arrangement of their bodies and conduct.

As seen from Fragment 2, the participants express their surprise or even shock one after another when the submarine makes the third turn ("EEEE," "EE," "AA" at Lines 2 to 4). The point I want to make here is that not only do they see what to see, but also they see it *in an appropriate way*. In the preceding segment of their interaction reproduced as Fragment 1, when they specified what to see and where to see it, they also specified *how* to see it, that is, how to react when they see what to see. It should be noted that what they should see is not only the submarine's third turn (and its subsequent course) but whether this attempt succeeds or fails, especially at the submarine's third turn. In A's uttering "*Yossha* [All right]" (which indicates the speaker's confidence in success) at the beginning (at Line 2) in Fragment 1 and B's assuring A that it will succeed by saying "*Daijoobu* [It will]" (at Line 3 in Fragment 1), they observably do expect it to succeed. That is to say, if they "see" that it fails, being surprised should be the appropriate reaction; they *should* see its failure with surprise. In fact, they did so, and by doing the "right thing," they display to each other that they now see what to see (see Figure 4). By being surprised, they make it mutually visible that they now see what runs counter to their expectation.[7]

---

[7]We may be reminded here of Goffman's (1981) observation that emotional expressions (or "response cries") are often used interactionally; although they are not addressed to others, they are very often intended to be heard by copresent others. The most relevant here is Goodwin's (1996) discussion. He remarked that emotional expressions are "organized as social phenomena that provide very powerful resources for shaping the perception and action of others" (p. 393). For the organization of emotional displays as social phenomena, see also Coulter (1979).

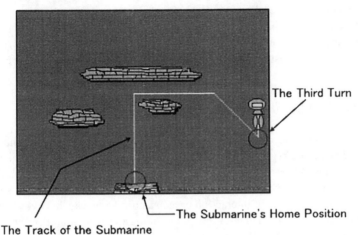

The Third Turn

The Submarine's Home Position

The Track of the Submarine

FIGURE 4   An image on the screen right after the submarine took the third turn at the second attempt. The submarine went in an unexpected direction.

Furthermore, it is remarkable that after expressing her surprise, A criticizes B, who took the initiative in designing the rearrangement of blocks at the second attempt, by talking as if she had not expected that the second attempt would succeed ("*Hora dakara … tte ittajan* [Look, so I told you that …]" [at Line 5]). Apparently, this contradicts her other conduct, that is, saying "All right" (with falling intonation) before the start and expressing surprise at seeing the failure. Note also that C's expression of her surprise ("A:::" [at Line 4]) is somewhat delayed. It looks as if they are surprised because they should.

Their being surprised together is an interactional resource for displaying and shaping their seeing in ways relevant to their activity in progress, rather than simply being "caused" spontaneously by what happens before their eyes. Being mutually surprised organizes the factual nature and sense of what they see within the historical context of the ongoing activity they are jointly involved in.

The game players saw on the computer monitor that they failed, that is, that the submarine did not go as they had programmed. This natural fact of seeing belongs within the normative order of activity.[8] They saw what they should see in the way they should see it. What to see and how to see it depend on what they are doing. Their seeing can only be meaningful within the actual context of the ongoing activity; it is embedded within the activity they are currently engaged in. Indeed, during the interaction reproduced in Fragments 1 and 2, they turned their faces in various directions, and various patches of light and color must have struck their eyes, but they cannot be said to have *seen* all these things. Seeing must be relevant to the development of the current activity and oriented to by the participants as a part of their activity in progress; their seeing that they failed is rel-

---

[8]I mean by "normative" what Sacks (1964–1972/1992) calls "programmatically relevant" or "protected against induction." In so far as one sees is what one should see, not just what one see as a matter of fact, the absence of one's seeing becomes observable and accountable. Indeed, if a participant of the computer game had not seen what she saw, that is, that they failed again in the second attempt, she might have been blamed for not seeing it (e.g., "You should've paid attention to the monitor") and some remedial practices might have been in order.

evant both to the failure of their first attempt and to their prospective next attempt; their seeing is retrospectively sensitive to the previous steps of the development of their activity and also prospectively gives them directions as to what and how to do in the next steps. That is to say, what one sees and how one sees it must be appropriate to the actual development of the ongoing activity.

Instructions for Seeing and the Sequential Organization of Emotion

Here we see that seeing is accomplished interactively and sequentially. The exchange between A and B at Lines 2 and 3 in Fragment 1 functions as instructions for seeing. It projects what to see, when to see it, and how.[9] These instructions for seeing make the sequence of the participants' emotional expressions an appropriate response to what they see then. Instructions for seeing generally organize the subsequent course of interaction in such a normative way that even less conventional emotional expressions are provided with specific meaning and accountability in reference to those instructions. In fact, vision and other perceptions, emotion, (verbal and nonverbal) conduct, and other phenomena are mutually organized in and through the actual development of interaction to build an "activity system." How emotion and vision are mutually organized is clearer in another fragment, which is excerpted from an audio-visual recording of a private Japanese word-processing lesson.

In this lesson, the instructor gives tasks to the learner, and the learner attempts to complete them. The result of each attempt by the learner is commented on by the instructor, that is, the proper way of operation is described, why she has failed is explained, and so on. The task in the fragment being reproduced in the following is to input the string of letters "IBM" into a computer in a special way. The instructor was a part-time instructor at the Information Center at a university when the session was recorded.

Fragment 3 starts when the instructor (A) gives the learner (B) a new task: Input a "half-sized IBM." The task given just prior to this one, which the learner has just completed, was to input a "full-sized IBM." All the Japanese word-processing devices have two types of Roman letters, full-sized and half-sized. What we call half-sized letters are ones we use when writing in English or other European languages; full-sized ones are specially used for Japanese kana and kanji characters. ("Full-sized" means "of the same size as normal Japanese characters.") Therefore, as long as writing in Japanese with a computer, we usually use full-sized letters, and inputting half-sized ones requires one extra operation. In these terms, it is quite reasonable to give the task of inputting a half-sized IBM only after that of inputting a full-sized one in a Japanese word-processing lesson. The interactional relevance of this point is mentioned shortly.

#3 (WP: 0:42:50)

Transcript 1-a (A Free Translation of the Japanese Transcript)

1 A: Then now la(rge [?])- This is (.) a full-sized "IBM," right?
2 B: Yes
3 A: Then, try to input a half-sized "IBM." An application.

---
[9]See Goodwin's (1996) discussion on what he called "prospective indexicals."

4 : (7.4)
5 A: Yeah. (.) O?
6 B: O?
7 : (0.2)
8 B: (*ne*)
9 A: *Aaaa:::*. That's the way. So because pressing key number 8 first doesn't work, …

*Transcript 1-b (The Original Transcript and a Phrase-by-Phrase
Translation; see Figure 5)*

1 A: *Jaa   ima   oo- Korettesaa, (.) zenkakuno "IBM" desu yone::.*
    then now   this   full-sized   is
2 B: *Hai*
    yes
3 A: *Hankakuno "IBM" jaa   irete   mite.   Ooyoo*
    half-sized   then input try   application
4   (7.4)
5 A: *Un   (.) Are?*
    yeah   o
6 B: *Are?*
7   (0.2)
8 B: (*ne*)
9 A: *Aaaa:::. Soodesne.   Dakara,   ikinari (.) hachi   banwo (.)*
            that's the way so   first   eight   number
    oshi   temo   ( )   kara::
    press though   because

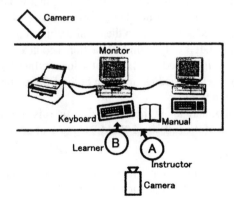

FIGURE 5   The participants' positioning of their bodies and tools on the table.

At Line 3, A, the instructor, gives B, the learner, an exercise, which functions also as instructions as to what to see and how to see it.[10] At Line 9, A reacts (to what he sees) in an appropriate way with an emotional expression "*Aaaa:::,*" which has a unique sound contour, that is, starting with a high pitch and ending with the pitch falling down sharply. This expression achieves a special interactional job here precisely through being produced at a particular sequential position, and precisely in doing this job it is provided with special accountability.

Before going on to a closer examination of the sequential organization of emotion, it should be noted that the force of those instructions for seeing is interactively and sequentially achieved as such. In the case of Fragment 1, as we saw, the exchange of talk between two participants constituted instructions for seeing. Moreover, the exchange was positioned in the actual context of interaction; that is, the exchange was made right after a shared visual field where the thing they should see was established and the play button was pressed. The exchange is also embedded within (while at the same time activating) the local history of the joint activity in progress. In Fragment 3, too, the instructions for seeing are positioned in the actual context of interaction in some way:

#3 (WP: 0:42:50)

Transcript 2[11]

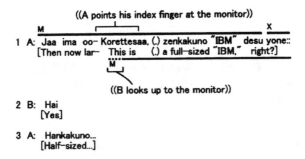

2 B: Hai
       [Yes]

3 A: Hankakuno...
       [Half-sized...]

When A starts to give B an exercise, B looks down at the table or the keyboard. Then A interrupts his own utterance and points his index finger at the computer monitor in front of B (see Figure 5) while restarting his utterance with the demonstrative "*kore* [this]." This self-interruption and pointing at the monitor induces B's gaze to the monitor, and B gives A an explicit verbal response ("*Hai*") to A's utterance. It is only in this interactional context that A moves on to giving B the exercise ("*Hankakuno* ... [Half-sized ...]"). Thus, the instructions for seeing in Fragment 3 are also produced in the arrangement of bodies in which both of the participants display to one another their orientation to the monitor.

It should be noted, too, that here again the exercise A gives is contrasted to what has already been attained. In A's mention of the full-sized "IBM," the task of inputting a half-sized "IBM" is

---

[10]The words "*Hankakuno* [half-sized] IBM" function as what Goodwin (1996) called a "prospective indexical." As seen later, their "referent" will have to be fixed on the monitor in a specific way, that is, as a successful outcome of the learner's operation.

[11]Solid lines led by M's and X's just above or under each utterance indicate that A's or B's face is directed to the monitor and their coparticipant respectively.

made prominent as a next step against the full-sized one already on the monitor screen. Furthermore, I guess that the self-interrupted phrase should be "*ookii* IBM" or "*ookina* IBM," which means "large IBM" or the like; as you see now, full-sized letters are larger-sized compared with half-sized ones. Taken together, A's and B's gazes are jointly focused not just on one visual field, but on the visual field specifically relevant for the next step of their activity. Again, instructions for seeing are provided in a relevant fashion and at a particular place and time in reference to the historical context of the ongoing activity the participants are jointly engaged in.

Now, let us turn to the responses with emotional expressions. As for Fragment 2 (from the AlgoBlock material), I indicated previously that all the participants expressed their surprise in the special bodily arrangement (where they can display to each other their orientations to the monitor) in an orderly way, that is, that their being surprised was finely attuned to each other's conduct rather than a spontaneous, natural expression of a mental state. A's production of an emotional expression in Fragment 3 (from the word-processing lesson) is also very precisely coordinated with B's conduct:

#3 (WP: 0:42:50)

Transcript 3

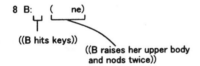

8 B: (ne)
((B hits keys))
        ((B raises her upper body
        and nods twice))

9 A: Aaaa::::::. Soodesu ne. Dakara ikinari hachiban wo ...
     [That's the way. So, hitting #8 first   ...]

After hitting some keys, B, the learner, raises her upper body, looking at the monitor, and nods twice, while saying something (inaudible from the recording). This conduct, it looks, marks out the completion of her operation. (In doing so, the learner shows that she recognizes those letters as the ones she was assigned to input and ties them back to the task assigned by the instructor.) It is only immediately after the completion of the current task has thus been marked out that A, the instructor, produces the emotional expression "*Aaaa*". This precise coordination of conduct marks out exactly what they see.

Certainly, A must have seen the "IBM" independently of B's recognition of it, because he had been looking at the monitor while she was operating on the keyboard. However, the string of letters "IBM" is not all they see. Insofar as their seeing is linked up to B's performance of the exercise, they do not see a mere string of letters "IBM" any more than those game players in Fragment 2 saw just a mechanical movement of the submarine. They see that B has succeeded in inputting a half-sized IBM and completing the assigned task, just as did those game players see that they had failed in letting the submarine come back to its home base again. Both a mere string of letters in this case and a mechanical movement of the submarine in Fragment 2 would be rather an artificial abstraction detached from our lived world.

In this connection, attention should be drawn to those remarks A made subsequently to his emotional expression ("*Aaaa*"). He starts his remarks with "*Soo desune. Dakara* ... [That's the way. So …]." Those words, referring by a kind of demonstrative ("*soo* [that]") to what has been in their perceptual field of mutual orientations, mark out that A is now going to give a review of what A and B have jointly perceived (with what can be called a "summing-up" token, i.e., "*dakara* [so]"). Then A goes on to comment on, in a general way, what was wrong and what was right in B's operation (i.e., that pressing key number 8 first does not work and that key number 9 should be pressed first, etc.). In this way, what he and B have just (visually) perceived on the monitor screen is accounted for and formulated as a result of B's operation on the keyboard.

A's production of an emotional expression achieves an interactional job of marking out the visibility of B's success in inputting a half-sized IBM, not just the mere string of letters "IBM," and precisely in doing this job, the sound with that unique contour ("*Aaaa:::*") can be an expression of being impressed by B's performance.

Seeing Through Being Embarrassed Together

Of course, it is quite rare for the instructor to express his being impressed in such a marked way in response to the learner's success in completing a task. There is a reason why he did so there. The following is a detailed transcript of the middle part of Fragment 3:

#3 (WP: 0:42:50)

Transcript 4

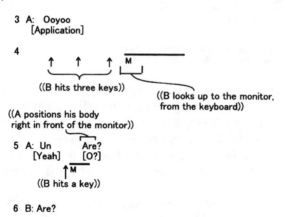

```
3  A:  Ooyoo
       [Application]

4
           ↑    ↑    ↑   M
          ⎵_____⎵  ⎵__⎵
          ((B hits three keys))
                              ((B looks up to the monitor,
                               from the keyboard))
    ((A positions his body
    right in front of the monitor))

5  A:  Un        Are?
       [Yeah]    [O?]
                ↑ M
          ((B hits a key))

6  B:  Are?
```

Here, too, producing an emotional expression plays an interactional role in the organization of seeing. After hitting three keys in response to A's assignment, that is, making three letters appear on the monitor, the learner (B) shifts her gaze from the keyboard to the monitor screen. Here some delay in hitting function keys has become noticeable. A's "*Un* [Yeah]" marks it out, encouraging B to go ahead while claiming there is no problem so far.[12] In this interactional context, not just some string of three letters, but an "incomplete state of operation" becomes visible on the monitor.

---

[12]See Schegloff's (1982) discussion on continuers.

FIGURE 6A   The learner has just hit a key and looked up
to the monitor (at Line 5).

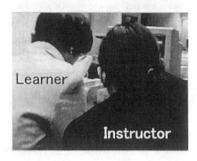

FIGURE 6B   The instructor has brought his upper body in.

Then B hits a key. Immediately A and B say "*Are?*" one after another in response to what has been made on the monitor by B's hitting the key. "*Are?*," a rather conventional expression of surprise, especially used when something unexpected has happened, indicates that something is wrong. A and B are, as it were, jointly being embarrassed at what is going on, which is, in reference to the given instructions for seeing, an appropriate thing to do when a half-sized "IBM" did not appear.

Their production of the expression "*Are?*", too, is interactively and sequentially finely coordinated. A, while saying "*Are?*," brings his upper body in front of the monitor, as if he were inspecting what is going on (see Figure 6A & 6B). The real reason for his bodily movement is not important. What is important is that he is searching for the problem publicly and observably in front of B. B produces "*Are?*," it seems, in response to this whole conduct of A's. By doing this, B shows that she understands A has seen something wrong on the monitor screen at the same time as she shows she recognizes something wrong for herself (and in so doing, displays that, despite having made an error, she knows what counts as competent performance in this task). A's and B's being embarrassed together now makes the visibility of B's failure in her operation available and embodied on the monitor. This visibility of B's failure encourages her to make another attempt on the keyboard.

Back to A's expression of being impressed (at Line 9): It apparently responds to this publicly visible failure. In reference to this visible failure, his expression of being impressed is organized such that B's success is now visible against that failure that was visible a moment ago.[13] Both the visibility of success and that of failure are relevant and useful in unfolding the ongoing activity A

---

[13]In this way, emotional displays "are embedded in local contexts of social action" and in those contexts, "achieve meaning and import" (Whalen & Zimmerman, 1998, p. 158). The demonstration in this section is another example of "the integration of the study of emotional display with the sequential organization of talk-in-interaction."

and B are now jointly engaged in, and emotion is organized in the same sequential order of the on-going activity in which vision is organized. Vision and emotion are mutually organized within the actual context of an activity.

SEEING AS A VISIBLE PHENOMENON

Seeing Relevant to the Ongoing Activity

We have seen that seeing is a public and normative phenomenon, which is achieved in and through the actual course of a distinct activity. I do not deny that when one sees something, some physiological processes or events take place under one's skin and that these processes or events are a very important area of the study of visual perception. I do deny that those processes or events *are* seeing or visual perception. What puzzles me about the orthodox conception of vision is that it seems to fail to take into consideration the fact that we can see the lack or absence of something; indeed, the game players in Fragment 2 *saw* that the submarine had *not* gone the way that they expected it to go, and the instructor and the learner in Fragment 3 (at Lines 5–6) *saw* that a half-sized "IBM" did *not* appear on the monitor. It is implausible that there are physiological conditions *specific* to the lack of something or some fact, although there might occur some physiological changes.

Probably, Harvey Sacks is the first sociologist who was seriously surprised at the fact that we often use such expressions as "is not," "do not," "none," "nothing," and the like. Generally speaking, there are an infinite or indefinite number of things that someone does not or did not do. Therefore, when one says "He did not do …" or "She is not doing …," one does not say this just because it is true (Sacks, 1964–1972/1992). For example, we sometimes say something like this: "She did not greet anyone." It is also true that I have not greeted anyone for the past couple of hours; I have been by myself at my office. Do we say, however, "I did not greet anyone"? It is when the statement is embedded in the specific context of an activity, such as the distinct activity of opening up an encounter, for example, when some people have just greeted her, that we can say she did not greet anyone.

The same holds true also for other kinds of statements. In one lecture held in 1966, Sacks (1964–1972/1992) cited the following example. In midst of a group therapy session, one boy uttered the words "We were in an automobile discussion." It is true that they had been discussing automobiles. Obviously, however, he did not produce this statement precisely at that time just because it was true; indeed, there must have been an indefinite number of things the participants had been doing prior to his statement. The statement was produced just after a newcomer had been introduced by the therapist to those present. According to Sacks, automobiles are generally (or normatively) expected to be accessible as a common topic for teenagers and, by uttering those words precisely at that time, the boy invited the newcomer, who was also a teenager, to join their discussion, showing him that they had been talking about very ordinary things any teenager could be interested in even if that one may not be interested in automobiles at all actually. Thus, the fact that he said what he said right there and then is embedded in the distinct activity of inviting a newcomer to the ongoing interaction.

In the same way, although it is possible to say that the participants in the word-processing lesson saw that a string of words did not appear, it does not make any sense to say that they saw that

Mozart did not appear, even though it is true that Mozart did not. What one sees is embedded in the activity one is engaged in, for example, performing an exercise or whatever. I saw my colleagues at a faculty meeting today, but did I see their eyelids? When voting last time, I saw a quadrangular space surrounded by black lines on a slip of paper, inside which I wrote down a candidate's name; but did I see those lines were slightly crooked at several places if they were actually so? A young baby saw a ball rolling up to her and tried to hold it, but did she see also a lot of stains on the surface of the ball?

This said, however, an activity is not something like a container for seeing. Not only is seeing lodged in an encompassing activity. What I have demonstrated is that seeing is organized through the precise and fine coordination of the participants' conduct. It is not that the participants' current activity, for example, playing a computer game jointly, lies somewhere above and over their actual conduct and constrains it from the outside; playing a game is accomplished jointly in, through, and as the spatiotemporal arrangement of their bodies and conduct. An activity is organized as a distinct one through the mutual organization of (visual and other) perceptions, emotions, and other various kinds of things in which the participants display and manage their orientations to that very ongoing activity. Although seeing is accomplished within the actual arrangement of bodies and conduct that constitutes the ongoing activity, seeing is also an interactional resource for (re)organizing the actual arrangement of bodies and conduct.[14]

The Fallacy of Reification

The orthodox conception considers the verb "see" to refer to some process or event or some state inside an individual. However, the word is not the name of a process or occurrence, a state, or even an activity. The orthodox conception is caught up in what Coulter (1989) called "the fallacy of reification." In Ryle's (1949/1963) terms, the verb "see" is an achievement word: "'see', 'descry', and 'find' are not process words, experience words, or activity words. They do not stand for perplexingly undetectable actions or reactions, any more than 'win' stands for a perplexingly undetectable bit of running, or 'unlock' for an unreported bit of key-turning" (pp. 145–146). One criterion for being an achievement verb is that "in applying an achievement verb we are asserting that some state of affairs obtains over and above that which consists in the performance, if any, of the

---

[14]In this connection, it is worth mentioning Coulter and Parsons' (1991) criticism of J. J. Gibson's ecological approach to visual perception. Gibson's (1979/1986) criticism of the orthodox psychology theory of visual perception was so radical that he went so far as to argue "perception of the environment is direct" and that "it is not mediated by *retinal* pictures, *neural* pictures or *mental* pictures" (p. 147). However, his approach is still so orthodox that he does not take into consideration the "embedded-in-activity" (i.e., normative) character of vision. At least in the human case, verbs covering visual perception vary very widely, including "see," "observe," "notice," "read," "examine," and so on. According to Coulter and Parsons, Gibson does not pay enough attention to this variety in modalities of visual perception. They remarked, "Regardless of which modality is invoked, displayed, or presupposed in members' activities, to stipulate a continuity in our visual orientations is to violate logical grammar" (p. 263). The various modalities of our visual orientations constitute what Wittgenstein (1958) called "family resemblance"; they do not have any characteristics in common; there are no general properties of visual orientations. Then, how should we be able to speak of visual perception in general? Any attempts to construct a general theory of visual perception seems doomed to failure. All that is left to us is to examine in detail how vision is organized in members' activities of various kinds. For a criticism of the Gibsonian approach, see also Ueno (1996). Ueno indicated a direction in which the Gibsonian ecological approach could develop in a productive way, emphasizing the social character of human vision.

subservient task activity" (Ryle, 1949/1963, pp. 143–144). The fallacy consists in searching inside the individual for the referent of the verb "see" because obviously the verb does not refer to any observable process or state. However, not only does it not refer to any *observable* process or state, but it does not refer to *any* process or state. As Coulter remarks, achievement words presuppose the demonstrable facticity or accuracy of what it is one is claiming to have seen, found, and so on. They "do not name discrete states, events or 'phenomena' susceptible to first-person 'revelation,' 'observation' or 'internal monitoring' of any kind. Claims to facticity are dismissible, defeasible, by public recourse to convincingly established counter-evidences of all sorts" (Coulter, 1989, p. 121). On the other hand, as I said previously, neural conditions for visual perception are not visual perception per se, but just its conditions. The verb "see" does not name any process or activity that takes place under an individual's skin.

Incidentally, it is very misleading to describe physiological processes accompanying seeing as a kind of information processing. It is well known that Kenny (1984) pointed out an absurdity resulting from applying to a part of a person or an organism (e.g., the nervous system) those predicates that can be only applied to a person or an organism as a whole in its ordinary use. He called this confusion "the homunculus fallacy." The trouble is this: If for us to do some activity, information has to be processed by the nervous system, that is, a homunculus, then for the latter to do this distinct activity of information processing, another homunculus has to process information inside the nervous system. It is easy to see here the absurdity of regress ad infinitum.

I will not go into philosophical arguments here. The point I want to make here is that we are often engaged in a distinct activity of information processing, the performance of which requires one to see various things. The game players in Fragments 1 and 2 saw the failure of their second attempt, that is, they extracted visual information from the environment organized through their coordinated conduct and processed and transformed it into information as to how to lay out the blocks. Information processing is a publicly *seeable* activity that the participants are mutually oriented to. Visual perception is not simply a discrete state resulting from information processing, but rather a resource for the activity of information processing. As Sharrock and Coulter (1998) emphasized, "to gather/obtain information of many kinds *presupposes* (and thus cannot *explain*) seeing" (p. 156). To call even metaphorically those physiological processes accompanying visual perception "information processing" seems to have caused unnecessary confusions and misconceptions. Particularly, it induces us to conceive the word "seeing" as a label of some hidden activity or its resulting state.

A Consequence to Human–Machine Interaction Studies

One should not suppose in advance of analyses that there are two different kinds of entities, that is, human beings on the one hand and tools and other objects on the other, and attempt to explore the interaction of these entities. As has been shown, even such a simple object as a half-sized "IBM" on the computer monitor has its visibility embodied in the actual arrangement of bodies and conduct in which the participants' visual and other orientations are displayed and managed. It is, as it were, the participants' "extended body." It does not stand by itself out in the world but constitutes, together with human bodies and other artifacts, talk and other conduct, and so on, an activity system. Seeing is not a processing of that information that comes from objects in the outer world into the human body, but a structural feature of an activity system.

ACKNOWLEDGMENTS

Many thanks to Dom Berducci, Jeff Coulter, Chuck Goodwin, John Hindmarsh, Mike Lynch, Lucy Suchman, and Naoki Ueno for their encouragement and helpful comments on earlier drafts. I am very grateful to Hiroshi Kato and Hideyuki Suzuki for their permission to use the AlgoBlock material, and to Satoyuki Morita for his corporation in collecting the word-processing lesson data. I wish to thank Chuck Goodwin also for his very detailed editorial comments, which were of great help.

REFERENCES

Coulter, J. (1979). *The social construction of mind.* London: Macmillan.

Coulter, J. (1989). *Mind in action.* Cambridge, England: Polity Press.

Coulter, J., & Parsons, E. D. (1991). The praxiology of perception: Visual orientations and practical action. *Inquiry, 33,* 251–272.

Gibson, J. J. (1986). *The ecological approach to visual perception.* Hillsdale, NJ: Lawrence Erlbaum Associates, Inc. (Original work published 1979)

Goffman, E. (1981). *Forms of talk.* Philadelphia: University of Pennsylvania Press.

Goodwin, C. (1981). *Conversational organization: Interaction between speakers and hearers.* New York: Academic.

Goodwin, C. (1994). Professional vision. *American Anthropologist, 96,* 606–633.

Goodwin, C. (1995). Seeing in depth: Space, technology and interaction on a scientific research vessel. *Social Studies of Science, 25,* 237–274.

Goodwin, C. (1996). Transparent vision. In E. Ochs, E. A. Schegloff & S. A. Thompson (Eds.), *Interaction and grammar* (pp. 370–404). Cambridge, England: Cambridge University Press.

Goodwin, C., & Goodwin, M. H. (1996). Seeing as situated activity: Formulating planes. In Y. Engeström & D. Middleton (Eds.), *Cognition and communication at work* (pp. 61– 95). Cambridge, England: Cambridge University Press.

Heath, C. (1986). *Body movement and speech in medical interaction.* Cambridge, England: Cambridge University Press

Kendon, A. (1990). *Conducting interaction.* Cambridge, England: Cambridge University Press.

Kenny, A. (1984). *The legacy of Wittgenstein.* Oxford, England: Basil Blackwell.

Lynch, M. (1988). The externalized retina: Selection and mathematization in the visual documentation of objects in the life sciences. *Human Studies, 11,* 201–234.

Lynch, M., & MacBeth, D. (1998). Demonstrating physics lessons. In J. G. Greeno & S. V. Goldman (Eds.), *Thinking practices in mathmatics and science learning* (pp. 269–298). Mahwah, NJ: Lawrence Erlbaum Assocites, Inc.

Nakayama, K., He, J. Z., & Shimojo, S. (1995). Visual surface representation: A critical link between lower-level and higher-level vision. In S. M. Kosslyn & D. N. Osherson (Eds.), *Visual cognition* (pp. 1–70). Cambridge, MA: MIT Press.

Ryle, G. (1963). *The concept of mind.* Middlesex, England: Peregrine Books. (Original work published 1949)

Sacks, H. (1964–1972/1992). *Lectures on conversation* (Vol. 1 & 2). Oxford, England: Basil Blackwell.

Schegloff, E. A. (1982). Discourse as interactional achievements: Some uses of "uh huh" and other things that come between sentences. In D. Tannen (Ed.), *Georgetown University roundtable on languages and linguistics* (pp. 71–93). Washington DC: Georgetown University Press.

Sharrock, W., & Coulter, J. (1998). On what we can see. *Theory & Psychology, 8,* 147–164.

Suzuki, H., & Kato, H. (1995). Interaction-level support for collaborative learning: AlgoBlock—an open programming language. *Proceedings of CSCL '95,* 349–355.

Ueno, N. (1996). Jokyo ninchi to Gibson [The situated cognition and Gibson]. *Gengo, 25*(1–6).

Whalen, J., & Zimmerman, D. H. (1998). Observations on the display and management of emotion in naturally occurring activities: The case of "hysteria" in calls to 9-1-1. *Social Psychology Quarterly, 61,* 141–159.

Wittgenstein, L. (1958). *Philosophical investigations.* Oxford, England: Basil Blackwell.

MIND, CULTURE, AND ACTIVITY, 7(1&2), 124–146

Patents, Promotions, and Protocols: Mapping and Claiming Scientific Territory

Michael Lynch
Department of Science & Technology Studies
Cornell University

Kathleen Jordan
Postdoctoral Fellow, Gerontology Center
Boston University

Scientific representations include a diverse and confusing array of maps, descriptions, diagrams, and protocols. This study examines and compares the practical and communicative uses of such artifacts. The main source of material is the authors' ethnographic research on the polymerase chain reaction (PCR), a laboratory routine that has numerous scientific, medical, and forensic applications. Contextually relative versions of PCR are examined: schematic diagrams for popular audiences, advertisements in biotech publications, patent descriptions, praxiological descriptions (recipe-like formulations), and material standards and references. These renderings do not exemplify a single type of cognition or information processing. Schematic diagrams, advertisements, patents, protocols, and material standards are differently formed, and the information they convey substantially differs from one form to another. This study contributes to a noncognitivist understanding of representation that emphasizes a plurality of material formats and communicative practices rather than an underlying mental process.

Suit the action to the word, and the word to the action; with this special observance that you o'erstep not the modesty of nature. (Shakespeare, *Hamlet*, Act III, Scene 2, ll. 17–19)

According to a popular conception of genetic reproduction, DNA is a sequential code that furnishes a set of instructions to a molecular factory, which then assembles an organism. When the assembly is complete, the mature organism's DNA, together with *messenger RNA*, instructs the factory on how to maintain and repair the organism's functions. According to this view, the code is relayed through a series of literary automatons, which inscribe, duplicate, edit, transcribe, translate, read, and express the code. By using such literary vocabularies, molecular biologists locate a whole series of representational functions within the cell itself. This conception of reproduction has been criticized for its deterministic, and even fetishistic, treatment of coded information, and for the way it projects managerial control of an industrial economy into a subcellular domain (Haraway, 1997; Kay, 1995; Keller, 1992; Lewontin, 1993). Criticisms of genetic reductionism

Requests for reprints should be sent to Michael Lynch, Department of Science & Technology Studies, 622 Clark Hall, Cornell University, Ithaca, NY 14853. E-mail: mel27@cornell.edu

partly overlap with criticisms of deterministic theories of human behavior in artificial intelligence and cognitive neurophilosophy, which also stress the governing role of internal instructions (Button, Coulter, Lee, & Sharrock, 1995; Coulter, 1995; Suchman, 1987). We sympathize with such criticisms, but our aim in this article is not to criticize, but rather to examine a more mundane context of scientific production and reproduction that surrounds, supports, and promotes molecular genetics. This article examines a series of representations of particular genetic phenomena and practices. By focusing on examples of maps, descriptions, diagrams, and protocols that have different roles in the practice, application, and public dissemination of molecular genetics, we intend to describe a few of the many ways in which human communicative actions set up, depict, and promote the representational functions that are said to be intrinsic to genetic reproduction. The study contributes to a developing understanding of "representations" that emphasize the diverse communicative objects and orders that are glossed by that term.[1]

PICTURES AND MAPS

There are a number of established prototypes of representation in science. Perhaps the best known is that of a picture of nature. This prototype is exemplified by Galileo gazing at the moon through his telescope and drawing a series of sketches (Galilei, 1610/1989). The resultant sketches synthesize and give stable form to *what* he saw, while indicating *how* he may have seen it. Almost four centuries later, the drawings, as well as faithful reproductions of them, enable historians and their readers to recognize the moon in Galileo's sketches and to assess the accuracy of the drawings and the measurements derived from them. The drawings also provide historians with a basis for investigating the conceptual and artistic resources that enabled Galileo to visualize the moon (Edgerton, 1991). Two representational relations are at work in such analyses: First, Galileo's sketches are treated as representations of a moon that we can now see, photograph, sketch, measure, and even visit; and, second, the sketches are treated as representations of what Galileo may have seen in his mind's eye. Simply put, sketches like Galileo's are conceptualized first as mirrors of nature and second as mirrors of perception. The two are intimately related. Retrospective assessments of the accuracy of the sketches lead naturally to questions about the power of Galileo's telescope, his artistic skills, and his conceptual preparation. There are, of course, ambiguities and uncertainties associated with both interpretive relations. A comparison of the sketches with modern measurements and depictions of the moon may get in the way of a more historically authentic understanding of Galileo's circumstances, and there is no assurance that his sketches stand proxy for what Galileo actually saw. Close study of Galileo's writings, comparisons of his sketches with those of his contemporaries and predecessors, investigations of his equipment and his background, and so forth can provide a basis for gaining a degree of confidence about one or another interpretation, although some questions are likely to remain unanswered.

---

[1]See Lynch and Woolgar (1990) for a collection of studies that examine the practical uses and interrelations of pictorial, verbal, and other perceptual and communicative modalities. Also see Goodwin (1995); Ochs, Gonzales, and Jacoby (1996); Kawatoko (1999); and Ueno (1998). The term *representation* carries considerable baggage in theoretical discussions and debates, and it is often used as a name for a process of one kind or another. We prefer to think of representation not as a single kind of process, or even a process at all, but as a gross characterization of the various practices and practical relations involved in speaking, speaking-on-behalf-of, writing, depicting, graphing, transcribing, and so forth. For further discussion see Lynch (1994).

A related, though perhaps more general, conception of visual representations is that of a map. Polanyi (1958) asserted, "all theory may be regarded as a kind of map extended over space and time" (p. 4). Such maps are "objective" according to Polanyi, because their representational values, as well as their faults, are detachable from the particular persons who compose and use them. Polanyi observed that whenever formalisms like maps are "applied" to experience, "there is an indeterminacy involved, which must be resolved by the observer on the ground of unspecifiable criteria" (p. 81). This is a point taken up in social constructionist treatments of science. For social constructionists, representational conventions, situated rhetoric, and culturally specific tendencies among scientists in a community bridge the gap between abstract theory and situated application. In recent years, the idea that the features of maps correspond point by point to a depicted territory has undergone progressive deconstruction. Barnes (1977) pointed out that a map of the London Underground is organized for a specific purpose. The map simplifies, selectively distorts, and stylizes the routes depicted. The map's layout of routes and stations bears no consistent relation to the linear matrix of directions and distances in a typical road map. One would not want to read the map "literally" as a geographical plan of London, but in its own way the map provides a concise account of how to navigate the underground. Another kind of map is evident as we leave London Underground. In many stations, maps of the local district are positioned near the exits. Typically, a pointer and inscription indicates, "You are Here." Similar maps are placed strategically on college campuses, city parks, and elsewhere. Often they are made of hard material and fastened to a fixed signpost. The map's stationary place is indicated on the map itself by the existential pointer "You are Here." Even when no pointer is included on a stationary map, we sometimes find a smudge produced by a cumulative history of indexical touches that announces, "Here we are!" Like a footpath, the deictic erosion etches a collective trace in a virtual territory, an archaeological landmark that produces an intersubjective channel between a god's-eye view of the territory and a stream of embodied subjects entering into it from the Underground. Stepping into a car and setting out on a road leading out of the city, perhaps aided by an "occasion map"—a sketch-map drawn by a friend that shows us how to get from our existential "here" to the geographical "there" of our destination[2]—we can notice as we go along a proliferation of "You Are Here" announcements that inscribe the features of a road map on the surface of the roads themselves. When exiting a roundabout, we read, for example, "A-312 Heathrow" painted on the road surface to mark the appropriate turning for that route and destination, and this message is reiterated by signs fastened alongside and above the roadway. One still can find it easy to get lost in the midst of all this textuality. In their own mundane way, these signs and markings perform a function similar to the trained birds in Aldous Huxley's (1962) utopian island, which exclaim "Here and now!" to remind the inhabitants not to get lost in their daydreams. This literary architecture, with its reminders, directional indicators, and formatted lanes, integrates the built environment through which we travel with a paper map of the territory (Latour, 1987). The correspondence between a map's signifiers, the concrete territory, and the existential place in that territory differs profoundly from a realist version of representation, because it exhibits a partial, selective, and pointed collapse of the essential difference between the map's signs and the objective geography to which they correspond. Baudrillard (1983) presented the ultimate limit of such collapse when

---

[2]Harold Garfinkel's unpublished research on occasion maps was presented to his students in lectures (Department of Sociology, University of California, Los Angeles), colloquia, and in unpublished manuscripts since at least 1972. For a published source drawing on Garfinkel's insights, see Psathas (1979).

he borrowed Borges' vivid image of an immense map blanketing the territory it describes. This absurd asymptote satirizes the conventional idea that a map re-presents an already existing territory. Baudrillard suggests that the simulacrum (the map in this case) *precedes* the territory it describes. For him, the map prescribes, runs ahead of, and establishes the boundaries and parameters for realizing a territory.

One of Baudrillard's favorite examples of this "precession of simulacra" is molecular biology. The project of "mapping" DNA does not re-present a familiar territory; instead, it employs a set of coordinates, landmarks, and terminology that (re)define "the type organism and hence the species" (Gilbert, 1992, p. 85). Terminological and material continuities identify the map with the stuff it represents. Take, for example, different modes of physical mapping:

> Physical maps ... come in two types. One is created by measuring the distances along each chromosome in terms of the sequences at which restriction enzymes cut. That provides an abstract distance map for the size of the chromosomes and some points within them. The second type of physical map is called a *cosmid map*—it consists of DNA pieces each about fifty thousand bases in length, each cloned in a separate bacterial strain, and each overlapping other identified cosmids on either side. This map is actually a physical collection of bacteria, about a hundred thousand in number, containing the clones, known as cosmids, that span the entire genome. It is roughly equivalent to having the physical material in one's hand for each of the hundred thousand different human genes. (Gilbert, 1992, pp. 87–88)

To clarify what a cosmid map might be like from a bacterial point of view, imagine an epic poem that is recorded and preserved by the members of a large preliterate civilization. (We shall leave aside the question of how such a poem could come into existence in the first place.) The poem would be far too long and complicated for any individual to memorize. To assure retention of the poem, the society's members organize it into 100,000 consecutive segments, with each fragment of several stanzas being assigned to the members of a separate village. In each of the 100,000 villages, the members keep their fragment alive by rehearsing it, rectifying discrepancies in collective recitals, and then passing it down to their children. This goes on for generations, and the whole enterprise is sustained by the hope that at some future time, a novel method, or a higher intelligence, will enable the civilization to extract each village's segment, piece it together with the others, and gain a comprehensive understanding of the poem and its meaning.

In genomics, physical maps are intermediaries rather than ultimate ends. Gilbert and his fellow visionaries aim eventually to transliterate and digitize the sequences of base pairs in the DNA segments stored in the map. Nevertheless, the molecular biologist who builds a DNA library does not simply write down the relevant sequences on paper and file them away in a catalog; rather, he or she inserts segments of autonomous genetic writing into an organic matrix (e.g., a bacterial "vector"), which is classified, stored in vitro, and retained in a living state. The physical map confounds a conception of a map as a representation of a territory. Moreover, it confounds established concepts of representation and territory. It even complicates Baudrillard's idea of a hyperreal map that precedes the realization of a territory. Baudrillard takes DNA as emblematic of "digitality"—the reduction of life to code—whereas the cosmid map is a living matrix that embodies a code prior to its visualization and digitization.

Yet another analogy may help clarify the peculiarity of the cosmid map. In one of Garrison Keelor's (1986, pp. 98–100) monologues about Lake Wobegon, an imaginary Minnesota village, a crowd of celebrants reflexively embodies a "Living Flag" in the town square every July Fourth to celebrate Independence Day. Each member of the crowd is given a red, white, or blue cap, and, under the instructions of an overseer perched on a ladder, they arrange themselves in a grid to form of an American flag. The overseer then ascends four flights of stairs in the town's Central Building and photographs the Living Flag for the local newspaper. Keelor hilariously describes how, on a sweltering day, the citizens begin to resent the fact that they cannot see the flag their bodies compose, and so in a spontaneous rebellion each member takes a turn and ascends the four flights of stairs to view the Living Flag while the others "hold" the flag's shape. As the afternoon wears on, the flag gradually atrophies as members in the crowd of elderly gatherers grow weary and wander off. Like the good citizens who held their places, the bacterial constituents of a cosmid map "understand" the digital representation and keep it alive through sustained life-activity. The bacteria are not alone. Small armies of human technicians are necessary to produce, sustain, and organize the life-activities of the bacteria in a complex genetic mapping project. So, although the map may precede the territory, it is itself preceded and sustained by organized forms of life. The cosmid map is only one example, but it alerts us to the way that a concept of a map as a store of information reveals little about the material embodiments of life and labor that create and sustain representational functions. The same can be said about many of the other representational and communicative activities that have a role in molecular biology.

Representations of the genetic landscape are more than a collection of metaphors, because they are bound up in material forms and labor relations. For example, an autoradiograph—an x-ray photograph produced through the common laboratory practice of electrophoresis—is infused with a complex hybridization of material and semiotic figures: agarose gels arranged as a tabular matrix; molecular "scissors" (restriction enzymes), probes, and markers for isolating and identifying DNA fragments; and a complex progression of activities for graphically framing electrochemical processes and residues (Amann & Knorr-Cetina, 1990). Like directional signs and place markers inscribed on a roadway, genetic probes and markers are both signs and concrete constituents of the genetic landscape they make intelligible. There is no "rupture" between the things and the signs (Latour, 1995, p. 169). The signs denote, while also taking their places within, material realizations of molecular territory. The literary and representational metaphors associated with DNA and its activities are embedded in more familiar communicative practices associated with writing, reading, and following laboratory protocols, as well as disseminating results, tools, and products of laboratory industry.

Many of the classic oppositions and problems associated with representation become less salient when we consider pictures and texts as communicative artifacts. The fact that historians can examine and interpret Galileo's sketches already indicates that the preservation and duplication of the drawings, along with the writings with which they are associated, provide a communicative link between 17th-century activities and present-day commentaries about them. Moreover, the sketches and textual descriptions can be understood as Galileo's devices for forging communicative relations between his observations and his contemporaries. Representations and simulacra used by present-day scientists and their publicity agents also facilitate and embody communicative relations. Such linkages extend beyond the material properties and epistemic relations associated with traditional conceptions of representations as pictorial and verbal mediators between objective and subjective domains. It is sometimes said that laboratory science is a "messy" domain infused with "heterogeneous relations," but these are not very revealing terms. Even if we assume that there is no single dominant form of representation, it is still possible to get some clarity on the subject by proceeding case by case and examining how relations of production, communication, and dissemination are intertwined with different representational artifacts. To comprehend the role of representation and more specifically visual representation in scientific activity, we believe it is necessary to take account of a complex order of things and activities. There is no single way to do this, and the task involves more than a matter of isolating a single domain of, for example, "visual" representation and ascribing essential cognitive functions to the communicative artifacts associated with that domain.

A CASE—PCR

In the remainder of this article we lay out an inventory of different modes of textual representation and reproduction associated with a single molecular biological innovation, the polymerase chain reaction (PCR). PCR is apt case for examining some of the many ways a scientific innovation can be presented, represented, reproduced, and disseminated for different practical and communicative purposes.[3] We shall not focus in detail on any single type of representation, but will instead examine several different representational uses and occasions of use. This analysis will not produce a very "deep" ethnographic account of how representational artifacts are constructed or rendered, but it may have some preliminary value for gaining an overview of an array of communicative techniques and situations.[4]

PCR is a technique that in just a few years became widely used in many scientific, medical, and legal contexts of investigation. It is a technique with an established identity and pedigree as a patented invention for which the inventor, Kary Mullis, won the Nobel Prize. PCR straddles established distinctions between methods, facts, artifacts, and commodities, and it passes back and forth between science, engineering, and industry. PCR is not only a thing—a discovered object or an artifact—it is a method of genetic replication. It is a method in two, intertwined senses: a molecular process through which specific sequences of nucleotide bases are "amplified" through the action of specific enzymes and reagents, and a set of protocols for accomplishing such amplification (Lynch & Jordan, 1995). Molecular biologists describe PCR as a laboratory method that harnesses subcellular mechanisms of genetic reproduction.

Representations of various kinds come into play when PCR is performed, described, and disseminated. They are associated with different audiences, practical purposes, and epistemic demands. The following cases are arranged to exhibit some typical renderings while also instructing readers of this article on how PCR gene amplification works.

Schematic Diagrams

Starting in the early 1990s, PCR started to appear in popular magazines and newspapers. Diagrams explaining it to readers with relatively little background in molecular biology often accompanied

---

[3]For further treatments of PCR and its dissemination, see Jordan and Lynch (1993; 1998) and Lynch and Jordan (1995). For a highly readable story of the personal and organizational circumstances of PCR's invention, see Rabinow (1996).

[4]More intensive accounts of representational practices in particular settings are provided by Lynch (1985), Amann and Knorr-Cetina (1990), Goodwin (1995), and Ochs et al. (1996). For further discussion of the approach taken in this article, see Jordan and Lynch (1998).

articles about it. More specialized diagrams described PCR for practitioners and audiences who became involved with its use in paternity testing, prenatal diagnosis, and criminal investigation. Such diagrams often employed cartoon conventions for representing a series of steps or stages in the procedure. They also include visual analogies, such as a common likeness between the DNA double helix and a segmented zipper that can be unzipped along the bonds between the bases. Figure 1 is typical of the genre.

This figure uses the conventions of a cartoon to connote sequential and temporal development while also showing a strip of DNA that runs through the cartoon frames, weaving the story together. It employs a whole array of simplifications, icons, anthropomorphisms, visual fictions (Gilbert & Mulkay, 1984), and objectifications in order to make PCR readily intelligible. It is evidently simplified and unrealistic. There are relatively few steps in the picture compared to the protocols in a lab manual. Visual resemblance performs metaphoric functions. For example, icons are used to depict DNA strands as though they were strips of photographic film linked together by separable fasteners (a variant on the zipper analogy). DNA segments, such as the AIDS DNA segment in Frame 2, have little hooks on them that latch into complementary segments like jigsaw puzzle pieces.

At the time the diagram was produced, doing PCR required improvisational handiwork (it is now fully, or partially, automated in many research and industrial settings), and yet in Figure 1 there are no hands, bodies, or other visual references to the embodied performance of the procedure. Instead, the figure makes use of cartoon conventions to depict a series of material transformations. For example, a sequence of frames presents a step-by-step process through which a series of material changes is effected. There are no humans in the picture to handle the test tubes and combine the ingredients. Instead, the primers mentioned in Frame 2 are endowed with a capacity to "look for matching segments of AIDS DNA in the blood sample." This portrayal rhetorically enhances an objective effect with a common type of communicative device. In brief, the agency and logic of the procedure are exhibited by animating a molecular process. In some respects, the figure is like instructions for assembling a bicycle or adjusting a carburetor, which show a novice what to do by depicting an objective metamorphosis. A frame-by-frame sequence of exploded images provides an account of how the parts of the artifact fit together. Consequently, although the practitioners' bodies have been deleted from the portrayal, a practitioner's competence is implied in and through the depiction.[5]

The diagram in Figure 1 is not organized to instruct a potential practitioner. Instead, it explains a technical practice for readers who presumably have limited acquaintance with molecular biology. The cartoon includes various bridging devices that use what the reader may know and care about as a point of departure for displaying technical novelties. For example, the selection of AIDS DNA as the genetic phenomenon of interest associates the procedure with a familiar and important point of reference. Such points of reference are typical of science-news columns in daily newspapers, where potential medical applications are highlighted when scientific breakthroughs are discussed. The illustration also uses visual bridging devices. Much in the way a

---

[5]Halfon (1998) reproduced a similar diagram of another molecular biological technique (the single-locus probe technique of DNA profiling) and made note of the many practical contingencies that are not included in the diagram. Halfon's analysis effectively dramatized the difference between the diagram and an ethnographic account of the practices it glosses, but it would be misleading to conclude from it that the diagram was designed to give a more complete or comprehensive description than it does.

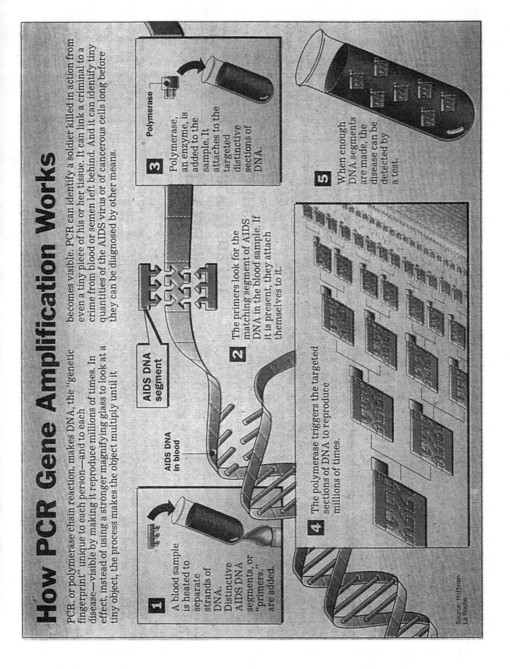

How PCR Gene Amplification Works

PCR, or polymerase chain reaction, makes DNA, the "genetic fingerprint" unique to each person—and to each disease—visible by making it reproduce millions of times. In effect, instead of using a stronger magnifying glass to look at a tiny object, the process makes the object multiply until it becomes visible. PCR can identify a soldier killed in action from even a tiny piece of his or her tissue. It can link a criminal to a crime from blood or semen left behind. And it can identify tiny quantities of the AIDS virus or of cancerous cells long before they can be diagnosed by other means.

1 A blood sample is heated to separate strands of DNA. Distinctive AIDS DNA segments, or "primers," are added.

AIDS DNA in blood

AIDS DNA segment

2 The primers look for the matching segment of AIDS DNA in the blood sample. If it is present, they attach themselves to it.

3 Polymerase, an enzyme, is added to the sample. It attaches to the targeted distinctive sections of DNA.

Polymerase

4 The polymerase triggers the targeted sections of DNA to reproduce millions of times.

5 When enough DNA segments are made, the disease can be detected by a test.

Source: Hoffman-La Roche

FIGURE 1   From "How PCR Gene Amplification Works" by Paul Gonzales, *Los Angeles*, January 18, 1992. Reprinted with permission.

bird-watcher's field guide uses everyday, backyard species (sparrows, robins, crows) as standards for calibrating the size and profile of less familiar specimens (Lynch & Law, 1999), Figure 1 implicates an average educated reader's familiarity with laboratory artifacts. For example, the test tube with a "blood sample" inside is juxtaposed with the Bunsen flame. The glass test tube and Bunsen flame are familiar items in the elementary chemistry lab as well as the movie set depicting a basement laboratory, but they differ from the small, opaque, plastic test tubes and thermal cyclers (finely calibrated electrical "ovens" with multiple heating elements in which the tubes are placed) used in PCR preparations. The copious amount of blood sample in the iconic test tube also differs from the minute, often colorless samples analyzed in a diagnostics lab. The test-tube icon, with its standard shape and orientation repeated throughout the depiction, can be likened to a re-petitively stamped character in a pictographic text. Note that molecular structures are drawn at the same scale as the test tube and flame.

The process is organized through a series of steps that (somehow) are performed by humans and machines in lived-time and lived-space. This portrayal of a macroscopic course of action is in-tegrated, both within and between frames, with an account of a molecular process, a series of ma-terial events correlated with the sequence of procedures. Some of the figures in the picture represent visible and palpable materials that comprise part of a practice performed on a human scale, whereas others gloss a domain of invisible phenomena. So, for example, in the cartoon we can see that applying heat to the stuff in the test tube separates (unzips) strands of DNA. Both heat-ing and unzipping are depicted in a coherent visual frame as elements of a single act. Molecular "primers"—depicted as puzzle pieces—are then added to signal the starting points for copying at each end of the gene (or DNA segment) of interest. (Note that in this popularization, the primers are shown to latch onto the DNA strip at opposite edges, which differs from more technical ac-counts of their action that show two primers latching onto the strand at opposite ends of a longer sequence of nucleotides.) The depiction thus describes PCR as a practice performed through a se-ries of visible changes in molecular space. The mode of reproduction is both practical and processual, achieved through interwoven human and molecular agencies.

As the caption enables us to see, the practice or process "works" by separating the DNA strands, isolating a continuous sequence of nucleotide bases with primers (short DNA segments that latch to complementary regions of the DNA at specified points), introducing an enzyme that initiates formation of a complementary DNA strand along the region bracketed by the base pairs, and iterating the procedure to multiply the number of copies in a geometric progression. The last two cartoon frames depict, through yet another visual metaphor, a multiplication of puzzle pieces identical with the primers shown in the earlier frame. Although this effectively illustrates the geo-metrical progression, it glosses over the material difference between the relatively short DNA segments in the primers and the longer sequence of DNA in the gene of interest bracketed by the two primers.

It is easy to make ironic remarks at the expense of this popularization, but it is not incidental that we have used it here for instructional as well as analytic purposes. The very simplified, and even inaccurate, features facilitate the task of introducing the practice or process to unacquainted readers. The place of the reader is implicated in the diagram, though in a different way than by the "You Are Here" inscribed on a stationary map. Many of the figure's apparent distortions act as iconic or pictorial bridges that evoke a reader's limited familiarity with scientific tools and prac-tices. For all practical purposes, it is enough to say that the material is heated somehow, even though the "how" is misleadingly depicted. Borrowing Neisser's (1981) terminology, it gives a "gist" rather than a literal account of the protocol. Moreover, it is an account designed for an audience that is, and is likely to remain, remote from the performance of the technique. If the article were used as a recipe or guideline for performing the technique, it would fail miserably. Nevertheless, the techniques and theoretical objects of a science are recognizable, unmistakably present, "in" the picture.

Commercial Advertisements

PCR kits, thermal cyclers, PCR applications, and PCR itself are commercial products, and they are advertised as such in science journals, trade magazines, and other specialized publications. In many respects, advertisements for molecular biological tools are akin to those for home remedies, small appliances, and kitchen utensils. Ads for products with names like the DNA Dipstick™, Stratagene®, and Designer PCR™ emphasize how these innovations improve quality, ease the performance, reduce error rates, and facilitate clean laboratory work. Technical references are framed by familiar ad slogans: "At last! A simple, fast, inexpensive way to purify plasmids without CsCl gradients, without waiting for the ultracentrifuge or struggling with an HPLC." A combination of speed and simplicity (at low cost and without sacrificing quality) is highlighted in many slogans: "Makes quantification fast & simple!"; "It's simple and it works!"; "Results ... Pure and Simple."; and "Remarkably simple process. Simply remarkable results." (See Fortun, 1999, for further discussion of the theme of speed in molecular biology.) Once in a while, such references to speed are (slightly) qualified: "Fast, Efficient, Trouble-Free (With the Right Choice of Primers)." More often, they are quantified: "Purify PCR* products in only 15 minutes with Spin Bind" (the asterisk after PCR is referenced to a note that states in fine print that PCR process is covered by U.S. Patents owned by Hoffman-LaRoche, Inc.). Non-clock time references to time of day are also used: "Make your primers after breakfast.... Use your primers after lunch." Competitive advantage in a world of continual and unlimited innovation is also a major theme: "Closes the gaps other markers leave behind."; "The Revolution Continues ..."; "There's no limit to what you can achieve with out thermal cyclers"; "Explore the Outer Limits Uxing Gibco BRL RT-PCR Products"; and (in an ad reproduced in Haraway, 1997, p. 64) "**At $2.80** *per base*, OPERON'S **DNA makes** *anything* POSSIBLE". Sci-fi imagery is sometimes used to illustrate these futures: a mysterious glow emerging from a starry sky illustrates the "Outer Limits" slogan, and, in another ad, a dinosaur evokes a Jurassic Park theme to illustrate the announcement: "Oligo 5.0 PCR Software. With 22 New Features, Who Knows What You Might Come Up With?" The exaggerated promise of a fast and simple end to drudgery in a world in which, as Haraway (1997) described it "anything is possible" (p. 64), is certainly not original to these ads. Such promise also can be found in ads for household kitchen and laundry products. Biotech ads sometimes refer obliquely to negative delays, difficulties, and sources of impurity that the product on offer promises to remedy: "Introducing the ONCOR® *Template-Tamer*™ Controls PCR Contamination"; "Clean up PCR Reactions." Some ads combine promise with entertainment, often with technical plays on proverbial phrases: "Not all *Taq* DNA Polymerases are Created Equal"; "A Mutation is a Terrible Thing to Miss ... Don't"; and "The 5' End is Near." Punning is often achieved through an interplay of verbal and visual imagery. For example, the slogan "Stratagene Brings Back The Big Bands" with a PCR "Optimization Kit" is superimposed against a photograph of a Big Band era jazz orchestra, and an ad for a "fast and simple" aid to DNA sequencing is illustrated with an image of a model racing car whose chassis is made out of a test tube. A series of ads from a Japanese company, Takara, employs cartoon figures of Sumo wrestlers to represent its product "Power PCR," and in one of these ads the figure is shown in a series of overlapping images receding to a vanishing point. A similar pun on PCR amplification is shown in an ad in which duplicate photographs of inventor Kary Mullis illustrate a claim about a product for purifying PCR duplication.

Promises of speed, efficiency, quality, and competitive advantage are tied to automation. The advertisements promote the actual elimination of the human handiwork that is virtually eliminated from "hands-off" diagrams like Figure 1: "CircumVent™ DNA Sequencing Kit ... For Fast, Hands-Off Processing Directly in your Thermal Cycler."; and in language that would thrill proponents of actor-network theory, "PCR Primer Selection ... It's Not For Humans."

The kitchen analogies used in biotech advertising are no accident. In universities and many companies, labs are relatively small, inhabited by a director and a crew of staff scientists and technicians (a master chef, often male, and a crew of cooks and kitchen staff, frequently female). Production is decentralized, disaggregated, rather than organized around a massive facility like a large observatory or particle accelerator (Knorr-Cetina, 1992). The advertisers appeal to an end-user who manages a small and relatively bounded practical domain. As in the case of the household kitchen, the end-user is invited to partake in the use of packaged products that commodify what was once a routine part of the work (Cowan, 1985; Fujimura, 1992).

Some advertisements for molecular biology products—and, more generally, some modes of promotion—take on a distinctive cast as "scientific" communications. Although they are designed by advertisers in an attempt to attract customers, they appear to be written by scientists for other scientists. For example, several years ago, a Dupont ad for Repliprime™, a product associated with the PCR method, assumed the form of a one-page technical publication, complete with a list of references. The ad also mentioned a series of technical precautions (and products). Unlike a research article, it did not identify its author and was presented under the heading "Molecular Biology Products." Interestingly, although the Repliprime™ ad listed a series of technical publications associated with the invention of PCR, it never mentioned Cetus, the corporate holder of the original patent (see Rabinow, 1996, for an account of the invention of PCR at Cetus). In the initial paragraph, the ad noted that "[t]he theory behind PCR was originally described in 1971," and cited a reference in a footnote. This was a key claim in Dupont's unsuccessful challenge of Cetus's patent (Cetus Corporation later dissolved, and sold the PCR patent Hoffman-LaRoche and the right to use the Cetus name to Perkin-Elmer). The ad quickly moved to a discussion of "variations of the basic procedures" that have been "developed into state-of-the-art methodology." Not incidentally, Dupont offered for sale a "kit" that packaged key ingredients and instructions for such a methodology.

This mode of advertising is familiar in other print and electronic media that use the format of a news article or television program as a vehicle for advertising (such convergence has become familiar in the United States where children's television programs have been developed around particular products marketed by toy manufacturers). The very distinction between commercial advertising, journalism, and, in this case, technical publication, becomes difficult to maintain in some instances.

In molecular biology, a growing service industry has taken over some of the practices that were once performed in situ by staff scientists and technicians working in university and industrial laboratories. If Walter Gilbert's (1992) vision of molecular biology's future proves correct, we should expect to see an increasing number of laboratory routines delegated to external commercial services. This would comprise an accelerated version of the historical trend toward exporting household kitchen (and more recently restaurant) production to commercial services. This trend was illustrated by an advertisement for the Perkin-Elmer Cetus "DNA Amplification System."

Like many ads, it employed typical biotech conventions like an iconic DNA double helical strand running across the page. It also included a visual display—an open briefcase containing an array of test tubes, representing a PCR kit of prepared reagents—which merged scientific and corporate iconography. The ad also included a testimonial by a "Senior Technical Specialist," and much like ads for fast food, laundry, or other delivery services, there was a message at the base of the page: "For Fast Overnight Delivery Call TOLL FREE: 1-800-762-4002." The ad made clear that the company was selling a service and not simply a set of products. The ad copy listed a series of technical services available to the purchasing lab. Such services connect the user to a communal support system in which PCR is the central theme, and companies like Perkin-Elmer become central nodes that disseminate technical information and facilitate relations among users. Perkin-Elmer's ads frequently mention guarantees of pure results and the company's "commitment" to assuring quality. Customers on the company's mailing list receive a steady stream of invitations to seminars, workshops, and other quasiacademic meetings designed to promote products and instruct practitioners on their effective use.

Contrary to a popularization like Figure 1, in which a science is presented from a standpoint unreachably above the heads of the readers and is brought down to their level of understanding through a series of bridging devices, trade advertisements address potential partners in a service relation. This relation is not bridged by common understanding; rather, it is transacted through the sale and purchase of a black box. Unlike ads, like the Dupont ad discussed earlier, which take the form of a "scientific" publication for a community of investigators, commercial services promote the technique as a commercial kit. The kit is a particular type of black box in which a lab can obtain a set of products that were once "homemade" by the lab's own kitchen staff.

Patent Documents

Another distinctive account is provided by patent applications (see Bowker, 1994; Cambrosio, Keating & MacKenzie, 1990; Myers, 1995). For example, consider the "summary of the invention" section of one of the patents filed by Mullis et al. (1987, p. 2). Like the newspaper depiction in Figure 1, this account is written to convey an innovation to a broader audience than a community of technical specialists. Patent examiners and civil courts include some participants who are educated in the relevant specialties, but they include many who are not expected to have an ability to reproduce the technique. Unlike a popular audience, the examiners and courts must gain a deeper appreciation of what is being claimed, how it works, and what is novel about it. Compared to the newspaper account or advertisement, the patent application is highly prolix (Shapin & Schaffer, 1985). The sentences are long, multiclausal, technical, and exhaustive, not only because they are designed to convey a virtual sense of an actual practice. Like a number of areas in which legal and scientific competencies are intertwined (Jasanoff, 1996), patenting involves both a novel technique and a regulatory context. In accordance with U.S. patent regulations, the claim is oriented not only to a lay reader, but also to an ideal–typical practitioner who has attained "average skill in the art" (for practical purposes, a postdoctoral researcher in the relevant science). In principle, such a practitioner should be able to replicate the innovation from the description. This double agenda—to make the technique intelligible to a legally informed "lay" reader and to enable a practitioner to replicate it—places severe demands on writers and readers.

A distinctive feature of the patent is its explicit constructionist language. Again, there is a legal consideration: A discovery cannot be patented in the United States, whereas an invention can.

Mullis et al. (1987) freely spoke of their "invention," while at the same time they naturalized it. They used the terms *invention, method,* and *process* in close proximity when speaking of what was invented. The invention "relates to a process," "resides in a process," and "provides a process" for amplifying specific nucleic acid sequences (Mullis et al., 1987). It is also "a method [that] is expected to be more efficient" than alternative methods for amplifying samples of DNA. The patent describes different "embodiments" of this process or method in stepwise fashion. One such embodiment

> relates to diagnostic kits for the detection of at least one specific nucleic acid sequence in a sample containing one or more nucleic acids at least one of which nucleic acid is suspected of containing said sequence, which kit comprises, in packaged form, a multicontainer unit having
> (a) one container for each oligonucleotide primer for each strand of each different sequence to be detected, which primer or primers are substantially complementary to each strand of each specific nucleic acid sequence such that an extension product synthesized from one primer, when it is separated from its complement, can serve as a template for the synthesis of the extension product of the other primer;
> (b) a container containing an agent for polymerization;
> (c) a container for each of four different nucleoside triphosphates;
> (d) a container containing means for detecting hybrids of said probe and said sequence. (Mullis et al., 1987, p. 3)

If taken out of context, this multiclausal sentence might strike a reader as symptomatic of a peculiar obsession. However, it is not written to inform a novice or instruct a practitioner. Instead, it responds to a legal demand to describe, with a single sentence, the "essential features" of the technical embodiment that is being claimed. The phrases "one or more" and "at least one" specify particular elements of the technique while leaving open a range of potential applications covered by the claim. Essential elements, such as primers, the DNA sequence of interest, and the "agent for polymerization" are described generically. The language of the claim provides readers with an account of a definite set of things at hand, combined with an indefinite range of unspecified contextual variations and future applications (see Myers, 1995). The account uses a series of reflexive clauses to weave together the various elements in a single sentential frame ("at least one of which nucleic acid"; "which kit comprises"; "a container containing"). This language conveys a sense of auto-authorization and self-containment. It is a sociological description of a very particular kind. Although it makes no explicit mention of human actions, the passage describes a reproducible method that "relates to" an arrangement of materials and processes in diagnostic kits that have an unspecified range of future applications. The patent's reflexive sociological description weaves together an objective molecular process and a human practice.[6] There is no strict demarcation between the two:

---

[6]*Reflexivity* in this sense is not synonymous with direct reference to self or to one's own actions; quite the opposite, it is produced through the text's passive implication of a set of practices accomplished through the use of the tools and ingredients described. These implications are necessary to an understanding of the text's praxiological description of a reproducible method. Given the more established identification of *reflexivity* in the sociology of science with direct mention of the circumstances of human inquiry and writing, the passage is likely to seem conspicuously unreflexive or even designed to "delete" all reference to the contingencies of human action. But when we keep in mind that any passage of speech or writing necessarily communicates more than it says in so many words (Garfinkel & Sacks, 1970), we can begin to appreciate that reflexivity (like virtually all other analytic features of language) is not confined to literal features of sentences or statements. In this case we must ask "What does the passage require us to take into account in order to make sense of it, as a patent

the instrumentality of the description "relates to a process" that is described in molecular biological terms.

Praxiological Descriptions

Unlike the examples discussed thus far, some descriptions are designed to enable practitioners to perform the technique. There are many different modes of praxiological description, and they often are used in combination. (As noted previously, the patent description includes this as one of its aspects.) Typically, such descriptions take the form of step-by-step recipes. The recipes can be simple or elaborate in design, depending on the circumstances. When given to a skilled and trusted practitioner, instructions are often minimized. For example, when giving an example of a practitioner with "golden hands," a lab director described a staff scientist who

> is the kind of person that I don't have to sit down on a daily basis and say "today I want you to do this and this." What I do with [name of practitioner] is informally every couple of weeks, I'll say where we are going, "Let's look at this and this." And all of the details of the experiment she does herself. I can walk into the lab and look at the notebook, look at what's running ..., she doesn't even need to be there. What bands are coming up in the tray. And I know exactly what she's doing and why she's doing it, and it's a very comforting position to be in when you don't have to do daily supervision.[7]

In this account, the lab administrator links together minimal instructions and the transparency of the research assistant's work. In this particular account, a technician's work is "invisible" (Shapin, 1989) because her competence at implementing a plan is taken for granted and trusted without need for elaborate specification. (Technically speaking, this research assistant was not a technician: When asked if his assistant was a technician or a scientist, initially the administrator responded, "No, she's a master's degree chemist." When asked further if this implied that she is a "scientist," the response was, "She's a scientist.") A different, although in some respects related, kind of invisibility is produced by rationalizing the technician's work to such an extent that the work is presumed to involve nothing but the rote execution of a managerial plan. This classic mode of deskilling is evident in many of the larger government and corporate laboratories, and it is often followed by further innovations that automate procedures previously done by hand.

Initial instructions given to novices and low-grade technicians take a more elaborate form. Typically, the sort of rote "first you do this, and then you do that" instructions are accompanied by rationales and explanations expressed to varying degrees of depth. Especially under conditions where it is recognized that a technician or staff scientist will need to adapt or "tweak" the protocol under different circumstances, an effort is made to explain why one step follows another, or why particular ingredients, temperature settings, and latency periods are used.

Material ingredients of PCR typically include the following: small plastic test tubes with labels for types and amounts of primers, buffers, and enzymes; pipettes with disposable tips for transfer-

---

claim?" Although there is no shortage of things that can be said about the language in the passage, for that very reason much of what can be said about it is likely to be misleading or distracting. Ethnomethodological reflexivity, understood as a specification of the social "logic" of language, refers to the way linguistic expressions arise from, presuppose, and are referred back to (without necessarily referring to) actual routines and singular occasions of use (see Lynch, 2000).

[7] Interview of manager from a biotech corporation, conducted by Kathleen Jordan (December 24, 1993).

ring measured amounts of ingredients from one container to another; a thermal cycler for repeatedly heating and cooling a batch of preparations; and an electrophoresis gel apparatus for visualizing the product. For example, during a session in which a staff scientist shows a novice how to perform PCR, the protocol states

1. Label the tubes.
2. Add appropriate volume of water.
3. Make reaction mix for 10 reactions.
4. Add 30 microliters of reaction mix to each tube.
5. Add appropriate volume of appropriate DNA sample to each tube.
6. Overlay with two drops, 50 microliters of sterile mineral oil.
7. Place tubes in thermal cyclers set for 90 degrees C, 50 degrees C, and 72 degrees C.
8. Run 40 cycles.

This version of PCR exemplifies what Schutz (1964) called "cook book knowledge" (p. 71), a practical know-how that requires a limited understanding of the physical or chemical mechanisms that are employed. This recipe is incomplete in many respects, and the performance is accompanied by further instructions about what is in the various test tubes, what happens when the materials are heated in sequence and at the different temperatures, and so forth. In one instance, when it was used to instruct a novice, the recipe was accompanied by more detailed instructions referenced to the "thisses and that's" in the unfolding scene:

Let's go to the freezer.
    First thing, is I take a bunch of tubes— we're going to need and label them. I usually label them with the name and then the primers that I'm using. These are just "1" plus "2" and the date. ...
    So, you want water or the 10x buffer which we've taken out of the freezer and these are the primers, and these are the volumes. The way this is figured out is I add water and DNA to a total of 20 microliters, so that leaves a remainder of 30 microliters of volume for the total of 50 microliter reaction.

Unlike the "cookbook" protocol statement, this continuous set of instructions includes references to the immediate scene and participants, as well as "steps" that are not mentioned in any protocol ("Let's go to the freezer"). These mundane incidentals embed the protocol statement into the immediate field of instructed action. Even the "DNA" has a tangible point of reference to a visible, palpable container whose contents can be "picked up" in a pipette.

The recipe and running commentaries given to the novices in this case were further supplemented by the graphic description of PCR in Figure 2. This was a variant of a sketch map, in this case drawn on a computer, to help the novices navigate the territory.

The left-hand column describes in vernacular language what the procedure does and how it works at each of several stages. The right-hand column pictographically represents the described molecular arrangements and rearrangements.

The left-hand column glosses what a practitioner sees, says, smells, and handles when performing the technique, and it goes into brief molecular rationales. The account provides a concise way of presenting a molecular rationale for the various "handed doings" (Sudnow, 1978) that make up the procedure. Note the way the molecular constituents are depicted as linear strips of nucleotides. They are arrayed as pictographic sequences to be read from left to right. Alongside the

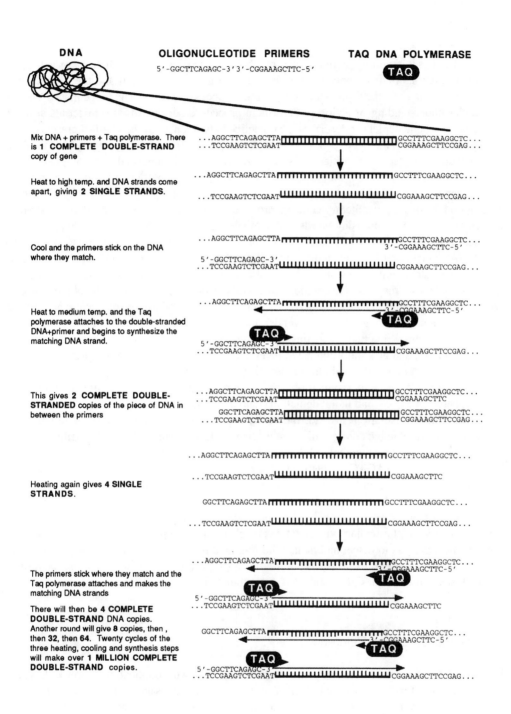

DNA   OLIGONUCLEOTIDE PRIMERS   TAQ DNA POLYMERASE

5'-GGCTTCAGAGC-3' 3'-CGGAAAGCTTC-5'   TAQ

Mix DNA + primers + Taq polymerase. There is **1 COMPLETE DOUBLE-STRAND** copy of gene

Heat to high temp. and DNA strands come apart, giving **2 SINGLE STRANDS.**

Cool and the primers stick on the DNA where they match.

Heat to medium temp. and the Taq polymerase attaches to the double-stranded DNA+primer and begins to synthesize the matching DNA strand.

This gives **2 COMPLETE DOUBLE-STRANDED** copies of the piece of DNA in between the primers

Heating again gives **4 SINGLE STRANDS.**

The primers stick where they match and the Taq polymerase attaches and makes the matching DNA strands

There will then be **4 COMPLETE DOUBLE-STRAND** DNA copies. Another round will give **8** copies, then , then **32**, then **64**. Twenty cycles of the three heating, cooling and synthesis steps will make over **1 MILLION COMPLETE DOUBLE-STRAND** copies.

FIGURE 2   Diagram.

139

graphic sketches is a running set of instructions about how to proceed through the steps in the procedure. The textual division between step-by-step instructions on the left and the depictions of molecular correlates on the right exhibits two parallel modes of writing. The first enlists a reader's vernacular understanding of action to describe a procedure performed with materials at hand, whereas the second depicts or describes the objective in two senses of the word: It presents a pictographic account of an objective process at each stage in the procedure, and it provides an idealized account of the technical "objective"—what the technique is supposed to accomplish.

The "molecular sequences" on the right are hybrid objects of a particular kind: They provide a graphic rendering of an object that facilitates a literary presentation and analysis (Lynch, 1990). This hybrid is not simply a literary code; its production and reading is not delimited by a domain of written communication using words and symbols. Much of the burden placed on laboratory practices is to import material extracts into the lab and modify them locally to isolate, purify, and read DNA sequences. Many techniques, including PCR, are used to untangle DNA, to separate strands, to isolate definite segments, to decode the sequence of base pairs, to store these in genetic libraries, to develop maps, and to compose data bases. Alongside the penetration of the molecule with literary metaphors (DNA code, RNA transcription, genetic libraries, physical maps, etc.) is the proliferation of technologies that engender material modifications that rectify material orders and facilitate literary practices. "Writing up" is not just an end product of laboratory research. More constantly, and at a more intensive level, an entire series of laboratory preparations and modifications fashions and refashions the legibility of molecular residues.

The hybrid object—pictographic molecular sequences—can be shifted about in an intermediate zone between writing and literal depiction (Latour, 1995). Verbal description and raw data are rarely presented in isolation; instead, molecular organizations are presented and re-presented through partly translatable configurations of writing, pictorial form, and material artifact. For example, a single-stranded fragment of DNA can be represented (and digitally stored) as a sequence of nucleotide "letters" (AGTC), but to get to that point it is necessary to perform a lengthy series of operations for extracting and denaturing DNA strands, isolating selected fragments, and sequencing those fragments. Molecular models (Francoeur, 1997), three-dimensional images, and video demonstrations can be used to re-naturalize the place of the strand within the coils of a chromosome, and various intermediary visualizations (such as autoradiographic bands) are used during the analytical process to detect and isolate the fragment of interest. Such praxiological descriptions are not stand-alone exhibits, like museum displays, popular illustrations, and advertisements. Instead, they are designed and used in combination as elements of a practice.

Material Standards and References

Because PCR is a technique, it may seem natural to suppose that the publication of protocols would be a major means for disseminating it. Numerous laboratory manuals are available, and patent documents include protocols for several embodiments of PCR. As has been frequently noted in social studies of science, laboratory protocols are notoriously difficult to follow. Moreover, protocols tend to vary even within the confines of a particular lab, as practitioners build in precautions, incorporate different ingredients, experiment with parameters, and settle for one or another routine that works "for me" or "for us" (Cambrosio & Keating, 1988; Jordan & Lynch, 1992). In some laboratory environments, concerted efforts are made to establish and administer standard protocols, but at a more massive scale standardization appears to be accomplished through a different route.

An official at a national laboratory responsible for standardizing DNA fingerprinting techniques informed us of a particular method for calibrating techniques among a consortium of forensics laboratories.[8] This official described the following list of considerations:

1. A forensics specialist worked for a year in the organization's lab, developing methods for transferring PCR and validating different applications.

2. This resulted in the production of "standard reference material" to be sent out to participating labs. The most important component of this standard reference was samples of DNA from a male source and a female source. According to the official interviewed, the reference material became "sort of the standards for the world." By means of the samples, measurements were transferred "by means of an artifact, the artifact being a well-defined material."

3. The male and female samples came from two distinct sources: The female sample "was derived originally from a female with chronic melogenous leukemia. So it's a standard cell line, you can trace it back to American-type culture collection, so that person lives on in perpetuity." The reference here is to the famous "Hela" cell line. These cells were selected for use as a standard because they had been so intensively studied and mapped in molecular biology. The male was selected for different reasons. "The male happens to be an individual who lives in the state of Colorado. He was chosen because ... he's heterozygous, that is, he has two allelic bands on nearly every DNA probe known to man. He's a true mongrel." He is also a "forensic urologist" whose DNA had been developed by a company for use as a control sample.

4. Using expensive, state-of-the-art techniques, the standards laboratory developed a precise account of the visible result to be achieved by running the samples through laboratory methods for visualizing the molecular weights of the constituents.

5. Small samples of these reference materials were prepared for distribution, for a fee, to participating labs. The material standards were distributed, together with a "certificate" that described the analytical results to be obtained. Protocols were not specified. Instead, the participating labs were free to work out their own protocols by reference to the certified result. As a way of controlling for the fact that samples degrade over time, the standards lab limited the amount of sample sent to each participating lab to a small portion that would be used up by one or a very few test runs. The samples produced at the centralized facility were periodically checked and refreshed (cf. O'Connell, 1993; Schaffer, 1992).

CONCLUSION

Although a conception of scientific representations as documentary mediations between nature and human experience opens up numerous familiar (and still interesting) questions, a more complicated set of relations becomes perspicuous when pictures are situated among various contemporary methods for disseminating facts, product information, and technical services. When considered as communicational devices, sketches, descriptions, recipes, and material standards no longer

---

[8]Telephone interview of official from U.S. National Institute of Standards, conducted by Michael Lynch and Kathleen Jordan (May 12, 1993).

provide the incidental grounds for conveying information. Instead, they become materially significant as devices that mediate fields of social relations.

Our inventory exhibits a whole variety of modes of representation, agency, dissemination, and reproduction associated with a single innovation, PCR. As we have seen, to speak of PCR as a single innovation glosses over many variations of the procedure. Superficially described, such representations indicate that a scientific invention was successfully reproduced by different means and in a number of different institutional circumstances. However, when we consider how the different modes of reproduction and dissemination were produced, we can begin to appreciate that we are not dealing with a single process or a unitary form of information. Schematic diagrams, advertisements, patents, protocols, and material standards are differently formed, and the information they convey substantially differs from one form to another.

Readers of schematic renderings gain an appreciation that has little to do with a practical mastery of the procedure. Nevertheless, this appreciation is not nothing; it is a specific kind of understanding, albeit not one that is vindicated through an act of replication. Advertisements presuppose specialized audiences and, to a variable degree, technically competent readers, but even the Du Pont advertisement discussed earlier does not exhaustively instruct its reader about how to use the product or technique in question.[9] Some ads are designed less as representations of a product than as invitations to a business transaction organized around a methodological theme and commercial service. In such cases, the leading edge of dissemination advances into the professional form of life of a science to the point that relations of scientific production and communication become established channels for commercial market transactions. In the case of a patent, a description (sometimes illustrated with diagrams) targets a legalistic reading divorced from a scientific performance. For a patent examiner, a claim is vindicated when a person of "ordinary skill in the art" can, if he or she so chooses, reproduce the innovation described in the patent application. The basis of understanding need not be demonstrated in a performance. Protocols can be specified elaborately, or when disseminated among colleagues who know what to do they can be glossed with a few words or a sketch. In such cases, the text does not contain the means for reproducing the procedure, nor is the appropriate way to "see what it says" confined to reading and understanding. Compared to a patent document, a protocol is not written to control future uses and contexts of use. It can bear the lighter burden of prompting practitioners to set in motion a ready-to-hand assemblage of skills, ingredients, kits, instruments, and routines. A material standard facilitates yet another kind of informing. The standards lab exports a hybrid object that includes a set of materials and a certificate. Together these provide materials, describe results to be obtained, and lend legitimate authority for the method in question. This, in turn, presupposes that the participating labs are able to work out for themselves how to approximate the certified standard. Discussions, seminars, and show-and-tell demonstrations sponsored by the standards lab (and also carried out independently by the participating researchers) establish a communicative and practical infrastructure that provides a basis (and, not incidentally, a clientele) for achieving a coherent community of practice with respect to the material reference.

---

[9] A remarkable advertisement for Quadrant restriction enzymes, which is reproduced in Haraway (1997, p. 65), uses a fanciful cartoon of a molecular biology shop floor in which the technicians work on a series of spiral segments that are depicted on the scale of automobile bodies in a machine shop. Whereas this ad is unusual for its depiction of practices for assembling macromolecules, it is not so unusual in the way it emphasizes the ease and simplicity of the procedures: "all you have to do is add your DNA and incubate.... There is no loss of activity, no risk of contamination and no wastage."

It is difficult to think of PCR without relying on the specialized discourse of molecular biology, and the technique is perhaps best understood and most precisely described in molecular biological idioms. Nevertheless, it can be described in other ways, for example in the manner of a recipe. Just as a cook can prepare a recipe without knowing the chemical composition of the ingredients, a laboratory technician or even a machine can perform various phases of PCR without knowing anything about molecular processes. Readers and writers of advertising copy and patents can be, and often are, not trained in molecular biology, although the texts they read and write can require a variable degree of technical familiarity. In any case, what texts, writers, and readers can be said to be doing is not limited to conveying the specialized knowledge of molecular biology. They can be setting up a commercial transaction, staking out a potential market, or supplying a "yardstick" for assessing and calibrating routine procedures. Science and knowledge do not disappear in the bargain, but they can become highly diluted when commercial, legal, and other, more local relevancies predominate.

Genetic reductionism treats the DNA code as a primary, natural foundation of organic reproduction. From the point of view of genetic reductionism, the maps, diagrams, protocols, and descriptions discussed in this article are of secondary importance: They are mediators, practical artifacts, and surface representations. They are way stations and stopgaps that play a mundane role in genetic practice. They serve to reveal and represent natural information, which is said to be intrinsic to DNA. From our point of view, the genetic code and the assumption of its primacy are secondary, in the sense that they arise from and are extracted from practices that make use of various forms of information that are independent of the genetic code. Practitioners, audiences, and consumers of genetic research can see and know the genetic code only by working with the maps, protocols, and other devices that make DNA visible and accountable for various practical and communicative purposes.

When we speak of "information," we are not referring to an intrinsic property of a natural object. As Coulter (1995) pointed out in a critical discussion of cognitive neurophilosophy, it is all too easy to confuse the ordinary, communicative sense of the word "information" (for example, calling the phone company to get directory information) with a theory of an abstract and unitary code that underlies diverse forms of communicative action. The ordinary concept of information has diverse uses. What counts as information varies with the situation and is not reducible to an intrinsic property of a signal, stimulus, or cosmological stuff. To speak of DNA as an informational code may be appropriate in some contexts, as long as it remains clear that the relevant conception of information is a technically restricted one, and that genetic information must be embedded in cellular and intercellular processes before it can produce organic products. Moreover, as the examples in this article suggest, genetic information must also be embedded in fields of practical and communicative action that enable it to be made visible and intelligible. The extent to which the idea of a genetic code has currency and cogency depends on the production and exchange of more mundane kinds of information.

Many of the communicative situations discussed in this article lend themselves to a characteristic form of misunderstanding. For example, popular representations of DNA tend to depict genetic information as a determinate code that is intrinsic to the chromosome. It is all too easy to forget that the extent to which the code and its consequences are understood depends on a complex array of practical actions and textual formats that visualize the code and set up its accountability. It is all too easy to conflate DNA information with familiar connotations of that word and to conclude that DNA profiles tell us directly about the guilt or innocence of criminal suspects, or that DNA sequences tell us how to decide questions about normality and pathology. What is too easily forgotten is that how DNA analysis informs our judgements is not a direct consequence of an abstract code, but a matter of assimilating laboratory techniques into legal, medical, commercial, and other contexts of practice.

ACKNOWLEDGMENTS

The research presented in this article was supported by a 1992–1993 National Science Foundation research award, "The polymerase chain reaction: The mainstreaming of a molecular biological tool," (NSF SBE–9122375). While preparing the article, Michael Lynch was partly supported by a grant from the UK Economic and Social Research Council, "Science in a Legal Context: DNA Profiling, Forensic Practice and the Courts" (R000235853). While preparing this article, Kathleen Jordan was supported by a multi-disciplinary training grant from the National Institute of Aging (T32AF00220). Michael Lynch presented earlier drafts of the article at two conferences: Visual Representation in Science, University of Texas, Medical Branch (Galveston, TX, April 29, 1994) and Postgenomics? Historical, Techno-Epistemic, and Cultural Aspects of Genetics, Max Planck Institute (Berlin, July 8–11, 1998). We are grateful to John Douard, Mary Winckler, Lily Kay, Hans-Jorg Rheinberger, and others who attended and helped organize the conferences.

REFERENCES

Amann, K., & Knorr-Cetina, K. (1990). The fixation of (visual) evidence. In M. Lynch & S. Woolgar (Eds.), *Representation in scientific practice* (pp. 85–122). Cambridge, MA: MIT Press.

Barnes, S. B. (1977). *Interests and the growth of knowledge.* London: Routledge & Kegan Paul.

Baudrillard, J. (1983). *Simulations* (P. Foss, P. Patton, & P. Bitmap, Trans.). New York: Semiotext(e).

Bowker, G. (1994). *Science on the run: Information management and industrial geophysics at Schlumberger, 1920–1940.* Cambridge, MA: MIT Press.

Button, G., Coulter, J., Lee, J. R. E., & Sharrock, W. W. (1995). *Computers, minds and conduct.* Oxford, England: Polity.

Cambrosio, A., & Keating, P (1988). 'Going monoclonal': Art, science, and magic in the day-to-day use of hybridoma technology. *Social Problems, 35,* 244–260.

Cambrosio, A., Keating, P., & MacKenzie, M. (1990). Scientific practice in the courtroom: The construction of sociotechnical identities in a biotechnology patent dispute. *Social Problems, 37,* 275–293.

Coulter, J. (1995). The informed neuron: Issues in the use of information theory in the behavioral sciences. *Minds and Machines, 5,* 583–596.

Cowan, R. S. (1985). The industrial revolution in the home. In D. Mackenzie & J. Wajcman (Eds.), *The social shaping of technology* (pp. 181–201). Milton Keynes, England: Open University Press.

Edgerton, S. Y. (1991). *The heritage of Giotto's geometry: Art and science on the eve of the scientific revolution.* Ithaca, NY: Cornell University Press.

Fortun, M. (1999). Designed for speed: Accelerating genomics. In M. Fortun & E. Mendelsohn (Eds.), *The practice of human genetics. Sociology of sciences yearbook* (Vol. 21). Dordrecht, Netherlands: Kluwer.

Francoeur, E. (1997). The forgotten tool: The design and use of molecular models. *Social Studies of Science, 27,* 7–40.

Fujimura, J. (1992). Crafting science: Standardized packages, boundary objects, and "translation." In E. A. Pickering (Ed.), *Science as practice and culture* (pp. 168–211). Chicago: University of Chicago Press.

Galilei, G. (1989). *Sidereus Nuncius* (A. Van Helden, Trans.). Chicago: University of Chicago Press. (Original work published in 1610)

Garfinkel, H., & Sacks, H. (1970). On the formal structures of practical actions. In J. McKinney & E. Tiryakian (Eds.), *Theoretical sociology* (pp. 338–366). New York: Appleton-Century-Crofts.

Gilbert, W. (1992). A vision of the grail. In J. J. Kevles & L. Hood (Eds.), *The code of codes: Scientific and social issues in the human genome project* (pp. 83–97). Cambridge, MA: Cambridge University Press.

Gilbert, G. N., & Mulkay, M. (1984). *Opening Pandora's box: An analysis of scientists' discourse.* Cambridge, England: Cambridge University Press.

Goodwin, C. (1995). Seeing in depth. *Social Studies of Science, 25,* 237–274.

Halfon, S. (1998). Collecting, testing, and convincing: Forensic DNA experts in the courts. *Social Studies of Science, 17,* 801–828.

Haraway, D. (1997). *Modest_witness@second_millennium. FemaleMan©_Meets_OncoMouse™: Feminism and technoscience.* London: Routledge & Kegan Paul.

Huxley, A. (1962). *Island, A novel.* London: Chatto & Windus.

Jasanoff, S. (1996). *Science at the bar: Law, science and technology in America.* Cambridge, MA: Harvard University Press.

Jordan, K., & Lynch, M. (1992). The sociology of a genetic engineering technique: Ritual and rationality in the performance of the plasmid prep. In A. Clarke & J. Fujimura (Eds.), *The right tools for the job: At work in twentieth-century life* (pp. 77–114). Princeton, NJ: Princeton University Press.

Jordan, K., & Lynch, M. (1993). The mainstreaming of a molecular biological tool: A case study of a new technique. In G. Button (Ed.), *Technology in working order: Studies in work, interaction and technology* (pp. 160–180). London: Routledge & Kegan Paul.

Jordan, K., & Lynch, M. (1998). The dissemination, standardization, and routinization of a molecular biological technique. *Social Studies of Science, 28,* 773–799.

Kawatoko, Y. (1999). Space, time and documents in a refrigerated warehouse. *Human Studies, 22,* 315–337.

Kay, L. E. (1995). Who wrote the book of life? Information and the transformation of molecular biology, 1945–1955. *Science in Context, 8,* 609–634.

Keelor, G. (1986). *Lake Wobegon days.* London: Faber & Faber.

Keller, E. F. (1992). *Secrets of life, secrets of death: Essays on language, gender and science.* London: Routledge & Kegan Paul.

Knorr-Cetina, K. (1992). The couch, the cathedral, and the laboratory. In A. Pickering (Ed.), *Science as practice and culture* (pp. 113–138). Chicago: University of Chicago Press.

Latour, B. (1987). *Science in action: How to follow scientists and engineers through society.* Cambridge, MA: Harvard University Press.

Latour, B. (1995). The 'pédofil' of Boa Vista: A photo-philosophical montage. *Common Knowledge, 4,* 144–187.

Lewontin, R. C. (1993). *Biology as ideology: The doctrine of DNA.* New York: HarperCollins.

Lynch, M. (1985). Discipline and the material form of images: An analysis of scientific visibility. *Social Studies of Science, 15,* 37–66.

Lynch, M. (1990). The externalized retina: Selection and mathematization in the visual documentation of objects in the life sciences. In M. Lynch & S. Woolgar (Eds.), *Representation in scientific practice* (pp. 153–186). Cambridge, MA: MIT Press.

Lynch, M. (1994). Representation is overrated: Some critical remarks about the use of the concept of representation in science studies. *Configurations, 2,* 137–149.

Lynch, M. (2000). Against reflexivity as an academic virtue and source of privilged knowledge. *Theory, Culture, & Society, 17,* 27–56.

Lynch, M., & Jordan, K. (1995). Instructed actions in, of and as molecular biology. *Human Studies ,18,* 227–244.

Lynch, M., & Law, J. (1999). Pictures, texts and objects: The literary language game of birdwatching. In M. Biagioli (Ed.), *Routledge science studies reader* (pp. 317–341). London: Routledge & Kegan Paul.

Lynch, M., & Woolgar, S. (Eds.). (1990). *Representation in scientific practice.* Cambridge, MA: MIT Press.

Myers, G. (1995). From discovery to invention: The writing and rewriting of two patents. *Social Studies of Science, 25,* 57–105.

Mullis, K., Erlich, H., Arnheim, N., Horn, G., Saiki, R., & Scharf, S. (1987, July). *Process for amplifying, detecting, and/or cloning nucleic acid sequences.* U.S. Patent No. 4,683,195.

Neisser, U. (1981). John Dean's memory: A case study. *Cognition, 9,* 1–22.

Ochs, E., Gonzales, P., & Jacoby, S. (1996). When I come down I'm in the domain state: Grammar and graphic representation in the interpretive activity of physicists. In E. Ochs, E. A. Schegloff, & S. Thompson (Eds.), *Interaction and grammar* (pp. 328–369). Cambridge, England: Cambridge University Press.

O'Connell, J. (1993). Metrology: The creation of universality by the circulation of particulars. *Social Studies of Science, 23,* 129–173.

Polanyi, M. (1958). *Personal knowledge.* Chicago: University of Chicago Press.

Psathas, G. (1979). Organizational features of direction maps. In G. Psathas (Ed.), *Everyday language: Studies in ethnomethodology* (pp. 203–225). New York: Irvington.

Rabinow, P. (1996). *Making PCR: A story of biotechnology.* Chicago: University of Chicago Press.

Schaffer, S. (1992). Late Victorian metrology and its instrumentation: A manufactory of ohms. In R. Bud & S. Cozzens (Eds.), *Invisible connections: Instruments, institutions and science* (pp. 23–56). Bellingham, WA: Optical Engineering Press.

Schutz, A. (1964). The problem of rationality in the social world. In A. Schutz (Ed.), *Collected papers II: Studies in social theory* (pp. 64–88). The Hague, The Netherlands: Martinus Nijhoff.

Shapin, S. (1989). The invisible technician. *American Scientist, 77,* 554–563.

Shapin, S., & Schaffer, S. (1985). *Leviathan and the air pump: Hobbes, Boyle, and the experimental life.* Princeton, NJ: Princeton University Press.

Suchman, L. (1987). *Plans and situated actions.* Cambridge, England: Cambridge University Press.

Sudnow, D. (1978). *Ways of the hand.* Cambridge, MA: Harvard University Press.

Ueno, N. (1998, June). *Technologies of mutual accountability of society, social organization, and activity for collaborative activity.* Paper presented at Fourth Congress of the International Society for Cultural Research and Activity Theory, Aarhus, Denmark.

MIND, CULTURE, AND ACTIVITY, 7(1&2), 147–163

Invisible Mediators of Action:
Classification and the Ubiquity of Standards

Geoffrey C. Bowker and Susan Leigh Star

Department of Communication
University of California at San Diego

This article is a methodological think piece about the ways in which classifications (and standards) impinge in myriad ways on our daily lives. We argue that although they are frequently invisible to us, they are highly political and ethically charged. We suggest 4 principles garnered from our own research and that of others that can together be used to give a picture of their scope and reach: recognizing their ubiquity, analyzing their material texture, examining ways in which they reconfigure our understanding of the past, and exploring their practical politics. Together, the principles suggest a "reverse engineering" of classification systems to reveal the multitude of local political and social struggles and compromises that go into the constitution of a "universal" classification.

INTRODUCTION

A classified and hierarchically ordered set of pluralities, of variants, has none of the sting of the miscellaneous and uncoordinated plurals of our actual world. (Dewey, 1929, p. 49)

Classifications are powerful technologies. Embedded in working infrastructures, they become relatively invisible without losing any of that power. Classifications should be recognized as the significant site of political and ethical work that they are. They should, in a word, be reclassified as key sites of work, power, and technology.

For all this importance, classifications and standards occupy a peculiar place in studies of social order. Anthropologists have studied classification as a device for understanding the cultures of others—categories such as the raw and the cooked have been clues to the core organizing principles for colonial Western understandings of "primitive" culture. Some economists have looked at the effects of adopting a standard in those markets where networks and compatibility are crucial. For example, videotape recorders, refrigerators, and personal computer software arguably embody inferior technical standards, but standards that benefited from the timing of their historical entry into the marketplace. Some historians have examined the explosion of natural history and medical classifications in the late-nineteenth century both as a political force and as an organizing rubric for complex bureaucracies. A few sociologists have done detailed studies of individual categories linked with social movements, such as between the diagnosis of homosexuality as

Requests for reprints should be sent to Geoffrey C. Bowker, Department of Communication, University of California at San Diego, La Jolla, CA 92093. E-mail: gbowker@ucsd.edu

an illness and its demedicalization in the wake of gay and lesbian civil rights. Information scientists work every day on the design, delegation, and choice of classification systems and standards, yet few see them as artifacts embodying moral and aesthetic choices that in turn craft people's identities, aspirations, and dignity.[1] Philosophers and statisticians have produced highly formal discussions of classification theory but few empirical studies of use or impact.

We all know and make banal assertions such as "We do many things today that a few hundred years ago would have looked like magic." And if we don't understand a given technology, it looks like magic: We are perpetually surprised by the mellifluous tones read off our favorite CDs by (we believe) a laser. Even engineers black-box and think of technology "as if by magic" in their everyday practical dealings with machines and their management (Star, 1995). A common description of a good waiter or butler (one thinks of Jeeves in the Wodehouse stories) is that he or she clears a table "as if by magic." Are these two kinds of magic, or one, or none?

The question is of import for activity theory, in that it links the (often forgotten and ignored) technical mediation of action with the performance of (often invisible) work. In more prosaic terms, we pose the problem here as

• What work do classifications and standards do? We want to look at what goes into making things work like magic: making them fit together so that we can buy a radio built by someone we have never met in Japan, plug it into a wall in Champaign, and hear the world news from the BBC.
• Who does that work? We want to explore the fact that all this magic involves much work: There is a lot of hard labor in effortless ease. Such invisible work is often not only underpaid, it is severely underrepresented in theoretical literature (Star & Strauss, 1999). We discuss where all the "missing work" that makes things look magical goes.
• What happens to the cases that don't fit? We want to draw attention to cases that don't fit easily into our created world of standards and classifications: the left-handers in the world of right-handed magic, chronic disease sufferers in the world of allopathic acute medicine (Strauss, 1970), the onion-hater in McDonalds (Star, 1991b), and so forth.

These are issues of great epistemological, political, and ethical import. It is easy to get lost in Baudrillard's (1990) cool memories of simulacra. The hype of our times is that we don't need to think about work anymore: The real issues are scientific and technological— in artificial life, thinking machines, nanotechnology, and genetic manipulation. Clearly each of these *is* important. However, there is rather more at stake—epistemologically, politically, and ethically—in the day-to-day work of building classification systems and producing and maintaining standards than in these philosophical high-fliers. The pyrotechnics may hold our fascinated gaze; they cannot provide any path to answering our questions. We first consider what kinds of things classifications and standards are and then elucidate four principles for their analysis.

---

[1]Two notable exceptions are Lucy Suchman and Sanford Berman. Suchman's article challenging the categories implicit in a popular software system was entitled "Do Categories Have Politics?" (Suchman, 1994). This article and critique has helped open up the discussion of values and categories in the field of computer-supported cooperative work. It is, importantly, a gloss on an earlier article by Langdon Winner (1980), "Do Artifacts Have Politics?," which similarly drew attention to the moral values inscribed in aspects of the built environment. Berman (1984, 1993) has done invaluable work in the library community with his critiques of the politics of cataloguing. See also *Library Trends,* Special Issue on How Classifications Work: Problems and Challenges in an Electronic Age, edited by Susan Leigh Star and Geoffrey C. Bowker (Fall 1998, Vol. 47:2).

TWO DEFINITIONS

We begin by clearing away some of the theoretical brush surrounding the very notions of categories and classification. Many scholars have seen categories as coming from an abstract sense of "mind," little anchored in the exigencies of work or politics. The work of attaching things to categories, and the ways in which those categories are ordered into systems, is often overlooked (except by theorists of language such as Harvey Sacks, 1975, 1992). A *classification* is a spatial, temporal, or spatiotemporal segmentation of the world. A *classification system* is a set of boxes, metaphorical or not, into which things can be put in order to then do some kind of work—bureaucratic or knowledge production.

Classifications arise from systems of activity and, as such, are situated historically and temporally. Categories—our own and those of others—come from action, and in turn from relationships. Ethnomethodologists and phenomenologists have shown us that what is often the most invisible is right under our noses. Everyday categories are precisely those that have disappeared—into infrastructure, into habit, into the taken for granted. These everyday categories are seamlessly interwoven with formal, technical categories and specifications. As Cicourel (1964) noted

> The decision procedures for characterizing social phenomena are buried in implicit common sense assumptions about the actor, concrete persons, and the observer's own views about everyday life. The procedures seem intuitively "right" or "reasonable" because they are rooted in everyday life. The researcher often begins his classifications with only broad dichotomies, which he expects his data to "fit," and then elaborates on these categories if apparently warranted by his "data." (p. 21)

The hermeneutic circle is indeed all around us.

Much of the philosophical and cognitive literature on classification ignores both the historical situation and the basis of classification in practice. Such treatments of classification systems demand an internal consistency of classificatory principles, based on an idealized notion of how things should work. For example, many demand that such systems be solely *genetic*, or classified by origin (Tort, 1989). Others demand mutual exclusivity of categories, or completeness (total coverage of the world being described). No working classification system that we have looked at meets these "simple" requirements, and we doubt that any ever could (Desrosières & Thévenot, 1988).

For example, consider the International Classification of Diseases, a list of causes of morbidity and mortality administered by the World Health Organization. The full title of the current (10th) edition of the ICD is *ICD–10: International Statistical Classification of Diseases and Related Health Problems* (1992). Note that it is designated a "statistical" classification. This means that only diseases that are statistically significant are to be entered in (it is not an attempt to classify all disease). It calls itself a "classification," even though many have said that it is a "nomenclature," because it has no single classificatory principle (it has at least four; which are not mutually exclusive; Bowker & Star, 1994, 1999). In many cases it represents a compromise between conflicting schemes: "The terms used in categories C82–C85 for non-Hodgkin's lymphomas are those of the Working Formulation, which attempted to find common ground among several major classification systems. The terms used in these schemes are not given in the Tabular List but appear in the Alphabetical Index; exact equivalence with the terms appearing in the Tabular List is not always possible" (*ICD–10,* 1992, pp. 1, 215). However, it presents itself clearly as a classification scheme and not a nomenclature. Since 1970, there has been an effort underway by the World Health Organization to build a distinct International Nomenclature of Diseases, whose main purpose will be to provide "a single recommended name for every disease entity" (*ICD–10,* 1992, pp. 1, 25). The point here is that we want to take a broad enough definition so that anything that is consistently called a classification system can be included. If we took a purist view, the *ICD* would be a nomenclature (and who knows what the International Nomenclature of Diseases would be).

With a broad definition, we can look at the work that is involved in building and maintaining a family of entities that people call classification systems, rather than attempt the Herculean, Sisyphian task of purifying the (un)stable systems in place. Howard Becker (1996) made the point here:

> Epistemology has been a ... negative discipline, mostly devoted to saying what you shouldn't do if you want your activity to merit the title of science, and to keeping unworthy pretenders from successfully appropriating it. The sociology of science, the empirical descendant of epistemology, gives up trying to decide what should and shouldn't count as science, and tells what people who claim to be doing science do. (pp. 54–55).

STANDARDS AND CLASSIFICATION SYSTEMS

We take a "standard" to be any set of agreed-upon rules for the production of (textual or material) objects. There are a number of histories of standards that point to the development and maintenance of standards as being a key to industrial production. Thus, as David Turnbull (1993) pointed out, it was possible to build a cathedral like Chartres without standard representations (blueprints) and standard building materials (regular sizes for stones, tools, etc.). However, it is not possible to build a modern housing development without them: Too much needs to come together—electricity, gas, sewer, timber sizes, screws, nails, and so on. The control of standards is a central, often underanalyzed feature of economic life (for an exception see the work of Paul David—for example David and Rothwell, 1994—for a rich treatment). They are key to knowledge production as well. Latour (1987) speculated that far more economic resources are spent creating and maintaining standards than in producing "pure" science. Central dimensions of standards are

• They are often deployed in the context of making things work together; for example, computer protocols for Internet communication involve a cascade of standards (cf. Abbate & Kahin, 1995), which need to work together well for the average user to gain seamless access to the web of information. There are standards for the components to link from your computer to the phone network, for coding and decoding binary streams as sound, for sending messages from one network to another, for attaching documents to messages, and so forth.

• They are often enforced by legal bodies, be these professional organizations, manufacturers' organizations, or the State. We can say tomorrow that volapük (a universal language that boasted some 23 journals in 1889) or its successor Esperanto shall henceforth be the standard language for international diplomacy; without a mechanism of enforcement we shall probably fail.

• There is no natural law that the best (technically superior) standard shall win; the QWERTY keyboard, Lotus 123, DOS, and VHS are often cited in this context. Standards have significant inertia and can be very difficult to change.

An aside about the relation between classifications and standards: Some classifications become formally standardized, as with race categories on a census form or intelligence categories as measured by standardized tests. Others are more informal, or ad hoc. Where they are formal, categorizing becomes a kind of situated action embedded in bureaucratic, institutionalized practices.[2] At other times, classifications mark context for decisions or things; or they may be treated as bins, holding things or people. Standards, such as technical standards for operating the Internet, are agreements about procedures—dimensions, rates, ordinality—that have reach and scope across settings. Every successful standard imposes a classification system, in the sense that it forms boundaries around objects and activities.

WHAT SORT OF THING IS A CLASSIFICATION?

In so far as the coding scheme establishes an orientation toward the world, it constitutes a structure of intentionality whose proper locus is not the isolated, Cartesian mind, but a much larger organizational system, one that is characteristically mediated through mundane bureaucratic documents such as forms. (Goodwin, 1996, p. 65)

Classification is a core topic within anthropology, especially cognitive anthropology, and within computer science, as the quote from Goodwin attests. Recently, there has been a move to understand the practical, work-related aspects of classification as part of a larger project of revisioning cognition (e.g., Hutchins, 1995; Keller & Keller, 1996). Ascher (1981) and Roberts and Roberts (1996), discussing in turn the Quipu string code system and the Luba memory system, explored the technology and practice of classificatory infrastructures in nonmodern settings. In each case, and especially Goodwin's work, classification is a local and situated achievement—embedded in an institutional set of practices and arrangements. No classification or standard, of course, holds for all time. Things left out of classification schemes or made residual often disturb purists who would classify for all time. Things and processes that are standardized must be customized to fit particular situations; the customization threatens the standardization, and so on, recursively.

A difficulty in conceptualizing classifications is the heritage of idealism and Cartesian dualism in traditional cognitive approaches. We face here a problem similar to Cole's (1996) search for the nature of artifacts in mediated action. Cole noted that

An artifact is an aspect of the material world that has been modified over the history of its incorporation into goal-directed human action. By virtue of the changes wrought in the process of their creation and use, artifacts are simultaneously *ideal* (conceptual) and *material*. They are ideal in that their material form has been shaped by their participation in the interactions of which they were previously a part and which they mediate in the present. (p. 117)

The materiality of categories, like that of other things associated with the purely cognitive, has been difficult to analyze. The Janus-faced conceptual and material notion of artifacts suggested by Cole, combined with the attention to the use in practice of categories (Keller & Keller, 1996), is a

---

[2]We are grateful to Naoki Ueno for helping clarify these points.

good way to begin. Classifications are both conceptual (in the sense of persistent patterns of change and action, resources for organizing abstractions) and material (in the sense of being inscribed, transported, and affixed to stuff).

Cole's intent is to emphasize the conceptual and symbolic sides of things often taken as brute material, tools, and other artifacts. For example, being a left-handed tool-user in a right-handed world means not only that it's more difficult to open a can or to use scissors, but that the left-hander is reminded of the symbolic articulation of left-handedness with awkwardness. It is similarly felicitous to emphasize the material force of that which has been considered ideal, as with categories. Thus, if Foucault's *The Archaeology of Knowledge* is classified in the "archaeology" section of the library (as we have seen on occasion), it will frequently be materially inaccessible to students browsing the shelves in search of "philosophy of the social sciences." At the same time, the double nature imagery risks instantiating another Cartesian divide, and one that isn't really necessary to make both these valuable points.

THE PRAGMATIST TURN

The most radical turn taken by pragmatist philosophers such as Dewey and Bentley, and closely followed by Chicago School sociologists such as Thomas and Hughes, is perhaps the least understood. Consequences, asserted Dewey against a rising tide of analytic philosophy, are the thing to look at in any argument—not ideal logical antecedents. What matters about an argument is who, under what conditions, takes it to be true. Carried over into sociology, Thomas used it (as Becker would some decades later) to argue against essentialism in examining so-called deviants or problem children. If as a social scientist you do not understand people's definition of a situation, you do not understand it at all. That definition—whether it is the label of deviant or the performance of a religious ritual—is what people will shape their behavior toward.

This is a much more profound cut on social construction than the mere notion that people construct their own realities. It makes no comment on where the definition of the situation may come from—human or nonhuman, structure or process, group or individual. It powerfully draws attention to the fact that the materiality of anything (action, idea, definition, hammer, gun, or school grade) is drawn from the consequences of its situation.

The pragmatist turn, like its cousin the cultural historical turn, emphasizes the ways in which things perceived as real may mediate action. If you take someone to be a witch, and develop elaborate technical apparatus with which to diagnose him or her as such, then the reality of witchcraft exists in the consequences—perhaps death at the stake. Classification systems are one form of technology, used in the sense Cole (1996) employed, linked together in elaborate informatic systems and enjoining deep consequences for those touched by them.

From the point of view of learning as membership and participation, the illegitimate stranger is a source of learning. Someone's illegitimacy appears as a series of interruptions to experience (Dewey, 1916, 1929), or a lack of a naturalization trajectory. In a way, then, individual membership processes are about the resolution of interruptions (anomalies) posed by the tension between the ambiguous (outsider, naive, strange) and the naturalized (at home, taken-for-granted) categories for objects. *Collectively,* membership can be described as the processes of managing the tension between naturalized categories on the one hand, and the degree of openness to immigration on the other. Harvey Sacks (1992), in his extensive investigations into language and social life, noted that categories of membership form the basis of many of our judgments about ordinary action:

> You can easily enough come to see that for any population of persons present there are available alternative sets of categories that can be used on them. That then poses for us an utterly central task in our descriptions; to have some way of providing which set of categories operate in some scene—in the reporting of that scene or in its treatment as it is occurring. (p. 116)

Sacks (1992) drew attention to the ways in which being ordinary are not pre-given but are in fact a kind of job—a job that asserts the nature of membership:

> Whatever we may think about what it is to be an ordinary person in the world, an initial shift is not to think of an "ordinary person" as some person, but as somebody having as their job, as their constant preoccupation, doing "being ordinary." It's not that somebody *is* ordinary, it's perhaps that that's what their business is. And it takes work, as any other business does. And if you just extend the analogy of what you obviously think of as work—as whatever it is that takes analytic, intellectual, emotional energy—then you can come to see that all sorts of normalized things—personal characteristics and the like—are jobs which are done, which took some kind of effort, training, etc. So I'm not going to be talking about to an "ordinary person" as this or that person, or as some average, i.e., a non-exceptional person on some statistical basis, but as something that is the way somebody constitutes themselves, and, in effect, a job that they do on themselves. Fate and the people around and may be coordinatively engaged in assuring that each of them are ordinary persons, and that can then be a job that they undertake together, to achieve that each of them, together, are ordinary persons. (p. 216)

The performance of this job includes the ability to choose the proper categories under which to operate, to perform this ordinariness. The power of Sack's work, like that of John Dewey (e.g., 1929), is that he draws attention to the ways in which the ordinary—and the interruption to the expected experience—are delicate constructions, made and re-made every day.

The following section discusses the problems of scaling up, from boundary objects and classifications systems to a notion of boundary infrastructure. This draws together the notions of multiplicity and the symbolic and material aspects of categories as artifacts discussed previously.

HOW ARE CATEGORIES TIED TO PEOPLE? FILIATIONS

> The frequency with which metaphors of weaving, threads, ropes and the like appear in conjunction with contextual approaches to human thinking is quite striking. (Cole, 1996, p. 135)

Categories touch people in a variety of ways—they are assigned, they become self-chosen labels, they may be statistical artifacts. They may be visible or invisible to any other group or individual. We use the term *filiation* here—related via Latin to the French "fil," for thread—as a thread that goes from a category to a person. This metaphor allows a rich examination of the architecture of the multiple categories that touch people's lives. Threads carry a variety of textural qualities that are often applied to human interactions: tension, knottiness or smoothness, bundling, proximity, thickness. We select a small number here to focus on in the following worked example.

LOOSELY COUPLED–TIGHTLY COUPLED

A category (or system of categories) may be loosely or tightly coupled with a person. Gender and age are very tightly coupled with a person as categories. One of the interesting aspects of the investigation of virtual identities in Multi-User Dungeons or Dimensions (MUDs) and elsewhere on-line is the loosening of these traditionally tightly coupled threads under highly constrained circumstances (e.g., Turkle, 1995). Loosely coupled categories may be those that are transient, such as the color one is wearing on a given day or one's position in a waiting line. Somewhere in the middle are hair color, which may shift slowly over a lifetime or change in an afternoon, or marital status.

SCOPE

Categories' filiations have variable scope. Some are durable threads that cover many aspects of someone's identity and that are accepted as such on a very wide or even global scale. (Noting for the record that none are absolute, none cover all aspects of someone's identity, and there is no category that is completely globally accepted.) The category alive or dead is quite thick and nearly global. So we can think of two dimensions of scope: thickness and scale. How thick is the individual strand: gossamer or thickest rope? With how many others is it shared?

WHAT IS ITS ECOLOGY?

Classifications have habitats. That is, the filiations between person and category may be characterized as inhabiting a space or terrain with some of the properties of any habitat. It may be crowded or sparse, peaceful or at war, fertile or arid. In order not to mix too many metaphors, two important questions about filiations and their ecology that may be visualized in threadlike terms are

How many ties are there? That is, how many other categories are tied to this person, and in what density?

Do these threads contradict or complement (torque vs. boundary object of cooperation)? That is, are the threads tangled or smoothly falling together?

WHO CONTROLS THE FILIATION?

The question of who controls any given filiation is vital to an ethical and political understanding of information systems whose categories attach to individuals. A first crude characterization concerns whether the filiation was chosen or imposed (an echo of the sociological standard, achieved or ascribed); whether it may be removed and by whom; and under whose control and access is the apparatus to do so. Questions of privacy are important here, as with medical information classifying someone with a social stigmatized condition. The nature of the measure for the filiation here is an important loci of control as well. For example, an IQ test may be an important way to classify people. Those who developed the test are at some distance from those who take it. The measure, IQ, is controlled from afar. Past criticisms of IQ tests charge that this control is racially biased and biased by gender on these grounds.

IS IT REVERSIBLE OR IRREVERSIBLE?

Finally, there is the important question of whether the filiation is reversible. The metaphor of branding someone is not accidental in this regard, branding meaning that a label is burned into the skin and completely irreversible. Some forms of filiation have this finality for the individual, regardless of how the judgment was later regarded (e.g., a charge of guilt for murder may mean permanent public guilt regardless of a jury's verdict, as with the decades' long attempt of Sam Shepard's son to prove his father's innocence). Many are somewhere between, but knowing how reversible is the filiation is important for understanding its impact.

The model of filiation presented here could be used to characterize a texture of information systems where categories touch either individuals or things. The aesthetics of the weave and the degree to which the individual is bound up or supported by it are among the types of characterizations that could be made. There are brute renderings, such as having two thick, irreversible threads tying one person to conflicting categories, as with the previous examples. More subtly, it is possible to think in terms of something like a myriad of Lilliputian threads, each weak in its own right, but collectively strong. Like Mark Granovetter's (1973) notion of the strength of weak ties, these sorts of filiations characterize the thousand and one classifications that weakly tie people to systems.

To summarize: The metaphor of filiation can be used to ask questions of working infrastructures in new and interesting ways. Two questions that rise directly out of our treatment of the metaphor for any individual or group filiation are

- What will be the ecology and distribution of suffering?
- Who controls the ambiguity and visibility of categories?

Both within and outside the academy, single categories or classes of categories may also become objects of contention and study. The demedicalization of the category "homosexual" in the *Diagnostic and Statistical Manual of Mental Disorders* (3rd ed. [*DSM–III*]; American Psychiatric Association, 1980) followed direct and vigorous lobbying of the association by gay and lesbian advocates (Kirk & Kutchins, 1992). During this same era, feminists were split on the subject of whether the categories of premenstrual syndrome and post-partum depression would be good or bad for women as they became included in the *DSM–III*. Many feminist psychotherapists were engaged in the bitter argument about whether to include these categories. As Figert (1996) related, they even felt their own identities and professional judgements to be on the line. (A researcher into the *DSM–III* made the complicating observation that psychiatrists increasingly use its language to communicate with each other and their accounting departments, although they frequently don't believe in the categories they are using; Young, 1995.)

More recently, the option of choosing more than one racial category was introduced as part of the U.S. Government routine data collection mission, following Statistical Directorate 15 in October 1997. The Office of Management and Budget issued the directorate, and, conservatively, its implementation will cost billions of dollars. One direct consequence was the revision of the U.S. Census form, an addition that was fraught with political passion. A march on Washington concerning the revision took the traditional ultimate avenue of mass protest for American activists. The march was conducted by people who identified themselves as multiracial and their families and advocates. At the same time, the change was vigorously opposed by many African-American and Hispanic civil rights groups (among several others), who saw the change as a "whitewash" against which important specific ethnic and policy-related distinctions would be lost (Robbin, 1998).

However, despite the contentiousness of some categories or systems, none of the previously named disciplines or social movements has systematically addressed the pragmatics of the invisible forces of categories and standards in the modern-built world, especially the modern information technology world. Foucault's (1970, 1982) work comes the closest to a thoroughgoing examination in his arguments that an archaeological dig is necessary to find the origins and consequences of a range of social categories and practices. He focused on order and its implementation in categorical discourse. The ubiquity described by Foucault appeared as an iron cage of bureaucratic discipline against a broad historical landscape. But there is much more to be done, both empirically and theoretically. No one, including Foucault, has systematically tackled the question of how these properties inform social and moral order via the new technological and electronic infrastructures. Few have looked at the creation and maintenance of complex classifications as a kind of *work practice*, with its attendant financial, skillful, and moral dimensions.

We have a moral and ethical agenda in our querying of these systems. Every standard and each category valorizes some point of view and silences another. This is not inherently a bad thing—indeed, it is inescapable. But it is an ethical choice, and as such it is dangerous—not bad, but dangerous. For example, the decision of the U.S. Immigration and Naturalization Service to classify some races and classes as desirable for U.S. residents and others as not resulted in a quota system that values affluent people from Northern and Western Europe above those (especially the poor) from Africa or South America. The decision to classify students by their standardized achievement and aptitude tests valorizes some kinds of knowledge skills and renders other kinds invisible. Other types of decisions with serious material force may not immediately appear as morally problematic. The collective standardization in the United States on VHS videotapes over Betamax, for instance, may seem ethically neutral. The classification and standardization of types of seed for farming is not obviously fraught with moral weight. But as Busch (1995) and Addelson (1994) argued, such long-term, collective forms of choice are also morally fraught. We are used to viewing moral choices as individual, as dilemmas, and as rational choices. We have an impoverished vocabulary for collective moral passages, to use Addelson's terminology. For any individual, group, or situation, classifications and standards give advantage or they give suffering. Jobs are made and lost; some regions benefit at the expense of others.

UNDERSTANDING CLASSIFYING AND STANDARDIZING

In our work on classification and categorizing, we have identified four major themes for understanding classifying, standardizing (and the related processes of formalizing), and their politics and histories. Each theme operates as a gestalt switch—it comes in the form of an infrastructural inversion (Bowker, 1994). Inverting our commonsense notion of infrastructure means taking what have often been seen as behind-the-scenes, boring, background processes to the real work of politics and knowledge production and bringing their contribution to the foreground. The first two, ubiquity and material texture, speak to the *space* of classifications; the second two, the indeterminate past and the practical politics, speak to their *time*. Taken together, they sketch out features of the historically creation of the infrastructure that (ever partially, ever incompletely) orders the world in such a way that actor–network theory becomes a reasonable description.

The first major theme is seeing the ubiquity of classifying and standardizing. Classification schemes and standards literally saturate the worlds we live in. This saturation is furthermore intertwined, or webbed together. Although it is possible to pull out a single classification scheme or standard for reference purposes, in reality none of them stand alone. So a subproperty of ubiquity is interdependence, if not smooth integration.

The second major theme is to see classifications and standards as materially textured. Under the sway of cognitivism, it is easy to see classifications as properties of mind and standards as ideal numbers or settings. But both have material force in the world and are built into and embedded in every feature of the built environment (and many of the borderlands, such as with engineered genetic organisms). When we think of classifications and standards as material, we can afford ourselves of what we know about material structures, such as structural integrity, enclosures, and confinements, permeability, and durability, among many others. We see people doing this all the time in describing organizational settings, and a common way to hear people's experience of this materiality is through metaphors. So the generation of metaphors is closely linked with the shift to texture.

The third major theme is to see the past as indeterminate. This is not a new idea to historiography, but it is important in understanding the evolution of ubiquitous classification and standardization and the multiple voices that are represented in any scheme. No one classification orders reality for everyone—for example, the red light–green light–yellow light categories don't work for blind people or those who are red–green color blind. In looking to classification schemes as ways of ordering the past, it is easy to forget those who are overlooked in this way. Thus, the indeterminacy of the past implies recovering multivocality; it also means understanding how standard narratives that seem universal have been constructed.

The fourth major theme is uncovering the practical politics of classifying and standardizing. There are two aspects of these politics: arriving at categories and standards, and, in the process, deciding what will be visible within the system (and of course what will thus then be invisible). The negotiated nature of standards and classifications follows from indeterminacy and multiplicity that whatever appears as universal or, indeed, standard, is the result of negotiations or conflict. How do these negotiations take place? Who determines the final outcome in preparing a formal classification? Visibility issues arise as one decides where to make the cuts in the system, for example, down to what level of detail one specifies a description of work, an illness, or a setting. Because there are always advantages and disadvantages to being visible, this becomes crucial in the workability of the schema.

Ubiquity

In the built world we inhabit, thousands and thousands of standards are used everywhere, from setting up the plumbing in a house to assembling a car engine to transferring a file from one computer to another. Consider the canonically simple act of writing a letter longhand, putting it in an envelope, and mailing it. There are standards for (inter alia) paper size, the distance that lines are apart if it is lined paper, envelope size, the glue on the envelope, the size of stamps, their glue, the ink in the pen that you wrote with, the sharpness of its nib, the composition of the paper (which in turn can be broken down to the nature of the watermark, if any; the degree of recycled material used in its production, the definition of what counts as recycling), and so forth.

Similarly, in any bureaucracy, classifications abound—consider the simple but increasingly common classifications that are used when you dial an airline for information (e.g., "If you are traveling domestically, press 1; if you want information about flight arrivals and departures, press 2..."). And once the airline has hold of you, you are classified by them as a frequent flyer (normal, gold, or platinum); corporate or individual; tourist or business class; short haul or long haul (different fare rates and scheduling applies); irate or not (different hand-offs to the supervisor when you complain).

A systems approach would see the proliferation of both standards and classifications as a matter of integration—almost like a gigantic web of interoperability. Yet the sheer density of these phenomena go beyond questions of interoperability. They are layered, tangled, textured; they interact to form an ecology as well as a flat set of compatibilities. There are spaces between (unclassified, nonstandard areas), of course, and these are equally important to the analysis. It seems that increasingly these spaces are marked as unclassified and nonstandard. How does that change their qualities?

It is a struggle to step back from this complexity and think about the issue of ubiquity broadly, rather than try to trace the myriad connections in any one case. We need concepts for understanding movements, textures, and shifts that will grasp larger patterns in this. For instance, the distribution of residual categories ("not elsewhere classified" or "other") is one such concept. "Others" are everywhere. The analysis of any one instance of a residual category might yield information about biases or what is valued in any given circumstance; seeing that residual categories are ubiquitous offers a much more general sweep on the categorizing tendencies of most modern cultures. Another class of concepts that are found ubiquitously, and that speak to the general pervasiveness of standards and classification schemes, concern those that describe tangles or mismatches between subsystems. For instance, what Strauss (Strauss et al., 1985) called a "cumulative mess trajectory" is a useful notion. In medicine, this occurs when one has an illness, is given a medicine to cure the illness, but incurs a serious side effect, which then needs to be treated with another medicine, and so on. If the trajectory becomes so tangled that you can't return and the interactions multiply, "cumulative mess" results. We see this phenomenon in the interaction of categories and standards all the time—ecological examples are particularly rich places to look. For example, the use of electric batteries in automobiles rather than gasoline often effectively displaces the pollution from one site to another. Although the streets of California might smell better, and air pollution be reduced by electric vehicles, the sites of manufacture of the batteries (in Mexico, say) themselves become more polluted from the manufacturing and disposal problems. Similarly, the chemicals used to recycle paper are toxic, and their disposal may offset the environmental gains from the recycling process meant to save trees. In each case, the remedy carries problems of its own, problems that may only be visible over large distances or lengths of time. There is no eagle's-eye view of these sorts of problems.

Texturing Classification and Standardization

How do we "see" this densely saturated classified world? We are commonly used to casually black-boxing this behind-the-scenes machinery, even to the point, as we noted previously, of ascribing a casual magic to it. All classification and standardization schemes are a mixture of physical entities such as paper forms, plugs, or software instructions encoded in silicon and conventional arrangements such as speed and rhythm, dimension, and how specifications are implemented. Perhaps because of this mixture, the web of intertwined schemes can be difficult to "see." In general, the trick is to question every apparently natural easiness in the world around us and look for the work involved in making it easy. Within a project or on a desktop, the seeing consists in seamlessly moving between the physical and the conventional. So when a computer programmer writes some lines of C code, he or she moves within conventional constraints and makes innovations based on them, while at the same time striking plastic keys, shifting notes around on a desktop, and consulting manuals for various standards and other information. If we were to try to list out all the classifications and standards involved in writing a program, the list could run to pages. Classifications include types of objects, types of hardware, matches between requirements categories and code categories, and meta-categories such as the goodness of fit of the piece of code with the larger system under development. Standards range from the precise integration of the underlying hardware to the 60Hz power coming out of the wall through a standard-size plug.

Merely reducing the description to the physical aspect such as the plugs does not get us anywhere interesting in terms of the actual mixture of physical and conventional. A good operations researcher could describe how and whether things would work together, often purposefully blurring the physical and conventional boundaries in making the analysis. But what is missing there is a sense of the landscape of work as experienced by those within it. It gives no sense of something as important as the texture of an organization: Is it smooth or rough? bare or knotty? What is needed is a sense of the topography of all of the arrangements—are they colliding? coextensive? gappy? orthogonal? One way to begin to get at these questions is to begin to take quite literally the kinds of metaphors that people use when describing their experience of organizations, bureaucracies, and information systems (Star, in press). So, for example, when someone says something simple like "things are running smoothly," the smoothness is descriptive of an array of articulations of people, things, work, and standards. When someone says, "I feel as though the whole project is moving through thick molasses," it points to the opposite experience. These are not merely poetic expressions, although at some level they are that, too. As Schön (1963) pointed out in his seminal book, *Displacement of Concepts,* a metaphor is something imported, meant to illuminate aspects of a current situation via juxtaposition. For example, the use of linguistic metaphors has proved very fruitful in the development of molecular biology over the past 30 years. Such metaphors are also a rich and often unmined source of knowledge about people's experience of the densely classified world.

The Indeterminacy of the Past

There is no way of ever getting access to the past except through classification systems of one sort or another—formal or informal, hierarchical or not. Take the following unproblematic statement: "In 1640, the English Revolution occurred; this led to a 20-year period in which the English had no monarchy." The classifications involved here include

- The current segmentation of time into days, months, and years. Accounts of the English revolution generally use the Gregorian calendar, which was adopted some hundred years later, so causing translation problems with contemporary documents.

- The classification of "peoples" into English, Irish, Scots, French, and so on. These designations were by no means so clear at the time—the whole discourse of national genius really only arose in the 19th century.
- The classification of events into revolutions, reforms, revolts, rebellions, and so forth (cf. Furet, 1978, on thinking the French revolution). There really was no concept of "revolution" at the time; our current conception is marked by the historiographic work of Karl Marx.
- The classification of a "monarchy." What is a monarchy? There is a strong historiographic tradition that says that Oliver Cromwell was a monarch—he walked, talked, and acted like one, after all. Under this view, there is no hiatus at all in this English institution; rather an usurper took the throne.

There are two major schools of thought with respect to using classification systems on the past, one saying that we should only use classifications available to actors at the time (authors in this tradition warn against the dangers of anachronism; Hacking (1995) on child abuse is a sophisticated version) and the other that we should use the real classifications that progress in the arts and sciences has uncovered (typically history informed by current sociology will take this path; for example, Tort's (1989) work on "genetic" classification systems, which were not so called at the time but which are of vital interest to the Foucaldian problematic). Whichever we choose, it is clear that we should always understand classification systems according to the work that they are doing and the network within which they are embedded.

When we ask historical questions about the deeply and heterogeneously structured space of classification systems and standards, we are dealing with a four-dimensional archaeology: Some of the structures it uncovers are stable, some in motion; some evolving, some decaying. An institutional memory, about say, an epidemic, can be held simultaneously and with internal contradictions (sometimes piecemeal or distributed and sometimes with entirely different stories at different locations) across (a given institutional) space.

In the case of AIDS, for example, there are shifting classifications over the last 20 years, including the invention of the category in the first place. There is then a backward look at cases that might have been AIDS before we had the category (a problematic gaze to be sure, as Bruno Latour (in press) wrote about tuberculosis; see also Star & Bowker, 1997). There are the stories about collecting information about a shameful disease and a wealth of personal narratives about living with it. There is a public health story and a virology story, which use different category systems. There are the standardized forms of insurance companies and the categories and standards of the census bureau; when an attempt was made to combine them in the 1980s to disenfranchise young men living in San Francisco from getting health insurance, the resultant political challenge stopped the combination of this data from being so used. At the same time, the blood banks refused for years to employ HIV screening, thus refusing the admission of another category to their blood labeling and thus, as Shilts (1987) told us, with many casualties as a result.

Practical Politics

Someone, somewhere, often a body of people in the proverbial gray suits and smoke-filled rooms, must decide and argue over the minutiae of classifying and standardizing. The negotiations themselves form the basis for a fascinating practical ontology—our favorite example is when is someone really alive? Is it breathing, attempts at breathing, movement? And how long must each of those last? Whose voice will determine the outcome is sometimes an exercise of pure power: We, the holders of Western medicine and of colonialism, will decide what a disease is and simply obviate systems such as acupuncture or Ayurvedic medicine. Sometimes the negotiations are more subtle, involving questions such as the disparate viewpoints of an immunologist and a surgeon, or a public health official (interested in even one case of the plague) and a statistician (for whom one case is not relevant; Neumann & Star, 1996).

Once a system is in place, the practical politics of these decisions are often forgotten, literally buried in archives (when records are kept at all) or built into software or the sizes and compositions of things. In addition to our archaeological expeditions into the records of such negotiations, we provide here some observations of the negotiations in action. Finally, even where everyone agrees on the way the classifications or standards should be established, there are often practical difficulties about how to craft their architecture. For example, a classification system with 20,000 "bins" on every form is practically unusable. (The original International Classification of Diseases had some 200 diseases, not because of the nature of the human body and its problems, but because this was the maximum number that would fit the large census sheets then in use.) Sometimes the decision about how fine-grained to make the system has political consequences as well. For instance, describing and recording the tasks someone does, as in the case of nursing work, may mean controlling or surveilling their work as well, and may imply an attempt to take away discretion. After all, the loosest classification of work is accorded to those with the most power and discretion, who are able to set their own terms.

These ubiquitous, textured classifications and standards help frame our representation of the past and the sequencing of events in the present. They can best be understood as doing the ever-local, ever-partial work of making it appear that science describes nature (and nature alone) and that politics is about social power (and social power alone). Consider the case discussed at length by Young (1995) and Kirk and Kutchins (1992) of psychoanalysts who, to receive reimbursement for procedures, needed to couch them in a biomedical language (the *DSM*) that was anathema to them but was the lingua franca of the medical insurance companies. There are local translation mechanisms that allow the *DSM* to continue to operate and to provide the sole legal, recognized representation of mental disorder.

CONCLUSION

This article is a methodological think piece about the ways in which classifications (and standards) impinge in myriad ways on our daily lives. The fact that they are frequently invisible to us ("transparency" being the highest goal in most information systems) does not make them any the less political and ethically charged. We have suggested four principles garnered from our own research and that of others that can together be used to give a picture of their scope and reach. Together, the principles suggest a "reverse engineering" of classification systems to reveal the multitude of local political and social struggles and compromises that go into the constitution of a universal classification.

ACKNOWLEDGMENTS

This research was funded in part by NSF Grant No. SBR 95147444, Ethics and Values Studies; and NSF/ARPA/NASA Digital Library Initiative, NSF–93–141 DLI. We gratefully acknowledge this support. We also thank Chuck Goodwin, Naoki Ueno, and Yasuko Kawatoko for very helpful comments on an earlier version of this article.

REFERENCES

Abbate, J., & Kahin, B. (Eds.). (1995). *Standards policy for information infrastructure.* Cambridge, MA: MIT Press.

Addelson, K. P. (1994). *Moral passages: Toward a collectivist moral theory.* Boston: Routledge & Kegan Paul.

American Psychiatric Association. (1980). *Diagnostic and statistical manual of mental disorders* (3rd ed.). Washington, DC: Author.

Ascher, M. (1981). *Code of the Quipu: A study in media, mathematics, and culture.* Ann Arbor: University of Michigan Press.

Baudrillard, J. (1990). *Cool memories.* New York: Verso.

Becker, H. S. (1996). The epistemology of qualitative research. In R. Jessor, A. Colby, & R. A. Shweder (Eds.), *Ethnography and human development: Context and meaning in social inquiry* (pp. 53–71). Chicago: University of Chicago.

Berman, S. (Ed.). (1984). *Subject cataloging: Critiques and innovations.* Binghamton, NY: Haworth Press.

Berman, S. (1993). *Prejudices and antipathies: A tract on the LC subject heads concerning people.* Jefferson, NC: McFarland.

Bowker, G. C. (1994). *Science on the run: Information management and industrial geophysics at Schlumberger, 1920–1940.* Cambridge, MA: MIT Press.

Bowker, G. C., & Star, S. L. (1994). Knowledge and infrastructure in international information management: Problems of classification and coding. In L. Bud-Frierman (Ed.), *Information acumen: The understanding and use of knowledge in modern business* (pp.187–216) London: Routledge & Kegan Paul.

Bowker, G. C., & Star, S. L. (1999). *Sorting things out: Classification and its consequences.* Cambridge, MA: MIT Press.

Busch, L. (1995, May). *The moral economy of grades and standards.* Paper presented at a conference on agrarian questions. Wageningen, The Netherlands.

Cicourel, A. (1964). *Method and measurement in sociology.* New York: Free Press.

Cole, M. (1996). *Cultural psychology: A once and future discipline.* Cambridge, MA: Harvard University Press.

David, P., & Rothwell, G. S. (1994). *Standardization, diversity and learning: Strategies for the coevolution of technology and industrial capacity.* Stanford, CA: Center for Economic Policy Research, Stanford University.

Desrosières, A., & Thévenot, L. (1988). *Les catégories socio-professionnelles.* Paris: Découverte.

Dewey, J. (1916). *Essays in experimental logic.* Chicago: University of Chicago Press.

Dewey, J. (1929). *The quest for certainty: A study of the relation of knowledge and action.* New York: Monton, Balch.

Figert, A. (1996). *Women and the ownership of PMS: The structuring of a psychiatric disorder.* Chicago: Aldine de Gruyter.

Foucault, M. (1970). *The order of things: An archaeology of the human sciences.* London: Tavistock.

Foucault, M. (1982). *The archaeology of knowledge* (A. M. Sheridan Smith, Trans.). New York: Pantheon.

Furet, F. (1978). *Penser la revolution Francaise.* Paris: Gallimard.

Goodwin, C. (1996). Practices of color classification. Ninchi Kagaku. *Cognitive Studies: Bulletin of the Japanese Cognitive Science Society, 3,* 62–82.

Granovetter, M. S. (1973). The strength of weak ties. *American Journal of Sociology, 78,* 1360–1380.

Hacking, I. (1995). *Rewriting the soul: Multiple personality and the sciences of memory.* Princeton, NJ: Princeton University Press.

Hutchins, E. (1995). *Cognition in the wild.* Cambridge, MA: MIT Press.

ICD–10 International Statistical Classification of Diseases and Related Health Problems. (1992). (10th rev., Vol. 1). Geneva, Switzerland: World Health Organization.

Keller, C. M., & Keller, J. D. (1996). *Cognition and tool use: The blacksmith at work.* Cambridge, England: Cambridge University Press.

Kirk, S. A., & Kutchins, H. (1992). *The selling of DSM: The rhetoric of science in psychiatry.* New York: deGruyter.

Latour, B. (1987). *Science in action: How to follow scientists and engineers through society.* Milton Keynes, England: Open University Press.

Latour, B. (in press). *Did Ramses II die of tuberculosis? On the partial existence of existing and non-existing objects.* Manuscript in preparation.

Neumann, L. J., & Star, S. L. (1996). Making infrastructure: The dream of a common language. In J. Blomberg, F. Kensing, & E. Dykstra-Erickson (Eds.), *Proceedings of PDC (Participatory Design Conference) '96* (pp. 231–240). Palo Alto, CA: Computer Professionals for Social Responsibility.

Robbin, A. (1998). *The politics of racial and ethnic group classification.* Unpublished manuscript, School of Information Studies, Florida State University, Tallahassee.

Roberts, M. N., & Roberts, A. F. (Eds.). (1996). *Memory: Luba art and the making of history.* New York: Museum for African Art.

Sacks, H. (1975). Everyone has to lie. In M. Sanches & B.G. Bount (Eds.), *Sociocultural dimensions of language use* (pp. 57–80). New York: Academic.

Sacks, H. (1992). *Lectures on conservation* (Vols. 1– 2). Oxford, England: Basil Blackwell.

Schön, D. A. (1963). *Displacement of concepts.* London: Tavistock.

Shilts, R. (1987). *And the band played on: Politics, people, and the AIDS epidemic.* New York: St. Martin's Press.

Star, S. L. (1991). Power, technologies, and the phenomunology of standards: On being allergic to onions. In J. Law (Ed.), *A sociology of monsters? Power technology and the modern world* (Sociological Review Monograph, 38, 27–57). Oxford, England: Basil Blackwell.

Star, S. L. (1995). *The cultures of computing* (Sociological Review Monograph Series). Oxford, England: Basil Blackwell.

Star, S. L., & Bowker, G. (1997). Of lungs and lungers: The classified story of Tuberculosis. *Mind, Culture, and Activity, 4,* 3–23.

Star, S. L., & Strauss, A. (1999). Layers of silence, arenas of voice: The ecology of visible and invisible work. *Computer-Supported Cooperative Work: The Journal of Collaborative Computing, 8,* 9–30.

Strauss, A. L. (Ed.). (1970). *Where medicine fails.* Chicago: Aldine.

Strauss, A. L., Fagerhaugh, S., Suzcek, B., & Wiener, B. (1985). *Social Organization of Medical Work.* Chicago: University of Chicago Press.

Suchman, L. (1994). Do categories have politics? The language/action perspective reconsidered. *Computer-Supported Cooperative Work: The Journal of Collaborative Computing, 1,* 177–190.

Tort, P. (1989). *La raison classificatoire: Les complexes discursifs: quinze etudes.* Paris: Aubier.

Turkle, S. (1995). *Life on the screen: Identity in the age of the internet.* New York: Simon & Schuster.

Turnbull, D. (1993). The ad hoc collective work of building gothic cathedrals with templates, string, and geometry. *Science, Technology, & Human Values, 18,* 315–343.

Winner, L. (1980). Do artifacts have politics? *Daedulus, 109,* 121–136.

Young, A. (1995). *The harmony of illusions: Inventing post-traumatic stress disorder.* Princeton, NJ: Princeton University Press.

THE EMERGENT ORGANIZATION
Communication as Its Site and Surface
James R. Taylor
Emeritus Professor, University of Montreal
Elizabeth J. Van Every
A Volume in LEA's Communication Series

Today's organizations face a wide variety of challenges, including such contradictions as maintaining unity of action while becoming increasingly diverse. Even the definition of organization is changing and evolving. In this monograph, the authors apply their academic and professional experience to address the notion of "organization," setting forth communication as the essential modality for the constitution of organization -- explaining how an organization can at the same time be both local and global, and how these properties which give organization continuity over time and across geographically dispersed situations also come to be manifested in the day-to-day of human interpersonal exchange.

As a radical rethinking of the traditional discourse approaches in communication theory, this book develops a conceptual framework based on the idea that "organization" emerges in the mix of conversational and textual communicative activities that together construct organizational identity. Applying concepts from the philosophy of language, linguistics, semiotics, system design, sociology and management theory, the authors put forth a convincing argument demonstrating the materiality of language and its constructive role in organization and society.

Contents: Preface. **Part I:** *Theory of Communication.* Organizational Communication: A New Look. Communication as Coorientation. How the A Priori Forms of Text Reveal the Organization. Language as Technology and Agent. **Part II:** *Theory of Organization.* Reinterpreting Organizational Literature. From Symbol Processing to Subsymbolic Socially Distributed Cognition. Conversation Transformed: Organization. Reenacting Enactment. Why "In"? of Maps, Territories, and Governance.
0-8058-2193-7 [cloth] / 2000 / 368pp. / $79.95
0-8058-2194-5 [paper] / 2000 / 368pp. / $39.95

Lawrence Erlbaum Associates, Inc.
10 Industrial Avenue, Mahwah, NJ 07430
201/236–9500   FAX 201/760–3735

Prices subject to
change without notice.

Call toll-free to order: 1-800-9-BOOKS-9...9am to 5pm EST only.
e-mail to: orders@erlbaum.com
visit LEA's web site at http://www.erlbaum.com

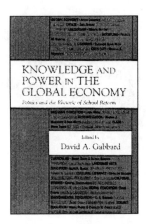

KNOWLEDGE AND POWER IN THE GLOBAL ECONOMY
Politics and the Rhetoric of School Reform

Edited by
David A. Gabbard
East Carolina University

A VOLUME IN THE SOCIOCULTURAL, POLITICAL, AND HISTORICAL
STUDIES IN EDUCATION SERIES

Advancing a three-fold political agenda, this volume:

❖ illuminates how the meanings assigned to a whole vocabulary of words and phrases frequently used to discuss the role and reform of U.S. public schools reflect an essentially economic view of the world;

❖ contends that education or educational reform conducted under an economized worldview will only intensify the effects of the colonial relations of political and economic domination that it breeds at home and abroad; and

❖ offers a set of alternative concepts and meanings for reformulating the role of U.S. public schools and for considering the implications of such a reformulation more generally for the underlying premises of all human relationships and activities.

Toward these ends, the authors, in Part I, critically examine many of the most commonly used terms within the rhetoric of educational reform since the early 1980s and before.

Part II links today's economized worldview to curricular and instructional issues. These essays are especially important for comprehending how the organization of school curriculum privileges those disciplines deemed most central to market expansion -- math and science -- and how the political centrality of the economic sphere influences the nature of the knowledge presented in specific content areas.

Given that language constrains as well as advances human thought, the twin tasks of deeconomizing education and decolonizing society will require a vocabulary that transcends the familiar terminologies addressed in Parts I and II. The entries in Part III cultivate the beginnings of such a vocabulary as the authors elucidate innovative concepts which they view as central to the creation of truly alternative educational visions and practices.

0-8058-2433-2 [cloth] / 2000 / 456pp. / $79.95
0-8058-2434-0 [paper] / 2000 / 456pp. / $39.95

Lawrence Erlbaum Associates, Inc.
10 Industrial Avenue, Mahwah, NJ 07430
201/236–9500   FAX 201/760–3735

Prices subject to
change without notice.

Call toll-free to order: 1-800-9-BOOKS-9...9am to 5pm EST only.
e-mail to: orders@erlbaum.com
visit LEA's web site at http://www.erlbaum.com

Subscription Order Form

Please ❑ enter ❑ renew my subscription to

MIND, CULTURE, AND ACTIVITY
Volume 7, 2000, Quarterly

Subscription prices per volume:

Individual: ❑ $35.00 (US/Canada)   ❑ $65.00 (All Other Countries)

Institution: ❑ $160.00 (US/Canada)   ❑ $190.00 (All Other Countries)

Subscriptions are entered on a calendar-year basis only and must be prepaid in US currency -- check, money order, or credit card. **Offer expires 12/31/2000. NOTE: Institutions must pay institutional rates.** Any institution paying for an individual subscription will be invoiced for the balance of the institutional subscription rate.

❑ **Payment Enclosed**

Total Amount Enclosed $_____

❑ **Charge My Credit Card**

❑ VISA   ❑ MasterCard   ❑ AMEX   ❑ Discover

Exp. Date_____ _____

Card Number _____

Signature _____
(Credit card orders cannot be processed without your signature.)

Please print clearly to ensure proper delivery.

Name _____

Address _____

_____

City _____ State _____ Zip+4 _____
Prices are subject to change without notice.

Lawrence Erlbaum Associates, Inc.
Journal Subscription Department
10 Industrial Avenue, Mahwah, NJ 07430
(201) 236-9500   FAX (201) 760-3735

ARTIFICIAL INTELLIGENCE AND LITERARY CREATIVITY
Inside the Mind of BRUTUS, A Storytelling Machine

Selmer Bringsjord
Rensselaer Polytechnic Institute
David Ferrucci
T.J. Watson Research Center

Is human creativity a wall that AI can never scale? Many people are happy to admit that experts in many domains can be matched by either knowledge-based or sub-symbolic systems, but even some AI researchers harbor the hope that when it comes to feats of sheer brilliance, mind over machine is an unalterable fact. In this book, the authors push AI toward a time when machines can autonomously write not just humdrum stories of the sort seen for years in AI, but first-rate fiction thought to be the province of human genius. It reports on five years of effort devoted to building a story generator -- the BRUTUS.1 system.

This book was written for three general reasons. The first theoretical reason for investing time, money, and talent in the quest for a truly creative machine is to work toward an answer to the question of whether we ourselves are machines. The second theoretical reason is to silence those who believe that logic is forever closed off from the emotional world of creativity. The practical rationale for this endeavor, and the third reason, is that machines able to work alongside humans in arenas calling for creativity will have incalculable worth.

Contents: Preface. Setting the Stage. Could a Machine Author Use Imagery? Consciousness and Creativity. Mathematizing Betrayal. The Narrative-Based Refutation of Church's Thesis. Inside the Mind of BRUTUS.
0-8058-1986-X [cloth] / 2000 / 264pp. / $59.95
0-8058-1987-8 [paper] / 2000 / 264pp. / $27.50

Lawrence Erlbaum Associates, Inc.
10 Industrial Avenue, Mahwah, NJ 07430
201/236–9500   FAX 201/760–3735

Prices subject to
change without notice.

Call toll-free to order: **1-800-9-BOOKS-9**...9am to 5pm EST only.
e-mail to: orders@erlbaum.com
visit LEA's web site at http://www.erlbaum.com